Behavioral
Architecture

Behavioral Architecture

TOWARD AN ACCOUNTABLE DESIGN PROCESS

Clovis Heimsath, AIA

MCGRAW-HILL BOOK COMPANY
New York   St. Louis   San Francisco   Auckland   Bogotá
Düsseldorf   Johannesburg   London   Madrid
Mexico   Montreal   New Delhi   Panama
Paris   São Paulo   Singapore
Sydney   Tokyo   Toronto

Library of Congress Cataloging in Publication Data

Heimsath, Clovis.
Behavioral architecture.

Bibliography: p.
Includes index.
1. Architecture—Human factors. 2. Architectural
design. I. Title.
NA2542.4.H44   729   76-47673
ISBN 0-07-027890-3

  3 4 5 6 7 8 9 0   VHVH   7 8 6 5 4 3 2 1 0 9 8

*The editors for this book were Jeremy Robinson and Tobia L. Worth,
the designer was Naomi Auerbach, and the production supervisor
was Frank P. Bellantoni. It was set in Palatino
by Progressive Typographers.*

Printed and bound by Von Hoffmann Press, Inc.

To Maryann

Contents

Preface

This book concerns behavior, systems, and the design process. It is written from the point of view of a practicing architect. In every sense it is a practical and pragmatic statement drawn from the pressures, frustrations, and sobering insight developed from practice.

The book is in three sections, which are similar to the stages I personally experienced in writing it. The problem dawned on me slowly, entrenched as I was in the latter-day excitement of the modern movement, concerned largely with aesthetic principles guiding the design process. Familiarity with closed environments brought the first queasy unease that something in the process of design was remiss; but the decision to write the book and begin what has become a 4-year arduous process of reeducation can be pinpointed to a moment of utter frustration. Working in St. Louis with the St. Louis Housing Authority in a plan to renovate the public housing development of Webbe, I was reconstructing the steps that led to the total abandonment of a nine-story high-rise in the center of the project. Copper flashing had been systematically torn from the roof, water had leaked through to the ninth floor, the tenants had been moved downward, and windows had been left broken. Waterpipes, exposed for economy, broke one cold January night and water filled the corridors of the floors below and froze. The fire department evacuated the remaining tenants on lower floors and they never returned. A vacant building stood as testament to good intentions unfulfilled.

The issue of reconstructing the building broadened to the issue of life patterns of the 2500 inhabitants of the three adjoining housing units: Darst, Webbe, and Peabody. This enclave could only be understood as part of a larger St. Louis, including the dreary wasteland of La Salle Place, scheduled (some day) for redevelopment, and Pruitt Igoe, almost completely abandoned in 1972, the scene of instant excavation by demolition, an explosion heard around the world.

The context expanded to other cities with similar plights, to other closed environments designed without the needs of the inhabitants in mind. The frustration increased—no one was to blame! It was not the architects, not the owners, not the government regulatory agencies, but the impersonal climate of opinion that divorced behavior from building, systematically and continually.

Born of frustration, the book project soon became reeducation. The bibliography is a personal one, not inclusive, but emphatic. One book led to the next, one sacred cow of architecture after another dropped away before the onslaught of behavioral psychologists intent on articulating the real impact of environment on human potentiality.

My particular thanks go to Dr. William Ittleson who early on read the manuscript and pointed up issues; to Dr. Bert Kaplan, the first psychologist to lend encouragement; and to Dr. Thomas Greening, a leader in humanistic psychology. A series of architects lent their support: Don Conway, an advocate of behavioral design within the American Institute of Architects (AIA); Charles Burnette, an author in his own right; Arnold Prima, Richard Kramer, Robert Shipley, Lawrence Spangler, all connected at one time or another with the innovative research effort in behavior at the U.S. Army Corps of Engineers. My appreciation extends to Wolfgang Preiser, one of the organizers of a symposium, "Programming for Habitability," which brought together 100 interested professionals in a forum for interchange. My own practice of behavioral architecture has been strengthened by the inputs of Mitch Mize, Emmett White, and Bob Bainbridge. The book is heavily laced with systems logic, learned by association with the Urban Systems Project Office at the Johnson Space Center, with particular involvement of Ted Hays and Jerry Craig. Systems logic became a part of the National AIA through the National AIA Systems Committee (during the years my book was forming) through process advocates Jonathan King, S. Porter Driscoll, Ezra Ehrenkrantz, Neal Mitchel, Stephen Diamond, to name only a few. All uncredited artwork was prepared by my own company, Clovis Heimsath Associates, Inc.

Many lent support. Particular thanks are extended to those who made the book technically possible: Kathy Chapman in typing and retyping, Cindy Shealor in endless photoresearching, and Dr. Richard H. Perrine, in reference material.

Clovis Heimsath

Behavioral Architecture

Introduction

Architecture, by definition, is built for people. Architecture is the enclosure in which people live their lives. Why then talk of behavioral architecture; why not architecture for people, or human architecture, or just architecture? The word "behavior" suggests people in action, with things to do, with other people to talk to and interact with. Behavior suggests an awareness of the social fabric of people, a moving together dynamically in time.

Buildings are static. The tragedy of architecture is seeing people as static, too. If a physical space will dimensionally accommodate a person, we feel that somehow that person has been provided for properly. Yet only by considering an individual's behavior in the space can we validate the design.

There is great interest today in people's behavior. Books are written on territoriality, linking the animal need for territorial definition with the same human need. Books on nonverbal communication are popular, documenting what we have all suspected for a long time, that people communicate by gestures and by attitudes as well as by using words. People's behavior in groups is being discussed, producing books on Transactional Analysis, the "I'm OK, You're OK" approach to social interaction, and books on role playing, like *Games People Play*.

More significant for my study is an increasing interest in the way the individual interacts with the environment—environment in the broadest sense as the total ecology and in the narrowest sense as the human engineering of a particular work station. There is a specific branch of psychology called environmental psychology and an alert group of investigators working to document how people interact. Schools of architecture have redirected their curricula to focus attention on people's behavior in buildings; some architecture schools have been renamed schools of environmental design.

At the same time there is a concerted effort to increase the systems methodology of design, leading to new tools such as life-cycle costing, value engineering, performance specifications, feedback, fast-tracking, construction management, logic diagrams, and computer applications. There has been a great deal of discussion of these various elements affecting design today, each one has been discussed either in the context of behavioral design or in the context of a systems approach to design. There has been little concerted effort to bring these two, seemingly divergent, directions together and present a synthesis for practicing architects.

This book attempts to bridge the gap between the current interest in behavior and systems and to coordinate them in a new design methodology. The accompanying logic chart for the book illustrates the point. The thesis is presented in three sections. Section 1 deals with the problem of the current state of affairs in design, stressing the symptoms of failure, the weakness of the current design process which leads to it, and the inadequacy of current theory. Section 2 discusses the issues raised by behavioral architecture, covering issues that relate to behavior, issues that relate to systems, and issues stemming from the building/behavior interface. Section 3 presents techniques currently available for implementing behavioral design, and the impact these new techniques will have on the

Outline logic diagram.

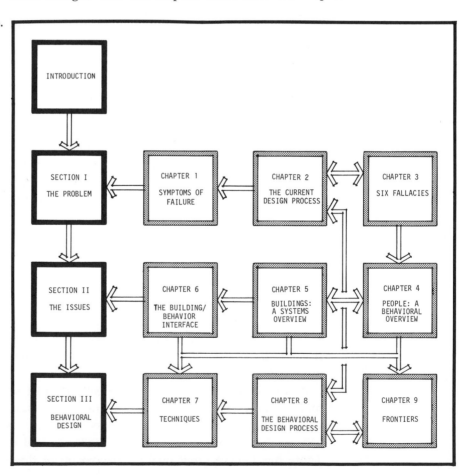

process of designing buildings. Finally, the book looks to the frontiers of thought and theory, past the status quo in the building world, and suggests the expanded role of behavioral design in a world of a rapidly nearing tomorrow, concerned on one hand with conservation, on the other with space habitation. It is admitted that the field of behavioral design is a new one, yet much can be done immediately to implant a new awareness of the individual in the environment.

In a sense the book is one practicing architect's synthesis. It is a working document written from the architectural viewpoint and directed toward professionals and administrators to explain and encourage behavioral design.

There is a pronounced need for accountability in architecture. The cybernetic view of interdependent systems in society has had an important effect on the climate of opinion. Administrators responsible for major social programs are under pressure to document, acknowledge, and monitor the decision-making process. The General Services Administration is encouraging systems design for precisely this reason—systems design brings accountability.

A movement toward accountability and systems leads logically to behavioral design. Behavioral design, in turn, directs attention to the total needs of people, recognizing that a container for activities can never be more successful than the activities themselves.

The Problem

1
Symptoms of Failure

A Cry to Be Heard

If a Bengal tiger were loose in Houston, it would be newsworthy, and a guest leaving my house after dinner would be careful about not only how he crossed the street but how he avoided places where tigers might hide. Bengal tigers would be newsworthy because they are an incongruity in a city in the United States. Newspapers have an obligation to report incongruities. They do their job well, which is the reason there is almost uniformly bad news in the papers. The public, on the other hand, makes a grave mistake in believing that items reported in the paper are the only ones out of kilter. Once the press has aired an issue, its coverage dies down and the public somehow assumes that the issue has been solved, that it has become congruous again.

In the 1970s there was widespread coverage of prison riots, following widespread coverage of psychiatric treatment abuses in the 1960s as part of the Kennedy administration's bid for the development of community mental health centers. Did the public assume that the problems of psychiatric treatment had been solved once the issue was no longer aired in the press? After prison riots, did the public assume that the issue of prisons was no longer incongruous and, therefore, no longer news?

The public forum in newspapers and in professional journals is vital in that it points out incongruities. But a desperate act that gets press coverage must be recognized for what it is, a desperate act, a cry to be heard. One can only infer from the act the level of frustration behind it and so the issue which caused the desperate act is clearly in the public's view for a short moment. But if the public assumes that the cry creates immediate change, it is unfortunately misled.

The cry for community mental health centers in the 1960s was a simple cry affirming what the vast majority of professionals in that field knew to be a need—the need to treat patients near home rather than in impersonal institutions separated from their families and friends. Now, after a number of years of progress toward the goal of community health, the issue has lost momentum in many states. The problem is complex and the reasons for failure are many, but one fact must not be overlooked. Large state hospitals built 100 and 200 miles from town are already built and paid for! The state hospital may be isolated, fortress-like, antiquated, and impossible to administer well, but the simple fact is that the building is there. In the eyes of the legislators, the buildings are free in the 1970s since they were paid for by earlier administrations in the 1920s, 1930s, and 1940s.

The problem of how the state or federal governments rationalize abandoning old psychiatric hospitals or old prisons must be considered when hearing the cry for help. If the cry is to be effective, it must be translated from a desperate act which gains attention to practical actions which can change the social and building process.

Two social issues have been much in the press during the 1970s: the issue of inhumane closed environments and the issue of "crisis ghettos." In 1971, George Jackson was slain along with three guards and two other inmates at San Quentin; a month later, eleven hostages and thirty-two inmates were killed in the Attica riots. In 1973, a convict murdered two guards at Lucasville Prison in Ohio. The Associated Press reported:

> The Lucasville prison, so new it still has not been officially accepted by the state from the contractor, has been the site of successive episodes of trouble. There have been guard strikes, inmate fasts, and a multitide of difficulties with the physical plant that is costing the state $23.5 million.[1]

Four days later *The New York Times* reported that three inmates were killed and more than twenty injured in a riot at the Oklahoma State Prison. A convict, Gibson, was allowed to meet with the Governor, and he was quoted as saying that the prison personnel have "absolutely no regard" for inmates. "We want to be treated like men," he said. "We have been treated like victims of a tribal system." The article goes on to state:

> Gibson, the convicted murderer, chosen to head the committee of inmates to negotiate with the Governor, said that the riot was the fourth reaction to the prison in recent months. He said that with overcrowding, poorly prepared foods, a "sadistic" medical system and no rehabilitation program this [the riot] just had to happen.[2] (See Figure 1.1.)

A 1973 report entitled "Prison 'Disaster' Warned" stated:

> Lake Butler Superintendent A. F. Cook said 1,305 inmates were at the reception center—about 100 more than when the doors were closed 13 months ago.

Fig. 1.1 Jails breed human degradation. (Ben Ross, photographer.)

[1] "Ohio Convict Slays 2 Guards," *The Houston Post*, July 25, 1973. Copyright © 1973.
[2] "11 Freed as Oklahoma Prison Riot Ends," *The New York Times*, July 29, 1973. Copyright © 1973 by The New York Times Company. Reprinted by permission.

(The prison closure by Florida Corrections Director Louie Wainwright shut down the system to new inmates for a second time.) Other officials said as many as four inmates are occupying 7 by 9 foot cells designed for one and many are sleeping on cement. Wainwright said state parole probation officials were dragging their feet in releasing prisoners and that a program to build 28 community correctional centers was behind schedule.[3]

In Texas, where correctional institutions have been well regarded by correctional professionals, continuing problems of violence at units, particularly at Ramsey, caused widespread concern in 1973 amid claims of systematic beatings of prisoners by "building tenders," special inmates used to control other inmates in violation of state law. Nationwide attention followed a series of accusations by young boys that the state school at Mountainview was inhumane. The *Houston Post* story,[4] "Boys Testify of Brutality at State Home," stated in part: "The five boys, ages 15 to 17, reported dozens of beatings including being hit in the head for minor rule infractions. All the groups charge that treatment at the [Texas Youth Center] Unit does not constitute rehabilitation." An expert on institutions for juvenile delinquents testified before a federal court hearing that he would close Mountainview.

> Miller also said brutality is almost impossible to stamp out in large institutions that are located far away from cities. Don't look for individual scapegoats. Brutality can become part of the bureaucracy, he said. Brutality is harder to get away with in small residential treatment centers where parents, probation officers and community workers are involved.[4]

Myriad press stories are available in every community sounding a cry to be heard. And whether all the facts are as they are stated during the riot or the civil suit for redress, the fact is that the public for a brief moment recognizes the problem. The problem of prisons is well summed up by Ronald L. Goldfarb, an attorney, who wrote in 1974:

> Presently in the U.S. there are about 5,000 city and county jails, 400 state and federal prisons, plus innumerable local lockups, work houses, camps, farms, ranches and detention centers. On an average day we confine *1.3 million offenders in these places.* [Italics ours] Over the course of a year, about 2.5 million offenders see the inside of prison. And all these prisoners in all these prisons only breed more crime. If the city slum is the high school of crime, prison is the university and a colossally expensive one at that.[5] (See Figure 1.2.)

In the 1960s a second kind of closed environment held public attention, if only briefly. Riots in Detroit, Los Angeles, and Washington, D.C., left

[3] "Prison 'Disaster' Warned," *The Houston Post*, February 10, 1973. Copyright © 1973.

[4] "Boys Testify of Brutality at State Home," *The Houston Post*, July 20, 1973. Copyright © 1973, The Houston Post. Reprinted by permission.

[5] Ronald Goldfarb, "American Prisons: Self-defeating Concrete," *Psychology Today*, January 1974, p. 20. Copyright © Ziff Davis Publishing Company.

Fig. 1.2 (right) An environment designed for control, not for human potential. (Joshua Freiwald, photographer.)

Fig. 1.3 (below) St. Louis housing being blown up. (Lee Balterman, photographer, Time-Life Picture Agency.)

the neighborhoods of the rioters in ashes. I drove through the area in Washington, D.C., a few weeks after the riot and I was not prepared for the extent of destruction I saw. People had set fire to their own neighborhoods and if not their own homes, at least the homes of their neighbors. It seemed to me very reminiscent of the prison burnings that followed riots. Perhaps the American public had never confronted so graphically the degree of frustration felt by those in ghettos; briefly perhaps they did gauge the frustration as they watched on television pictures of burning inner city streets.

In 1973, an event occurred that was televised around the world. A 12-story building at a public housing project, a black crisis ghetto, Pruitt-Igoe in St. Louis, was blown up, not by frustrated blacks but by the Department of Housing and Urban Development (HUD) of the United States Government. The experience had a particular impact for me, for I witnessed the action standing on the twelfth floor of an adjacent building with tenant representatives from the remaining housing projects in St. Louis. A spontaneous shout went up as the building collapsed and everyone clapped. It seemed briefly a festive moment and perhaps it was. Symbolically, it represented an end to the brave new world of public housing. (See Figure 1.3.)

LaClede Town and La Salle Place—Success and Failure

I had worked with a team in St. Louis preparing a plan for the renovation of vacant buildings of the Darst-Webbe-Peabody complex, projects lesser known than Pruitt-Igoe but nonetheless becoming abandoned as Pruitt-Igoe had been abandoned.

In a real sense our work was a feedback project, analyzing an environment already built. But the experiences of those months in St. Louis have left an indelible impression on me. The interdependence between decisions made in the building process and decisions made in the social process became most apparent. A study of one or more public housing projects led logically to a study of the whole system of public housing in St. Louis and the assumptions upon which it had been developed.

Two projects stood out in sharp contrast to one another: LaClede Town, the showplace of urban renewal in St. Louis (which in 1974 was adding Breakthrough units) and La Salle Place, just beginning the urban renewal process. (La Salle Place was particularly relevant to our study since it adjoined the Darst-Webbe-Peabody public housing complex.) When the Breakthrough units were completed, LaClede Town would encompass 1,700 units of housing, for families with incomes between $6,300 and

$10,400 per year. Under the 221-D3 interest subsidy, many of the homes were owned. The management was good; for example, derelict cars were towed away within 24 hours and broken windows were repaired in the same one-day time frame. All guards in the development were required to live there. A check on social services and activities revealed that the town center had a pub, coffee house, laundromat, beauty shop, general store, small restaurant, and children's play area. The Waring Elementary School, a laboratory school for Harris Teachers College, was the school for LaClede Town. Junior and senior high school students were zoned into city schools of recognized quality. The city maintained Vashon Community Recreation Center adjacent to LaClede Town and the Berea Church sponsored a variety of recreational activities, including four Little League Baseball teams and an adult softball team.

LaClede Town seemed to be working in 1972: the buildings were pleasant, the management and morale were good, and the social activities essential to community health were at least superficially viable. It was built on land bought and cleared through federal urban renewal financing. The city had directed that social services be placed nearby to support it, such as the Vashon Community Recreation Center. (Had not the Waring Elementary School been available, the city would have been involved in developing a school of recognizable learning value in order to maintain the middle class white population.)

Father Albert Prokes on South 11th Street in St. Louis was pastor of the oldest Czechoslovakian parish in the United States, part of the upcoming urban renewal area, La Salle Place. His parishioners, who had lived in his neighborhood for generations, had left in large numbers. He mentioned a survey that was made by HUD in 1969 indicating that 1,050 houses in the redevelopment area were rehabitable. Three years later a similar study made by HUD showed only 310 such houses. Some 700 families, predominantly white, had either abandoned their homes or lived on in them without maintenance. The church school was closed in 1969 and at that time there were fifty children to bus to the next (still healthy) parish in Compton Heights. In 1971 there were only ten children to bus.

La Salle Place in particular and urban renewal in general are complex problems and a few facts could not describe the whole community situation in any real perspective. But a simple, undeniable fact became clear: a largely white urban population, of strong ethnic and religious roots, was being systematically uprooted in the 1970s in the La Salle Place area in order that urban renewal could bring in stable ethnic, hopefully even religious, middle-class whites.

Federal sponsors would surely object to the color characterization of La Salle Place, but it was commonly understood in St. Louis in 1972 that the only hope for urban renewal in this area was a permanent white settlement to balance what had become almost totally black public housing at Darst-Webbe-Peabody.

The federal program of urban renewal was certainly not intended to destroy healthy urban communities; however, no one had considered the social side effects of urban renewal on communities adjacent to those being razed. Certainly the 700 families which were living in rehabitable dwellings had been scheduled, statistically, to remain. But the human fact that any family which can move, *will* move away from large areas of abandoned housing, was never computed. There was no process by which human behavior could be evaluated during the design process of razing and rebuilding.

Urban Apartheid

The problems surrounding abandoned public housing and urban neighborhoods were not unique to St. Louis, although Professor Murray L. Weidenbaum, in a report made to HUD in 1971 and entitled "Urban Decay in St. Louis," stated that no major American city approached the proportion of St. Louis' total population loss of 400,000 whites since 1950 with an immigration of only 16,000 blacks.[6] Statistics in the report of abandoned housing showed that while 24,596 living units had been destroyed by the city, the city's remaining vacant housing had increased from 4,426 to 22,962 since 1950.

The preliminary 1970 U.S. Census showed that New York City had lost 750,000 people since the 1960 census, Detroit, 157,000, and Cleveland, 136,000. Crisis ghetto situations surrounded public housing in many cities including Brooklyn, Newark, and Chicago. Rent strikes and mass abandonment had not occurred in other cities as they had in St. Louis, but social disintegration within public housing suggested it was just a matter of time. *Time* magazine in a December 1970 article called the 15,000-member black community of the Cabrini-Green housing project in Chicago a vertical ghetto. Although it has been described more comprehensively in professional literature, I was impressed with the wording of the opening paragraph:

> In mood and appearance, the vast complex resembles nothing so much as a maximum-security prison in dire need of both repair and reform. Its corridors are encrusted with grime and redolent with urine. Too many kids—too few adults. Fully 70% of the Cabrini population is under 18, and at least half of the families currently have no male parent in residence.[7] (See Figure 1.4.)

[6] Murray L. Weidenbaum, *Urban Decay in St. Louis,* HUD Report, 1971.
[7] *Time*, p. 76, December 7, 1970.

Fig. 1.4 Cabrini-Green housing in Chicago. (Paula Henderson, photographer.)

It is possible to go on and on quoting the cry to be heard, the incongruity of people suffering what they at least feel to be grave injustice in a country where the majority are well fed and well housed. Articles entitled "Ghettoes Claim Health Services are Inadequate," "County 'Deaf' to Pleas over Poverty Lines" ring in the ears of concerned Americans year after year as one area after another is spotlighted because of dramatic social disruption.

Many social scientists while acknowledging the problem cannot see its connection to architecture. Perhaps they are right if they conceive of architecture as the influence of a particular building or particular rooms on a particular group of people. But when architecture is conceived as a building process affecting the culture of society, then clearly the decision to locate 15,000 blacks in high densities and without significant social programs is of critical influence on subsequent behavior. What must be acknowledged is that the placement and size of Cabrini-Green *was determined as a design decision, not as a social decision!* The owner and the architect set the social organization in motion by deciding on the building, the location, the density, and the configuration!

Albert Mayer, writing in *The Urgent Future,* put the matter quite succinctly.

> We all naively thought that if we could eliminate the very bad physical dwelling and surroundings of slums, the new sanitized conditions would almost per se cure social ills. We know better now.[8] (See Figure 1.5.)

Architects perhaps know better but they are still building as before, largely on intuition, with little or no behavioral evaluation, and with no one willing to pay for it or respond to it. In its heyday, the Urban Development Corporation of New York State developed a major new complex in the East River at densities perhaps ten times those of Pruitt-Igoe. They were experimenting with a concept of scattering elementary schools on the first floors of apartment buildings. In short, they were setting in motion a physical organization in the name of building, with incalculable social and behavioral ramifications. Would it work? Who knew?

Stratification through Construction

Although society is considered *open* by many people (open in the sense that the vast majority of people have the unprecedented opportunity to change their physical and social surroundings), the architect concerned with the design of a variety of building types becomes impressed with the number of people stratified by the built environment. The extended fam-

[8] Albert Mayer, *The Urgent Future* (New York: McGraw-Hill, 1967).

ily, including old people as well as young, was once the hallmark of American social organization, particularly in the rural areas of the country. Today it is more common to find the elderly grouped in retirement homes or, still more commonly, in retirement cities.

Every major American city has its poor centralized in a common area or areas. Anthony Downs in *Opening Up the Suburbs*[9] explains this fact as the product of the American "Trickle-Down Process." "Wealthier households deliberately exclude the poorest people from their neighborhoods through laws requiring high quality housing plus police prevention of land expropriation." He points out that for "middle-income" families, those then earning between $8,000 and $15,000 a year, the system works well, securing them stable neighborhoods. In 1969, 60.4 percent of families in the United States had incomes of $8,000 or more; therefore, a majority found this system beneficial. But he continues,

> For millions of the poorest households in American metropolitan areas, the trickle-down process is a disaster. It compels households with the lowest incomes and often the least competence to live concentrated together in our worst urban housing. This concentration has a "critical mass" effect that [reinforces] the negative impacts of poverty, creating entire neighborhood environments dominated by conditions of poverty. These include certain problems and pathologies most intensively associated with indigence (although found in all income groups to some extent). The results are "crisis ghettos" marked by high rates of crime, vandalism, broken families, mental illness, delinquency, and drug addiction. These areas also have the lowest quality public schools, public services, and housing in urban society.[9]

While many others have described this phenomenon, Downs's statement is a concise summation of a stratification situation well understood by design and social service professionals. The extraordinary difference in the environment of communities is seldom recognized by the general public, however. A few examples of experiments set up to gauge these differences follow. Many more experiments are needed to demonstrate the extent of social deprivation.

A study to demonstrate the difference in social order between one community and the next was developed by P. G. Zimbardo (Nebraska Symposium on Motivation USA, 1969). Two parked cars were left in two different cities, one near New York University in the Bronx, and the other adjacent to Stanford University in Palo Alto, California. The license plates were removed and hoods were opened to provide "release cues" for potential vandals. Within 24 hours the car in New York was stripped of all movable parts, and much of the activity took place in broad daylight. In the next three days the car in New York was further stripped until all that remained

Fig. 1.5 Interiors of abandoned housing.

[9] Anthony Downs, *Opening Up The Suburbs* (London: Yale University Press, Ltd., 1973), pp. 2 and 9.

was a pile of rubble. In the same time frame, the car in California was left untouched.

Such a study can be used as a comparative indication of urban "overload." Meier did a study in 1962 which related the frequency of transactions in stores with the time expended on such transactions. Meier documented that when the customer volume and daily turnover increased, the time allocated for the human transaction dramatically decreased, leading to the brusqueness characteristic of urban centers such as New York. Other experimental studies related the feeling of tempos in a city to the number of times one must step aside to avoid a personal collision, or the lack of greeting in urban areas caused by the necessity of passing mostly strangers, unlike in a smaller community where the vast majority of individuals seen are known.

Kevin Lynch argues that a good city is highly visualizable. This hypothesis was tested by mechanically photographing particular intersections throughout the New York Metropolitan area. He then asked neighbors if they could identify the locations in the photographs. He found that a very much higher proportion of neighbors living in Manhattan were able to identify the photographs, than those living in the Bronx, Brooklyn, Queens, or Staten Island. The superior information value of the street environment in Manhattan could have been anticipated; the research project was important as a means of corroboration.

A considerable body of information is becoming available that maps areas of the city in human terms, indicating the kind of deviant behavior that is expected, the degree of visual chaos broadcast by the environment, and the lack of opportunity an occupant has to change the situation.

C. S. Doxiadis describes a 5-year study made in the Detroit area that designated and rated places having aesthetic or cultural value. He found that a person who lived in the city center and had a car could visit 582 units of aesthetic and cultural value, and a person living in the suburbs could visit 622. He continues:

> However, a person without a car has access to only 27 units—that is, less than $1/20$ the number of units to which the other person has access, even if his income is half as great. If we now remember that, in the past, poor and rich had equal opportunities to visit places by walking, we will see that modern technology has increased the gap between people relative to the choices they have for making contacts in their settlements.[10]

Separate and unequal environments are developing in spite of programs specifically set up to avoid social inequities. Are the social programs misdirected? In 1970 there were more than 600 federally funded programs for

[10] C. S. Doxiadis, "Ekistics, The Science of Human Settlement," *Science*, vol. 170, pp. 393–404, October 23, 1970.

urban improvement sponsored by seventy-eight different agencies and representing 15 percent of the federal budget. That these programs are to a large extent failing in their tasks can be seen from the dismal statistics of crime, deteriorating education, and urban abandonment.

Using techniques of systems dynamics developed by Professor Jay W. Forrester at The Massachusetts Institute of Technology, researchers have illustrated how areas of cities become less attractive on a relative base of alternatives. Since 5 percent of Americans move from one town to the next each year and three times as many move within a particular city, the degree of attractiveness, however quantified, operates to draw or repel individuals. The thesis is that the uncoordinated efforts of government may solve one problem and create another. For example, by increasing the amount of low-income housing, secondary problems can result. The effect of temporarily increasing the attractiveness of a city center to low-income families, in turn draws more families in and ends by creating a worse problem, for additional low-income families increase crime, unemployment, health needs, and so forth. The solution is to provide improvements that will not cause behaviorally counterproductive actions.

Unraveling the complexity of urban life is difficult, but the suspicion increases that much of the separation and inequality found in the urban structure is exactly what the majority of Americans want. Until 1954 there were "Jim Crow" laws that legally separated people, legally established public double-tracking for rest rooms, movie houses, restaurants, libraries, and schools. Today there is still substantial segregation, not only on racial grounds but also continuing the separation between rich and poor. As Arnold Toynbee states:

> It is this unhappy cultural consequence of poverty that moves the rich to shun the society of the poor; and poverty and lack of cultivation promote each other in a vicious cycle. The poor cannot afford to give as good an education as the rich can to their children, and consequently the children of the poor are handicapped at the start in their struggle to escape from poverty.[11]

The deprivation of poor persons is compounded logarithmically by their forced location. Others who are poor and hence uneducated are their neighbors constituting the largest percentage of their human contact; deviant behavior associated with the poor is enacted before their eyes on a daily basis; health needs go unattended. Poor individuals without cars have little opportunity to develop any cultural perspective. The symbolic language of their segregation and deprivation is broadcast by countless actions which become internalized metaphors of what they can expect from life: police who seem to arrest arbitrarily, crime that goes unpun-

---

[11] Arnold J. Toynbee, *Cities on the Move* (New York: Oxford University Press, 1970), p. 213.

ished, cruelty in human associations, to name only a few. Conversely, the positive socializing activities that are associated with healthy communities are lacking: football rallies, school dances, sports events, festivals, bazaars, political activities, and active religious participation.

For whatever reasons, be it a poor tax base or a lack of political representation, the same areas of the city will receive the poorest service in garbage collection, derelict car removal, vacant lot cleanup, abandoned house removal, street light or pavement repair. The visual language becomes a ready-reference to the social stigma of living in the "wrong place," on the "wrong side of the tracks."

The fact that such symbolic language is universally present in compounding the visual separations and therefore deprivations of the poor can be written off by some as a natural consequence of poverty itself. Or, it can be seen as a subtle and seldom discussed *technique of social and physical apartheid.* That behavior is part of the technique, that negative environments establish poverty cycles that return the children to the places of their parents does not invalidate the suspicion.

While double-corridor systems are found in buildings as a technique to support the social organization, the complex social techniques of double-corridor systems in urban areas support the status quo of social separations, a process that assures the middle class majority of comfortable and separated suburban neighborhoods.

Corridors from affluent neighborhoods into the central business district generally avoid the worst areas of blight so that a large proportion of the population does not witness on a daily basis any of the life patterns of the poor, or the use of high-speed freeways minimizes the impact upon drivers who see these areas only peripherally at 55 mph. Nor are many people anxious to become involved. In Houston, when a group of citizens banded together to achieve passage of a housing code, they offered a bus tour of the areas in question to demonstrate the need. As could have been expected, very few people took the tour.

The damage done in childhood is generally irreversible when the adult in such an environment does have an opportunity to move. The social actions thought acceptable to segregated individuals have been internalized and have become their ready-reference for action in adult life. The director of a halfway house for ex-convicts pointed to this internalization when he indicated that the major task he had was to reorder the life patterns of those leaving jail. Having served 30 years himself, he spoke with some authority when he indicated that few of his fellows understood even rudimentary socially acceptable behavioral patterns, that they were unaware that the majority of citizens are at home after 10:30 P.M., not on street corners and in bars.

It is the contention of this book that cities are a megastructure of the same basic geometries that define buildings. Cities cluster people, as in Pruitt-Igoe, and create what is essentially a closed environment. James B. Conant in his book, *Slums and Suburbs*, points to the disparity of communities within the same town:

> In a slum area of 125,000 people, mostly Negro, a sampling of the youth population showed that roughly 70 percent of the boys and girls ages sixteen to twenty-one were out of school and unemployed. When one considers that the total population in this district is equal to that of a good-sized independent city, the magnitude of the problem is appalling and a challenge to our society is clear. . . . It is a matter of geography in the last analysis. Three factors are significant: first, group size (the larger the group, the more dangerous); second, the density of the population (the number of frustrated youth per block); third, the isolation of the inhabitants from other kinds of people and other sorts of streets and houses.[12]

Although Conant is talking about urban ghettos, he might as well be talking about prisons or boys' homes. Of course there are differences, but the same forces that demand penal institutions be set apart from the mainstream of the community also demand clustering of the poor and frustrated in undermaintained areas of cities.

The Subcommittee on Housing and Urban Affairs (Committee on Banking, Housing and Urban Affairs, United States Senate) in publishing its report, *The Central City Problem and Urban Renewal Policy*, quotes the basic conclusion of the Kerner Commission report which emphasized racial inequality: "Our nation is moving toward two societies, one black, one white, separate and unequal."[13] And it admitted that one of the recent causes of out-migration of whites from the central city after World War II could be laid at the doorstep of the government itself. "It would cost less to move out than to renovate the older housing they occupied in the central city. New highways, widespread automobile ownership and favorable FHA and VA terms for financing new suburban property made the suburbs a better buy."[13] *The study found that the exodus occurred before the sharp rise in inner city crime and blight had reached its peak of severity and could not, therefore be traced to these conditions alone.*

Building Apartheid

Stratification is not only citywide, not only predicated on wealth. In addition to urban stratification there are a multitude of closed environments, defined as environments that hold the inhabitant on a reconstructed

[12] James B. Conant, *Slums and Suburbs* (New York: McGraw-Hill, 1961), pp. 34–35.

[13] *The Central City Problem and Urban Renewal Policy*, Subcommittee on Housing and Urban Affairs, U.S. Senate Committee on Banking, Housing and Urban Affairs.

24-hour schedule. Institutions include county jails, state and federal prisons, long-term chronic disease hospitals (including VA complexes across the country), reform schools, orphanages, homes for the retarded, psychiatric centers, and geriatric homes. Closed environments can be developed on very positive social values. Some of these include prep schools, monasteries, remote outposts, retirement home communities, and exclusive resort hideaways. Whether the quality of the social environment is negative, benign, or positive, the closed environment traditionally has similar elements:

1. There is a screening process for individuals arriving or leaving.

2. Individuals within the environment are either in a served role or in a service role. (An anomaly of many institutions, prisons for example, is that the served group is actually subservient to the service staff.)

3. Time is controlled, whether it be programmed for the convenience of the staff or for the pleasure of the participants.

4. There is invariably a physical separation from the rest of society. The separation is often doubly complete, one separation being accomplished by enclosing walls, the other by a physical separation from centers of social activity.

5. Historically, at least, the closed environment was built to be a symbol. While purporting to symbolize the philanthropic value of the organization sponsoring the building, the end result was a large, scaleless complex so unlike the residential scale of buildings around it that it became a symbol of the social ordering that occurred within its walls. The interior aspect of many closed environments manifested the same scaleless, repetitive format with long corridors and drab decor.

6. Institutions historically have been large complexes, particularly prisons and psychiatric centers, recreating in isolation not only the 24-hour day of the served inhabitant, but also the supporting services for the community as well in shops, sewer disposal systems, and even power generation.

Although closed and stratified environments do not represent the living condition of the majority of Americans, they do represent the living environments most often detrimental to personal growth and well being. In recent years some of these closed and stratified environments have come under increasing scrutiny, partly because a wave of riots have brought them into public attention, partly because behavioral psychologists have begun to quantify the psychological deprivations many institutions induce.

It is certain that these institutions and the stratification of society did not just occur by chance. If stratification is rampant, and if it is usually detrimental to healthy human behavior, the three building partners (the owner, the regulating government, and the architect) are each responsible. Owners, usually well-meaning but without considering the problems of human dynamics, have commissioned institutions of all kinds and arbitrarily placed them apart from communities. The federal and state governments have often been the clients for these institutions which increase stratification rather than inhibit it. The well-documented program of subsidized highways and FHA-mortgaged housing after World War II is a classic example of the government encouraging the abandonment of the inner city. Rather than accept the social implications of these first actions, the government then instituted programs for urban renewal for the rapidly deteriorating inner cities. Of similar social significance was the accelerated program of high-density public housing, located (until the Supreme Court prohibited it) in already predominantly poor sections of the city.

Given the current realization by many professionals and an increasing number of governmental agencies that the design process needs radical improvement, what alternatives are there? There are on the surface three approaches:

Choice One: Stop building, or delay building as long as possible until better data is available upon which to design buildings. Surely the issue between density and congestion ought to be clarified along with a host of other significant behavioral issues. There is merit to such an argument and the stop building movement has been launched informally, in any case, by the National Council on Crime and Delinquency (NCCD), by environmentalists, and by community groups. Ada Louise Huxtable in *Will They Ever Finish Bruckner Boulevard?*[14] describes the blocking of two projects by irate citizens: the Columbia Gym and the Harlem State Office Building. In essence the neighbors blocked these projects because they questioned the motives of Columbia University and the federal government in building these buildings; surely the wishes of those who would live adjacent to them were not adequately considered. A seemingly irrefutable human fact was brought up in the case of the office building: subtracting a full city block from an otherwise continuous residential neighborhood would radically alter the patterns of living in the blocks remaining.

A proper process of building must begin with the possibility of not building. Design requires that the building be justified in the first place. Certainly if "stop building" means thinking through building and alternatives to building, then it has merit. But building will continue regardless of the behavioral failures! A policy based on ceasing to build is bound

[14] Ada Louise Huxtable, *Will They Ever Finish Bruckner Boulevard?* (New York: Macmillan, 1970).

to fail. It is a necessary position to take for dramatic impact, just as studies of utopian solutions to tomorrow's city are important studies, if for no other reason than to dramatize options. But building will not stop; it will hardly even abate despite severe economic conditions.

Choice Two: Use the powers of the federal and state government to better regulate building. This proposal has merit as well, particularly at a time when the form of regulations is undergoing major revision. Codes have traditionally been "specification" codes, that is, they spell out in specific detail what can and cannot be done. (For example, concrete block is specified in certain fire zones for certain types of buildings.) Today, specifications may give the performance objectives without indicating any specific material. Further guidelines regulating building *design* are increasingly presented as Design Guides. A Design Guide describes what the intent of the building is in functional terms but avoids developing one definite plan that must be followed.

However, the governmental control mechanisms are almost useless in directing the design partners of the owner and the architect to a well-balanced, humane solution. For example, HUD developed Land-Use Intensity Charts, known as LUI, or the "Louie Scale," to determine acceptable amounts of open space for successful developments.

A number of years ago I attended a week-long seminar sponsored by the developers of the LUI scale to see if the scale could have a cost-of-building dimension. For example, the LUI scale suggested that high-rise buildings, which cost more to build than low-rise buildings, must have greater open space than low-rise buildings since they cover less ground area. Recreation space, parking space, open space were all calculated on the scale and a prospective owner of a high-density project (perhaps a housing authority or a private owner for middle-income housing) could use the LUI scale to determine how much space was required for different configurations, different land coverages, and different building costs. We assembled to add the cost dimension to the LUI scale so that a comprehensive tool would be available to the profession. After a week of violent disagreement the conference adjourned, realizing as a body that the project was not feasible. What I learned, personally, had until that conference been ambiguous. The LUI scale was not based on any systematic behavioral data! The original scale had been developed by compiling open-space areas from floor plans and site plans of "successful" high-density projects. Why projects were deemed successful was never made clear. Data covering even superficial social and activity patterns, such as those discussed at LaClede Town, were not part of the scale. Yet the LUI scale had operated for years as if there were a direct connection between space and social activity!

In fairness to the scale, it did serve to weed out the schemes that were patently unworkable, and perhaps that is all the LUI scale was intended to accomplish. What actually occurred in practice was that owners and architects used the LUI guidelines to judge when they had a socially acceptable project! It is interesting to note that Pruitt-Igoe, completely abandoned by HUD only 16 years after it was designed, *ostensibly met* the LUI scale, since with all its failures it had a land coverage of only 10.38 percent of its 12.27 acres. The fact that the elementary school that was scheduled to open along with Pruitt (which was predominantly white in the beginning) did not materialize for a number of years and hence forced white families with children out, does not show up on the LUI scale.

Sophisticated planning decisions cannot be legislated by negative constraints, for while one or more problems may be avoided, others such as social organization cannot easily be quantified.

Even the much heralded Environmental Impact Statements required of developers to justify a major project have turned into a new kind of political constraint, with some estimating that it costs upwards of $250,000 to prepare an impact statement for a major development.

Choice Three: Change the design process by which buildings are built. Clearly this is the direction with greatest potential. Public opinion can be used briefly to direct attention to behavioral ills, but when the next incongruity presents itself, the last one is assumed somehow to have been solved and social pressure moves on. The government continues to protect health and safety, yet sophisticated issues of psychological and social health are not easily legislated. The design process, however, is the arena of building decision making, and the design process can be changed to be more responsive to human needs.

Conclusions

There is a direct link between social and physical decisions in society; many decisions made in the context of physical requirements become socially debilitating. Seldom is this connection fully acknowledged, so that a code requirement may work against the very social end it was written to serve. A case in point is the stipulation in the New York State Hospital Code (1967) that the minimum size of a double bedroom for the elderly in wheelchairs be 200 ft^2. A goal of the hospital is rehabilitation, yet the size of the room makes it impossible for even one undersized wheelchair to move about the room, much less two. The code was written without regard for this need, nor is there a feedback mechanism available to change the code when it is found wanting.

Divisions within society that cut inhabitants off from contact with the open society around them are particularly damaging, for not only are individuals thereby deprived of a variety of opportunities for personal growth but they are forced to interact with others equally restricted. While the physical dimension is not the cause of inequities, too often it is the means of perpetuating such inequities.

The major changes that are needed to make cities more humane must come from the climate of opinion of the society as a whole. However, a major first step in that direction can be achieved by acknowledging the role that building and city divisions play in creating inequities. More positively, we must acknowledge that the real test for success in a building is how well it supports a positive social environment.

I suggest that all physical configurations ultimately will fail in human terms unless there are commonly held convictions related to the goals of life and the culture that hold most people together. If the family, the nation, and the church were the centers of such social cohesion in the past, what will happen if each of these institutions is eroded and nothing new appears to replace them? Will the city become a series of fortifications guarding class from class, from night marauders who have no fear of life or death? How should one react to an advertisement in *The New York Times* that reads:

> Here am I, your special island in Palm Springs. The view of desert and mountains is spectacular. The life style: privileged, the atmosphere quiet and serene. The Security: maximum (the only road by auto to our island is guarded 24 hours a day).

2
The Current
Design Process

Building Roles

Three roles must be defined if the building process is to come to life. One, that of the architect who designs the building for the owner. Two, that of the owner who commissions the building and manages it after it is built. Three, that of regulatory government, local, state, or federal. Simply speaking, the architect, operating for the owner, works within the constraints of regulatory government as expressed through deed restrictions, zoning laws, health, fire, and building codes. As every architect is well aware, the profession of architecture is licensed by the state to protect health and safety.

With the three major role players defined, it can be stated that each element in the physical environment, whether it be a building or a new highway system, is the product of three things:

1. The need of the owner, defined by the owner
2. The regulatory guidelines of the governmental agencies protecting health and safety
3. The experience and insight of the architect as expressed in the design.

If change is to occur within the building process, it is going to occur within the existing roles of these partners to design. (It is unlikely that social scientists, no matter how telling their observations, will influence the design of many buildings unless they influence one or more of the building partners.) A temporarily outraged public may clamor for reform in the building of detention homes in Texas following a series of grim exposés, but the clamor will be ineffective if it does not influence the owner, the architect, or the regulatory government. John Gardner, founder of Common Cause, stresses the need to identify the operating forces within the society that make activities occur. In the building industry architects, working within the constraints imposed by regulatory bodies, are situated in the key role of implementors of design needs developed traditionally by the owners.

Owners will ask that architects design what is economically sound, socially useful, aesthetically pleasing or some combination thereof. Regulatory agencies will control, through a series of prohibitions or incentives, the physical health and safety aspects of a building. Architects will design within the accepted norms of the profession and the aspirations of the community as a whole as they perceive them. If change is to occur in the building process, it could occur by a dramatic change in society's needs, or by a shift in economics that will make certain building forms more or less feasible. These shifts would influence owners in establishing their needs. Change could occur by legislation. Or change could occur by influencing the architects who are the active, on-going participants in building after building. Without belittling changes that have occurred through rapid shifts in the climate of opinion or through government regulations, it seems reasonable to assume that the major developments in design will continue to take place within the profession of architecture, defined broadly to include the field of design professionals.

How architects design is a product of the theory they use in design and the procedure society has established for producing buildings. Since theory can be changed or influenced without major upheaval, the question of theory will be discussed second. The question of procedures comes first.

The current design procedure is well illustrated by the standard contract document produced by The American Institute of Architects (AIA). While the document is basically sound, it exemplifies the two major weaknesses in the design process today, the lack of both a programming phase and a feedback phase. The omission of these phases in turn points to the physical bias of architecture, giving little direct attention to the needs of inhabitants as dynamic beings moving in time and space.

Programming is presented in AIA documents as the responsibility of the client. "The Owner shall provide full information, including a complete program, regarding his requirements for the project." The architect is required to confirm such a program in preparing schematic designs, but the word "confirm" hardly suggests a major role in developing a data base for alternatives that might include not building at all. Additional programming steps may be undertaken by the architect, if requested specifically by the owner. Payment for such services is listed as an additional service, under Article 1.3. It will be shown in discussing the behavioral design process in Chapter 8 that architects traditionally receive little remuneration for programming activities as currently envisioned. Yet it is precisely the programming phase that introduces behavioral data. If it is not introduced in the beginning, it cannot be effective in directing design, for basic and irrevocable decisions will have been made without considering behavior.

There is no feedback phase in the current process. Systems logic, increasingly effective in developing a cause-and-effect relationship between decision making and response, requires a feedback step. But there is not one in architecture! Not only is feedback lacking but there does not seem to be widespread understanding in the architectural profession of the role it might play. Award juries are not instructed to question the users of buildings. Awards are given when buildings are first occupied, and often data on use are not available. There is a 7-year cutoff date, so that buildings older than 7 years are not even eligible for many awards.

Similarly, architects interviewed for new jobs are asked to make verbal and visual presentations. Often three or more architects are interviewed by a board in one sitting, ostensibly to compare their abilities. Seldom are the buildings which architects design considered in terms of their social success. They are visited, perhaps, to see the physical characteristics of the building; they are seldom visited to find out how well they actually work. If a building leaks and the occasional review board visiting a building notices such leaks, it is an anxious moment for an architect although more often than not he has no responsibility for the leak. Whether or not the building is a positive or negative environment in human terms is difficult to compute in strictly visual terms, so the leak becomes more important than the social quality.

Feedback requires an orderly review of the building after it has been occupied and is functioning. A feedback document is not even mentioned as an additional service in the AIA standard contract documents.

During the design development and construction document phases, the architect is directed by a series of zoning and code regulations. Ostensibly these codes are written to protect health and safety and, in turn, the implication is that if health and safety are protected, the environment is healthy. Bringing this false logic to the surface is a vital step in clarifying the failure of the current design process. Codification may document all the things one should not do and still be far short of exemplifying what one should do. At best, codes avoid problem solutions; at worst, they compound problems by suggesting that all situations are the same.

One might feel that architects are trained to include behavior in all decisions and that the intuitive sensitivity of the designer can be relied upon. While I admit that there are many sensitive designers and that their intuition is considerable, it is also apparent that the architectural profession as a whole solves building problems by rules of thumb, few of which are ostensibly concerned with behavior, yet each of which indirectly and haphazardly affects behavior.

Listed below are some rule-of-thumb solutions. While every architect may not agree that these are the most important ones, surely each architect could develop a personal list that would endure.

Rules of Thumb—without Behavior

1. Spans between 20 and 30 ft are economical for structure loading; therefore bearing walls or columns should be placed between 20 and 30 ft apart.

2. Deep bays are more economical than shallow bays, for the ratio of usable bay space to corridor is improved.

3. Doubled-loaded corridors are more economical than single-loaded corridors, for the usable bay space to corridor ratio is twice that of a single-loaded scheme.

4. Rectilinear geometrics allow close-packing without wasted space, ease in repetition, ease in framing, and ease in dimensioning.

5. Grouping of like elements simplifies framing and simplifies servicing; for example, in grouping all bedrooms together, the bathrooms can be arranged back to back.

6. Corridors between spaces in a double-loaded scheme are ideally suited to carry the air-conditioning ductwork, which runs down the corridor and serves rooms on both sides.

7. A break on the exterior of a building is more expensive than a straight wall.

8. Changes of material require flashing details; hence, there is an additional cost in using more than one material.

9. Operating windows are more expensive than fixed glass. They also require screens if they are to be used extensively.

10. Windows come in standard sizes. It is more economical to keep all the window sizes standard to avoid a premium for custom sizes.

11. Use of a roof as a sitting deck requires a different structural loading than a roof not designed for people. Also, a sitting roof is more expensive to waterproof and requires a door rather than a window for access.

12. Underground parking, even half underground, is more expensive than surface parking.

13. Repetitive design is easier to build and easier to draw. Repetitive buildings are produced for less fee; thus a fee for a shopping center is less than the fee for a private home. The degree of repetition is implied even before the architect begins drawing, for the fee is based on the implied degree of complexity.

14. Codes, particularly in residential subdivisions, specify the following: setbacks, the size of house allowable, the number of stories allowable, the percentage of brick required (often 51 percent), the height of

fences (generally 5 ft), the homogeneity of housing (no variation in a particular housing or building zone).

15. In commercial and institutional buildings, every room on a floor above grade must have two separate fire exits, neither of which is more than 100 ft away from a given space. This regulation determines the placement of fire stairs.

16. Fire stairs must exit directly outside. Most decorative 2-story stairs do not count.

17. Low-speed hydraulic elevators will service five floors. For more than five floors more costly electric elevators are required; therefore 5-story buildings have an economic plus.

18. Mixed occupancy in a building is much more difficult to service than single occupancy; for example, placing a kitchen in a building requires a service drive and so forth. This fact, coupled with the fact that large central dining facilities are easier to administer than small scattered ones, tends to favor the large, single dining hall.

19. Many materials come in sheets 4 ft wide and 8 ft high. Most residential buildings use a standard 8-ft-high ceiling, partly because materials come in this size.

20. Air conditioning can extend approximately 30 ft without disturbing the air circulation in the room. This fact limits the width of rooms when air conditioning is placed in the vertical wall.

21. An individual thermostat in each room is more costly than one thermostat for a series of rooms.

22. Movable partitions are more costly than fixed partitions, aside from the cost of moving them.

23. Stacked baths are more economical than scattered baths for they can use a common vent.

None of these twenty-three rules of thumb *directly* involves behavioral considerations, yet each will affect some aspect of the behavior of people using the buildings designed by means of these rules. An architect may be the most responsive designer available; he or she may want to provide variety in the living environment by using more than one material, utilizing setbacks that stagger an otherwise monolithic and scaleless wall, using individual thermostats so the occupants can determine their own room temperature, and providing for flexibility, anticipating changes in the years to come. He or she may design with all these concepts based on anticipated behavior, yet each design idea could be canceled by any of the rules of thumb listed above. Cost will always be a factor in evaluating buildings and cost must be documented at each stage of building development. The point is, under the current design process, which has little or no quantification of behavioral data, there is no procedure for making human values coequal with physical constraints. A chicken coop is the cheapest building to build, because the chicken does not move from its cage throughout its life. If cost alone is the criterion for judgment of alternatives in design, "chicken coop," inhumane design prevails.

Funding

According to the current design process, appropriations for construction are made at a different time and by a different procedure from funds for programs or maintenance. Therefore, a federal or state agency may appropriate funds to build an institution with the anticipation that needed programs will be funded by the state or Congress to support the institution properly. It was suggested in Chapter 1 that a building once built generates its use, whether it is appropriate for the needs envisioned or not. Since appropriations can vary, the possibility exists that programs required to make an environment viable will never be funded; for instance, funds for education and counseling in a home for the retarded, or funds for rehabilitation in a veteran's hospital. The problem goes well beyond the architecture. It is an issue of social irresponsibility, brought on by the political vicissitudes of legislative bodies. Requiring accountability in the design process of architecture will not in itself solve the problem of inadequate or erratic funding. However, it will help remove architecture as a confederate in perpetrating inequities. A document that explicitly states particular social programs needed if the purpose of a building is to be served must be developed as part of the programming phase. If such programs are not forthcoming, feedback on the building will make the matter clear—an indication of how programming and feedback can work together to achieve social accountability.

Shortcomings

Recapping the failure of the current design process, the following elements are involved:

1. The program is specifically considered the owner's responsibility, suggesting strongly that a professional programming team including social scientists is superfluous.

2. When architects are asked to develop programs with the owner, the fee schedule for such work is insufficient to cover consultation.

3. Architects are often chosen on the informal precondition that they affirm the program, very often developed by others, leading to a superficial acceptance on the first and crucial decision, i.e., to build in the first place.

4. Users are not principal members of the design team, except as their role is interpreted through the administrative staff. While this is an acceptable format for uncomplicated buildings, it overlooks the profile of the actual users in institutions, a profile that may suggest goals different from those of the administration.

5. Most significantly, there is no feedback to check that the assumptions used in designing the building were indeed valid.

6. While the profession is becoming explicit in expressing physical design assumptions, quantification of behavioral information is almost universally lacking.

Advocacy Planning—Words and Weakness

Advocacy planning suggests that the user, if not represented personally, is represented through an advocate. The phrase, widely used in planning and design circles, suggests that the user has become represented in general building programs, when indeed only well-publicized experiments have actually materialized. The fact that advocacy planning has stirred such interest attests to the widespread recognition that behavioral failure has occurred in buildings and in cities and that one cause is the lack of proper user input.

The best-known experiment in advocacy planning was sponsored by the federal government in the 1970s through the Office of Economic Opportunity (OEO) and Model Cities programs dealing with design at an urban scale.

Six advocacy programs are described in detail in E. M. Blecher's *Advocacy Planning for Urban Development.*[1]

The term *advocacy planning* was coined by Paul Davidoff in his article "Advocacy and Pluralism in Planning."[2] Addressing himself to the planning profession and the then-current practice of urban planning, Davidoff rejected the notion of value-free planning. In tune with the new mood of the 1970s regarding urban decision-making and participation processes, he reiterated the idea that "appropriate planning action cannot be prescribed from a position of value neutrality, for prescriptions are based on desired objectives." He called for the development of a planning practice that "openly invites political and social values to be examined and debated" and stated that "acceptance of this position means rejection of

[1] Earl M. Blecher, *Advocacy Planning for Urban Development* (New York: Praeger, 1971), Special Studies in United States Economic and Social Development, pp. 121–122.

[2] Paul Davidoff, "Advocacy and Pluralism in Planning," *Journal of American Institute of Planners,* vol. 31, no. 4, November 1965. Reprinted by permission of the Journal of the American Institute of Planners.

prescription for planning which would have the planner act solely as a technician."[2]

The concept was that the user in an urban situation was most often poor and politically incapable. By organizing an advocacy planning approach the planner became an advocate; ideally if the advocate were powerful enough, he would build an organization to wield greater power. With these concepts in mind, six demonstration projects were funded to determine how effective funded advocacy planning could be in bringing about change. In order to test the effectiveness of various organizational formats, two different formats were developed.

> The existence of two distinct types of advocacy planning organizations (one controlled and operated by professionals and one controlled and operated by the non-professional poor) brought into focus for OEO a number of assumptions that needed to be tested. It was assumed that the professionals in the professionally based organizations possessed technical competence; what OEO questioned was their responsiveness to the poor. Where the planning was controlled and conducted by the poor, it was assumed that the organizations would be responsive to the client's needs; what OEO questioned was their competence and ability to carry out planning functions.[3]

Three models for advocacy planning organization were developed as illustrated by models A, B, and C in Figure 2.1. Success in achieving goals was greater in the model A format than in those of models B and C, because the model A format conformed more readily to the current operating format of professions and was thus able to attract greater support.

Formats B and C, which were developed by the government to test the abilities of the poor to administer, were less successful, partly because neither format conformed with accepted professional independence, partly because of bureaucratic slowness. In any case, the usefulness of advocacy planning activities was disappointing. It was summed up by Blecher who stated:

> The success of a client group in achieving the output of a specific urban development project is to a large extent a function of the environmental resources available. In addition, project success in this realm necessitates relatively long periods of time for implementation to become actualized. Thus, such specific achievements by the various advocacy planning programs were not as numerous or widespread as had been anticipated. . . .
>
> Success at this type of project impact was found in projects that were relatively small in size and scope and dealt primarily with issues in physical planning projects for parks and recreation, housing rehabilitation, and public works. The total number of such successes was few.[4]

---

[3] Ibid.
[4] Blecher, op. cit.

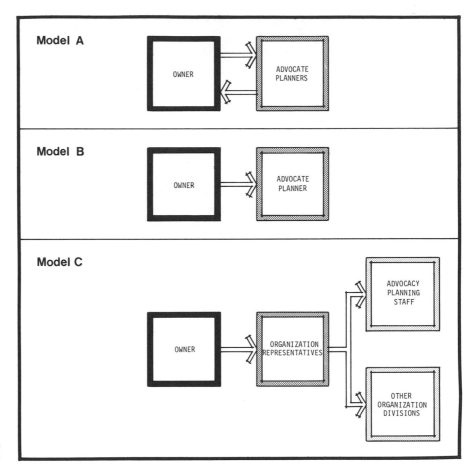

Fig. 2.1 Model advocate planner.

The comments above, while limited to one source, do confirm my personal experience with advocacy planning in a Model City area in Houston. Rather than dwell on situations of bureaucratic frustration, let me suggest that the advocacy planning process will surely fail if the user is represented by an advocate working apart from the design team.

Conclusions

The current design process involves three principal roles: the owner, the architect, and the regulatory government. Behavioral data are not currently developed and quantified for a building or planning project, nor is feedback a part of the process. The user of buildings is not, with rare exceptions, a participant in the design process. The owner often is represented by an agent in design meeting, but the agent almost always represents the administrative staff of a building, not the served occupants. Codes and zoning do not take the place of meaningful behavioral data, for a host of negatives does not define creative and sensitive design. Without justification for humane design concepts the cost efficiencies of "chicken coop" design maintain. Advocacy planning, looked to by some to solve the problem of user input, has not been successful. Even had experiments worked magnificently, the format of advocacy planning still placed the advocate outside the design process rather than as an integral part of it; the advocate became a critic not a doer. Advocacy planning, therefore, was not a format broad enough to affect the vast majority of buildings.

Procedures are interrelated with theory. It would be hard to argue which came first, the theory or the procedure that implements the theory. If there is social failure in the building field, and I feel it can be documented that there is, and if the current design process perpetuates such failures, then the theory behind the procedures and the product will also be found lacking.

3
Six
Fallacies

Theory in architecture is all-important, for it is the theory behind design that is taught in schools; hence it is theory that perpetuates theory. Changes occur, but normally not rapidly even though change may desperately be needed. Aside from behavioral interests, there are three main directions in today's theory. The first is a continuation of the Modern Movement with a largely aesthetic involvement. Jacquelin Robertson in an article commenting on one school of aesthetic theory states:

> Architect X has a field day with Corbusier's nautical motif, but with confusing results. Both his houses are literally crawling inside and out with a sort of nasty modern ivy in the way of railings, metal trellises, unexplained pipe, exposed beams, inexplicable and obtuse tubes—most to no apparent real or architectural purpose.

Finally, Robertson sums up the current trend in aesthetic architectural design style when he says:

> . . . As a result of all of the above, the style, unpopular from the outset, is not now in good health, and is only being maintained by the intravenous feeding of the "art world."[1]

A second, well-publicized direction in architecture is marked by a preoccupation with the banal. While it is necessary to recognize the visual signs of today for what they are, I find it hard to affirm the appearance of Las Vegas (see Figures 3.1 and 3.2). It leaves the issue of design theory in question at best, in abeyance at worst, and the effect is to dissipate in art terms what should instead be directed toward the practice of the profession.

A third direction is toward utopia. There has always been an architecture of utopia and it fulfills a particular niche in theory by exploring alternatives constrained only by the creative imagination. The danger of utopia, particularly in the followers who forget the context of the model, is

[1] Jacquelin Robertson, "Five on Five (Machines in the Garden)," *Forum*, p. 53, May 1973.

well expressed by John Lobel, of Pratt Institute, writing about Soleri. (See Figure 3.3.)

> Having learned these lessons, many humanists are now turning to Soleri's cities as solutions. But Soleri's cities compound every problem we know of. These gigantic, concentric, beehive structures will require rigid programmed conformity from their inhabitants in order to function safely. They will require a complexity of technology which may not even be possible, and the level of dependence on technology will imply a rule by the technocrats. A power failure would mean chaos for tens of thousands of trapped residents. Strikes and other antisocial actions and attitudes would have to be strictly outlawed, for they too could quickly lead to mass disruption.
>
> These giant cities are complete and closed systems. For example, there is no room to introduce a new transportation system if an existing one proves obsolete or unworkable. Worst of all is the symmetrical centrality of these designs. Once the center is occupied by an institution (government media, education, etc.), there is no way to replace that institution once it grows old and unresponsive. . . .
>
> I do not doubt the sincerity of Soleri and his supporters. I simply see something very different from what they see when I look at his architecture.[2]

Fig. 3.1 Fountain with statues, Las Vegas, Nevada.

Fig. 3.2 Pop art in Las Vegas, Nevada.

The purpose of this discussion is not to refute other directions in theory but to suggest that they are insufficient to guide a profession in a time of rapid change and increasing comprehensiveness.

At this point, I would *like* to present a simple theory of behavioral design that could succinctly supplant other theories of design. I cannot. In fact, one of the major stumbling blocks to implementation of behavioral architecture is the widespread misunderstanding about behavior in buildings. How *does* architecture affect behavior? What *is* the responsibility of the architect?

Listed below are six fallacies about architecture and behavior. To air the issues and build a positive climate for a new design process, we must put to rest the half-truths commonly held about behavior and design. In place of these fallacies what is espoused by this book is not a different configuration of words with a more precise meaning but rather a technique that quantifies behavior and a design process that implements behavioral techniques.

Fallacy 1—Designer Fallacy

The first fallacy I call the Designer Fallacy because architectural designers have fallen into this trap consistently over the years. Essentially it is the fallacy of architectural determinism which operates as if architecture directly determines behavior through design (with no influence from the

[2] John Lobell, "Editor's Comment," *The New York Times,* August 23, 1970. Copyright © 1970 by The New York Times Company. Reprinted by permission.

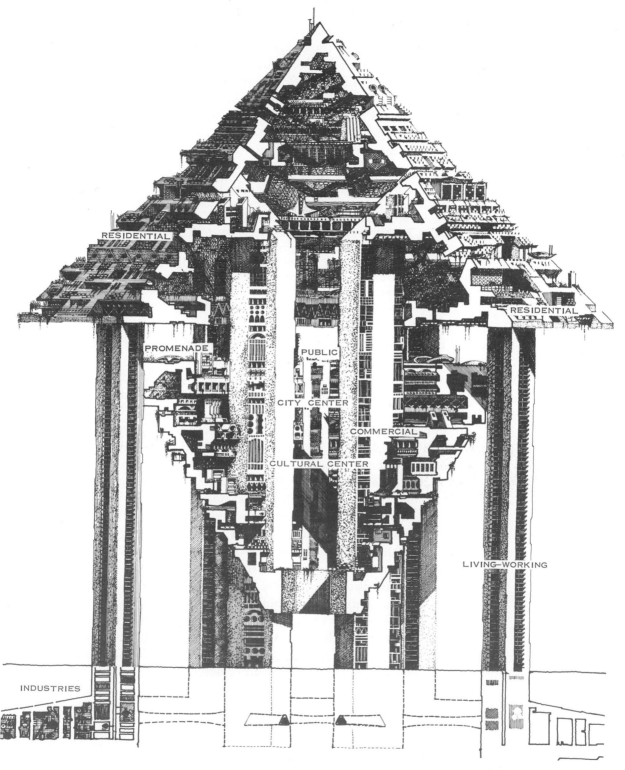

RESIDENTIAL

RESIDENTIAL

PROMENADE

PUBLIC

CITY CENTER

COMMERCIAL

CULTURAL CENTER

LIVING-WORKING

INDUSTRIES

Fig. 3.3 Arcology hexahedron, a scheme for a population of 170,000. [Ivan Pinter: Cosanti Foundation; from Paolo Soleri, Arcology: The City in the Image of Man (Cambridge: MIT Press, 1969).]

social mores directing behavior). In this fallacy social organization is not considered particularly important, and community mores, if considered at all, are considered fixed. While most readers will go far beyond this point of view in attitude and practice, it is essential to recognize that the profession of architecture is laced through with deterministic thought. A few blatant examples may clarify how pervasive this fallacy really is. In describing plans for the construction of jails, the following is stated concerning day rooms:

> All plumbing is located in the day room. The operational plan of this unit would call for vacating the sleeping room in the morning after which it would be closed. This immediately reduces the supervision area, keeps food out of the sleeping quarters, and permits free access to plumbing facilities, which include, in each unit a toilet, a lavatory, a urinal, one shower and a slop sink. The day room should be equipped with tables and chairs for eating, reading and such games as are permitted. By locating the plumbing fixtures at the front of the day room and limiting the utilities space for the piping to a height of 4 feet, and by enclosing the shower with transparent glass block, supervision is greatly facilitated. *Bad practices, always inherent around these facilities, can thus be minimized.*[3] [Italics mine.]

What is most dangerous about the Designer Fallacy is that the designer, as quoted above, somehow feels if he can conceive of behavior his design will assure it. The image the above quotation brings to mind is repugnant, an image of inmates defecating in public while others adjacent to them eat and play cards. It is repugnant when the human behavior of all those present comes to mind to replace the architect's conception. Behavior is no longer a neat package when the total population of the day room is superimposed on the theoretical behavior of an individual.

Fallacy 1 encourages architects to leave out any thought of the social organization of a building. They need not concern themselves with the staff of a building, their training, the scheduling of activities, or the variation of activities throughout the day or throughout the year. If it is possible for certain behavior to occur, it will, but the responsibility to consider social organization is seen outside the design process.

A second quotation from a more emancipated and well-meaning article on prisons I find equally disturbing. It is an admission that social organization does play a part in the neat package of architecture and behavior, but the statement implies that the architect has *no right* to assume good management practices will prevail in the building. The design described here might best be termed the result of defensive planning.

> The California "isolation promotion" cells, for which the inmates carry their own keys, are designed in a rather interesting manner for single occupancy.

[3] U.S. Bureau of Prisons, *Handbook of Correctional Institution Design and Construction* (Washington: U.S. Government Printing Office, 1949), p. 172.

These designs, officials advise me, were deliberately intended to make it difficult for a later administration to house more than one inmate in the cell, as an alternative to constructing additional housing units, if the prisons become overcrowded. The cells in the 'North Facility' at Soledad are square, with the wall which has a window (plumbing and the door prevent use of the other sides for the cot). Therefore replacing the single cot by a double deck cot would mean blocking the window.[4]

It is a sad commentary that defensive action seems to be an acceptable alternative to determining what is allowable use of architectural space. While it would be against the law for an administrator to burn down a building or destroy the air-conditioning plant, *it is not against the law to put more than one human being in a space designed for one human being* even though it may be immoral, unhealthy, and inhumane!

One cell can be designed to house one individual, but unless the cell is maintained for one individual and only one, it cannot function humanely. When the *possibility* of change is considered, then the social organization is considered and the fallacy of direct architectural behavior becomes apparent. The Designer Fallacy of a direct architecture/behavior link leads to a common practice in architectural design. Often the architect or owner will "make up" behavioral patterns to justify preconceived design ideas. When the building is completed, there is never a check to see if the assumed behavior did in fact occur; rather the building is evaluated aesthetically, that is, it is evaluated through photographs.

Another example seems in order. My firm was asked to design a Montessori school for young children on a narrow lot. The client arrived with a preconceived solution; to wit, the rooms for the younger children were placed directly behind the rooms for the older children. Since the lot was not wide enough to bring a drive past the first rooms (or so the owner thought), he had developed an imaginative solution. He proposed a second-level corridor that would run across the classrooms of the older children. Young children would arrive, go upstairs to the ramp and then downstairs into their space behind. I pointed out that by reproportioning the rooms a drive could be placed to give direct access to the rooms behind; the owner was crestfallen. His imaginative scheme of a raised corridor was no longer justified. In the next meeting, however, the owner for the first time presented a change in the program. In this meeting he made a great point of the need for viewing the children without the viewers' being seen. Having children in another Montessori school myself, I had been impressed by the visiting program our school had developed. It allowed a few parents at a time to come and to sit with the children on the little chairs and become inconspicuously part of the operation, allowing the

[4] Daniel Glaser, *The Effectiveness of a Prison and Parole System* (Indianapolis: Bobbs-Merrill, 1964). Copyright © 1964 by The Bobbs-Merrill Company, Inc. Reprinted by permission of the publishers.

children to show unselfconsciously what they were about. It seemed strange to me, therefore, that such a stress was being made on the newly arrived at requirement for *unseen* viewing. It became clear, however, when the owner enthusiastically suggested that the raised walkway (now discredited as a means of access) would be ideal as a means of private surveillance. The owner had changed the program to justify his design!

How many times does this happen? How often is the architect, rather than the owner, responsible for these shifts? It is my contention that such manipulation of behavioral needs is sadly widespread in the architectural profession. Needless to say the raised walkway would look great in photographs!

Architecture creates moods, architecture defines activity areas, but architecture by itself cannot determine behavior.

Fallacy 2—Genius Fallacy

It seems almost disloyal to suggest criticism of recognized geniuses but actually the Genius Fallacy is not involved with the genius in question as much as it is with the imprecision of his followers. I find blind emulation of a design figure objectionable largely because I am convinced that it cuts off creativity. Having thus stated my predilection, I feel free in suggesting that the Genius Fallacy is more common outside the design profession than in it. As a part of America's art-myth syndrome, the American public is generally uncritical of an architect who clearly has shown ability considerably beyond the ordinary.

To discuss again the behavioral flaws in Le Corbusier's Unité d'Habitation block may seem sophomoric to sophisticated professionals well aware of the issues involved. But a new generation of students and a continuing large percentage of the general public approach Corbusier's work uncritically. Others have traced the design concept of the Unité d'Habitation block to the general concept of high-rise urban towers built by architects in the United States generations later; but I was concerned to find in the Webbe high-rise building we analyzed in St. Louis a skip-floor scheme that seemed particularly reminiscent of the Marseilles apartment block. The brilliant solution he developed there used a skip-floor elevator and two-floor apartments he called Maisonettes. The alternate floors provided the bedrooms for the apartment entered on the floor below. In Webbe we found that a similar skip-floor scheme was used, with the elevator stopping on the first, fifth, and eighth floors of a 9-story building. But all apartments were single-floor apartments so that people going to the ninth, seventh, sixth, and fourth floors were required to enter an unsecured corridor, walk to unsecured fire stairs and go up or down one floor to their apartments (see Figure 3.4). In simplified terms, the inhabitability

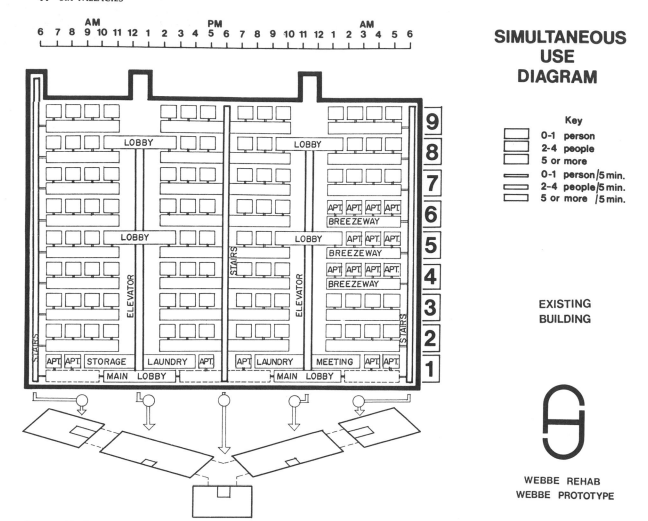

Fig. 3.4　Skip-floor elevator diagram showing the necessity of using unprotected fire stairs.

of these units could be traced directly to a scheme of elevators that created a behavioral disaster.

A bad adaptation of a recognized milestone design is certainly no basis for criticism of the milestone itself or of the genius creating it. However, the Genius Fallacy, does exist when each new generation of architects looks at the work of great designers uncritically. What it really points up is the lack of a recognized technique of feedback that could analyze buildings after they were built to ascertain if the assumptions were valid over time.

Fallacy 3—Common Man Fallacy

This fallacy is best stated in the simple phrase: ''Architecture has *no significant* affect on behavior.'' This position is held more widely than Fallacy 1, for Fallacy 3 is the Common Man Fallacy. The common man mouths this fallacy when he states, "Give poor people a good house and they will mess it up in no time." Or this phrase, thrown at architects in cynical disregard of their social good intentions: "Why do you architects keep talking about design? Poor people need jobs; they couldn't care less about where they live if they are unemployed and hungry." It is the Common Man Fallacy that architecture has *no affect* on behavior that leads politicians to separate building programs from social programs and to locate institutions politically instead of analyzing the behavioral implications of location. "Why provide a public room? It won't be used anyway," so the cynical legislator argues.

That there is a thread of truth to their cynicism makes the fallacy all the more difficult to refute. Time and again poor people do tear up their sanitized apartments. Jim Weber, a policeman in St. Louis who had the Pruitt-Igoe beat for a number of years, describes an incident pointing up this fact. He was called time and again to investigate a strong odor coming from one of the apartments. He investigated to find a very amenable black couple newly arrived in St. Louis who were more than anxious to be helpful. In the bathroom he found the toilet and tub filled to overflowing with excrement. He was furious that the seemingly cooperative couple had failed to report their plumbing failure, until he tried the flush valve on the toilet and found it worked perfectly. No one had told the family how to use the facilities and they were too docile to ask.

No one considered the necessity of explaining to the tenants how to use the building, for behavior and architecture were separate entities to the administration.

Lest I be accused of making up straw men by these fallacies the more easily to shoot them down, it is well to consider again the complete separation between building appropriations and social service appropriations in legislation written across the country. If the climate of opinion really accepted the interdependence of architecture and behavior, could it continue to thoughtlessly fund buildings and services separately?

During our investigation of Webbe, I became aware that an elevator serving twelve floors of an occupied building in the complex had been inoperative for 9 months. The social implications of this fact can only be imagined. In fact, everyone living in this wing of the building was required to walk across the floor to the other elevator shaft daily, or to climb up the fire escape, often the full height of the building. It seemed incredible to me at the time that a vertical corridor (which is what an elevator really is) could be left inoperative in a seemingly routine manner. Investigation pointed up a number of facts:

1. Teen-aged kids destroyed elevators ritually. One prize technique

was breaking the door of the cab, pulling the cables from under the cab, and sticking them through the window. When the kids pushed the "up" button and hopped out, the cab would rise and pull out its own cables!

2. There were so many entrances and exits at Webbe that there was no way of keeping surveillance on the elevator cabs.

3. The manufacturer guaranteed the elevator for normal service repairs and when the warranty ran out (or when teen-aged boys destroyed the elevator), there was no money to repair the elevator until routine maintenance funds could be allocated. (If, of course, repair of the elevator was given high enough priority for the limited funds available.)

4. I visited the research director of Otis Elevator Co., and strongly suggested that the current trend toward vandalism, mugging, and destruction in elevators in low-income housing projects would surely limit the number of elevators ordered for such projects in years to come. I cited the recent decision by the Missouri legislature after the disasters of St. Louis high-rise living to allow only small, scattered-site low-income projects in the future and no high-rise buildings except for the elderly. I suggested that a manufacturer might reverse this trend by *guaranteeing* service. The Otis executives immediately countered that this would put the manufacturer in the management business, and even if they were interested in setting up such a program, it would be useless, because the federal government made no provision for special maintenance features in awarding elevator contracts.

It is the author's contention that behind each step in such an investigation, beginning with the legislation that authorized the housing, provided for maintenance, and specified elevators, at each step the Common Man Fallacy was at work. Somehow there was no difference in hardware to middle-income families and the very poor. Hardware was one thing, behavior another. Poor people mess up nice buildings; if they wanted nice buildings they would keep them nice. In all such rationalization for a very distasteful status quo, no one considered the social implications of grouping 2,500 very poor families at a density of 44.4 units per acre, the essential social fact that the architecture created.

Fallacy 4—Open Society Fallacy

Fallacy 4 might be called the Open Society Fallacy. It is seldom implicitly stated any more for it is naïve. Unfortunately it is still behind a lot of rationalizations for the status quo, rationalizations that are easier to develop than significant change. The Open Society Fallacy says, "Yes, it must be tough to live in a slum, in a Webbe housing project, but it's still possible to make it. Look at Sammy Davis, Jr.!" This fuzzy argument says that there is enough choice even in an environment largely characterized as a jungle for the clean-cut, well-motivated to get ahead. *The geography of cities becomes a convenient method of establishing and maintaining separate and unequal social environments.* The refutation of the Open Society Fallacy is simply the statistics that relate areas of cities and indicators of human health and well-being. It is irrefutable that the vast majority of individuals growing up and being educated in deprived neighborhoods repeat the pattern of their parents. Recognition of this fact introduced the phrase ''the poverty cycle'' into social discussions. I believe that defining the problem in these terms has been a realistic step forward in understanding the dilemma of the poor. Perhaps the time will come when the extent of deprivation can be determined in graphic terms so that the inequalities built into the structure of cities can be recognized and eased.

In a society that did not end ''Jim Crow'' legal separations until 1954, it is regrettable but understandable that there is such difficulty in understanding the impact of physical location on human growth potential.

Fallacy 5—Manipulation Fallacy

In essence the argument of Fallacy 5 goes something like this: ''Sure, behavior is affected by architecture, sure, social organization is affected by architecture, but watch out, for planning creates cold, sterile environments and ultimately totalitarianism, the controlled world of 1984.'' Those espousing this Manipulation Fallacy point to the rigid regimentation of Fascist architecture or the endless repetition of housing blocks in the Soviet Union. (They overlook the equally rigid regimentation and endless repetition of housing in Queens, New York.)

I visited the City Planning Office for the City of Stockholm in 1973 and was shown a vast table full of high-rise buildings, which I assumed were the schematic models of *possible* land development. Later, in visiting new towns in the Stockholm area, I found that the models quite literally became the buildings; the planning was only slightly modified from cardboard to reality. The impression is hardly less totalitarian than housing built in the Soviet Union. Such experiences seem to lend credence to the Manipulation Fallacy that decries planning and its assumed concentration of power. The current interest in Las Vegas billboards and spontaneous architecture of all kinds seems to be a reaction against the overly ordered community.

In any case the Manipulation Fallacy is indeed just that: a mistaken view of planning. The basic repetitive constraints to the human environment, imposed not so much by human beings but by the geometry of existence and the force of gravity which keeps people two-dimensional, must be acknowledged. (That people can occasionally fly in a plane does not alter the constraint of their day-by-day two-dimensional environment.) The mystique of design has delayed the uncovering of systems of space definition, but they have been operational whether publicly understood or not. Manipulation of the environment has occurred throughout history: forts have been placed to control access through constricted passes; walls have been thrown around towns to protect the inhabitants from attack; undesirable people have been constrained in buildings that prevented escape; ghettoes have been maintained. History tells of towns being torn apart to provide greater public control as well as grandeur. Notable examples occurred when Pope Sixtus the Fifth restructured Rome to connect the Christian basilicas by straight avenues, and when Haussmann superimposed a radial pattern on Paris.

Each level of manipulation of space and the consequent control of behavior it imposed has been understood by *some* group of people. Many early Roman towns were engineered to have a dividing wall running down the center of the development. Slaves lived on one side of the wall, free men and Roman citizens on the other. The slaves were allowed access through openings reasonably adjacent to the households they served, yet were removed from sight and sound when not needed. The wall provided a simple, effective separation of the servant and the served. Rude planners of Roman communities were aware of this level of manipulation. In Early Christian churches the bones of martyrs were placed in the center of round buildings. One recognized value of the cross-in-plan format that developed in the Byzantine Church after the Early Christian era was that it made it possible to place the relics of the martyrs in niches, and thus place the altar of Christ in the center. Certainly the "better fit" of this church form was recognized by early church builders and priests.

Today these simple examples of manipulation of space and the subsequent effect of social organization/behavior have only historic value. What is needed in a highly urbanized society is an overview of systems and their effect on human activity developed for complex, urban situations. The development of a proper theory base for such planning design is a sure way of avoiding undue power, for it places the precepts of design in the public domain. The indirect way that behavior is affected today by the manipulation of buildings is a far more dangerous activity, for the premises are concealed, the motives obscure, and those controlling design anonymous. To pretend that complex cities can develop, grow, and change without a clear definition of the underlying systems that structure the city is romance not reality. Planning occurs; the challenge of this century is to make sure it is humane.

Fallacy 6—Know-Nothing Fallacy

The sixth fallacy is the Know-Nothing Fallacy. It is widely held by pragmatic administrators who were once idealistic and have had their fond dreams shattered by frustration. The premise of this fallacy is simply that it is all too complicated! Yes, there is merit to the basic thesis, some would say, but it is hard enough to get a building in on budget now, much less waste time contemplating whether or not there should ever be a building.

This Know-Nothing Fallacy becomes another rationalization for the current, haphazard status quo. Granting the difficulty of any change, I believe that the refutation of this fallacy can be seen within the professions themselves, where serious efforts are being directed to solving these considerable difficulties.

Summary

Theory in architecture has concentrated on aesthetics, or glorified the expression of the ordinary, or looked to utopian tomorrows. A more meaningful theory focusing on people's needs, seen dynamically, is hampered by half-truths about the relationship between behavior and buildings. Human beings are not directly affected by architecture, for the social organization that motivates them must be considered. On the other hand, it is false to suggest there is no connection between behavior and design decisions, for decisions determine lifetime configurations of people. And the genius cannot be uncritically followed, for genius in form giving does not automatically mean genius in social ordering. Other common fallacies suggest that the society is completely open, or accept the connection between form and behavior but fear regimentation, conveniently forgetting that regimentation occurs nonetheless but is unaccountable. Finally, it is easy when faced with the complexity of the problem to throw up our hands and look the other way, feeling there can be no solution.

Architects cannot stand still in the matter of theory, for they are forced to build; that is their role in society. They cannot stand aside. The question of behavioral architecture cannot be ignored. Hopefully, it will be both understood and implemented.

For me the most telling criticism of architectural theory and practice comes not from an architect but from a sociologist. It is his criticism that underscores most precisely the urgent need for change.

> As a sociologist, given my background and training, I find it amazing and wonderful that architects are willing and able to design buildings given the fragmentary character of the knowledge in terms of which they must proceed. I have asked myself how it is possible for them to do it. The answer I give to this question is itself sociological. Architects are able to be good designers because our society has thrown up the culture of architecture and created a social

role in which the individual who adopts this culture and fulfills its demands is rewarded. If the individual who is an architect manages to design buildings that work reasonably well, that stand up and are pleasant to the eye, he gets paid a regular salary, he can become a member of a chartered society, and he earns the respect of colleagues and the admiration of the nation. If he should prove incapable of proposing a building that meets these standards, if he balks at the fact that he is being asked to commit himself to a plan without sufficient knowledge on which to base that plan, then he doesn't get a job as an architect, he doesn't get the respect of his colleagues, and he cannot put the initials ARIBA or AIA after his name. To put it in another way, we can say that the social role, ''architect,'' and the culture, ''architecture,'' are organized in a way that is particularly appropriate for encouraging individuals to assume the responsibility of making design decisions.[5]

[5] Robert Gutman, The Questions Architects Ask, *People and Buildings* (New York: Basic Books, 1972), pp. 366–367.

section two

The Issues

4
People: A Behavioral Overview

Roles

In a restaurant there are distinctive roles performed by all those present: the patrons, the waitress, the manager, the cook, and the bus boy. Each participant has a specified place to be during working hours, and the interaction between individuals is in a repetitive format: the patrons sit at the table and the waitress and bus boy work around them. The manager moves from place to place but seldom performs any particular overt function, such as clearing the tables or taking an order. The manager's only accustomed role seems to be that of handing out menus and seating diners. The cook has a role and so does the kitchen staff (see Figure 4.1).

Patterns

Not only are there roles, there are patterns of action. For the purpose of this discussion I use the word "pattern" to refer primarily to individual movement. I refer to "activities" as group movement. The cook, manager, waitress, and patrons all perform their roles in set ways. These ways are culturally learned and culturally reinforced by the "rules of the house." We may feel that we move freely through society but in reality we do not. We move freely as long as we know the roles open to us and perform well in them. Recently in traveling with my daughter, aged four, I stopped at a restaurant and was greeted by a sign, "No shirt—no shoes—no service." She did not have any shoes on, but I knew that the sign was not intended for her, so we went in and no one questioned it. How did I know? The experience of performing the patron role in restaurants for years taught me the house rules to expect and the exceptions in force. The patterns of acceptable behavior cover every aspect of dress, place, and action. The same restaurant had a sign above the counter which read, "Please pay when served—no credit asked or given." The signs were directing my

Fig. 4.1 The kitchen becomes an archetypal place for activity.

dress and were directing my actions. A third sign stating, "Section closed," made the directions complete, directing my place as well as my dress and my actions.

I enter a restaurant and I become a patron. As a patron I move within an unwritten pattern of actions from finding a seat to paying my bill to leaving a tip, perhaps buying a candy on the way out. Concurrently, in the restaurant the manager is performing a role, the waitress is performing a role, and the cook, busboy, and more important, all of us together are performing roles. There are five waitresses, twenty-five patrons, three cooks in the kitchen, and so forth. By experience of trial and error the patterns of activity have been worked out so that the patron is served comfortably and well and in the process the business can be run at a profit.

Patterns suggest knowledge of the roles to be played. Patterns also suggest certain tools and sequences of tools that make my entry, action, and leaving smooth and pleasant.

Activities

Thus far the restaurant has been described as a series of patterns performed by the particular role players. Change the context from the individual role player to the group and different kinds of patterns emerge. Here the patterns are interweaving, bringing together all the players to function as a group in predetermined ways. The group patterns are here referred to as an "activity." There are thousands and thousands of activities, performed in a thousand individual settings.

Served Role/Service Role   In order to understand the structure behind activities it is necessary to distinguish between served and service roles. All role players in a particular activity can be defined as being in either a served or a service capacity. The restaurant illustration makes the distinctions easy, for the activity is one of service. The patrons are the served role participants and all the others are in a service capacity. There is a hierarchy in the service roles, with the manager in control, but the manager is no different from the other members of the service team when it comes to the goal of the activity. (See Figure 4.2.) A variety of building types is presented in Figure 4.2, beginning with those that are least complex, designated as group 1. (These designations will be discussed later.) The purpose of the chart is to illustrate the kinds of roles found in repetitive building situations.

Social patterns have form, some of them exquisite; they may or may not have a physical equivalent. Years ago in working on Lincoln Center there was a great desire to develop a structural form that was also acoustically correct. Why should a structure be both structurally correct and acousti-

		SERVED GROUPS →		PERSONNEL IN BUILDING				← SERVICE GROUPS	
BUILDING TYPE	GROUP	ROLE 1	ROLE 2	ROLE 3	ROLE 4	ROLE 5	ROLE 6	ROLE 7	ROLE 8
OFFICE BLDG.	1	Leasee	Visitor					Clean and Maintenance	Bldg. Mgr.
PUBLIC BLDG.	1	Visitors	Visitor in Groups				Guides	Clean and Maintenance	Bldg. Mgr.
STORE	2	Customer				Stock Employees	Salesmen	Clean and Maintenance	Store Mgr.
CHURCH	2	Worshiper Rel. School				Volunteer Teachers	Volunteer Workers	Clean and Maintenance	Minister
RESTAURANT	2	Guest				Service Help	Kitchen Help	Clean and Maintenance	Mgr./Owner
GRADE SCHOOL	2	Student	Parent			Teachers	Kitchen Help	Clean and Maintenance	Principal
MANU-FACTURING	2	Workers					Supervisors	Clean and Maintenance	Mgr./Owner
GEN. HOSPITAL	3	Patient	Family	Outpatient	Medical and Nurses	Nursing Helpers	Kitchen Help	Clean and Maintenance	Hospital Administrator
RESORT HOTEL	3	Guest			Recreation Help	Service Help	Kitchen Help	Clean and Maintenance	Manager
UNIVERSITY	3	Student				Teachers	Kitchen Help	Clean and Maintenance	President/ Business Staff
JAIL/PRISON	4	Inmate	Family	Other Visitors	Social Medical	Kitchen Help	Clean and Maintenance	Guards	Warden/Sherriff
JUVENILE HOME	4	Ward	Family		Foster Family	Teachers	Kitchen Help	Clean and Maintenance	Supervisor
HOME FOR RETARDED	4	Ward	Family		Foster Family	Teachers	Kitchen Help	Clean and Maintenance	Supervisor
PREP. SCHOOL	4	Student	Family		Faculty Family		Kitchen Help	Clean and Maintenance	Head Master
PSYCHIATRIC HOSPITAL	4	Patient	Family	Other Visitors	Medical Staff	Nursing Helpers	Kitchen Help	Clean and Maintenance	Hospital Administrator
REMOTE POST	4	Worker					Kitchen Help	Clean and Maintenance	Officer in Charge
SPACE STATION	4	Astronaut						Astronaut	Officer in Charge

Fig. 4.2 Service and served roles in buildings.

cally correct unless, of course, this were happenstance? These two physical characteristics were related, perhaps, but they were not synonymous. What finally evolved was the idea that certain forms were compatible with acoustic requirements but others were not. It was not intellectually a beautiful solution, but it was real. In a similar way I feel that it is valuable to discover in social activities their social patterns, for whatever meaning this discovery may or may not have in direct relation to building. Social patterns are handsome in themselves and once activities are seen in their full dimension as expressions of cultural norms as well as useful actions, they communicate meaning aside from the architectural setting.

The number of participants in an activity is important. Events such as the circus, a basketball game, or a dance are all group activities of perhaps 400 or more. Everyday activities more often involve between one and eight individuals. Even in the larger activities the social interchange breaks down into small groups.

It is possible to plot all the possible physical relationships between one and eight persons (see Figure 4.3). A person may stand, or sit for work, or sit for relaxation, or lounge, or sleep. The same five positions can be repeated for two people, three people, and so on up to our arbitrary cutoff point of eight people. The second aspect of these relationships cannot easily be shown graphically. This aspect is the social mores, or the "house rules," that govern acceptable behavior between participants, depending on number and mode. Very quickly one will recognize that the modes are only theoretically possible, that many of them are socially taboo. For example, only in extreme circumstances will eight men sleep together. Less often will a mixed group of men and women sleep together. In fact, an interesting study could be made demonstrating that each of the modes and each of the size groups has reasonably well-defined social connota-

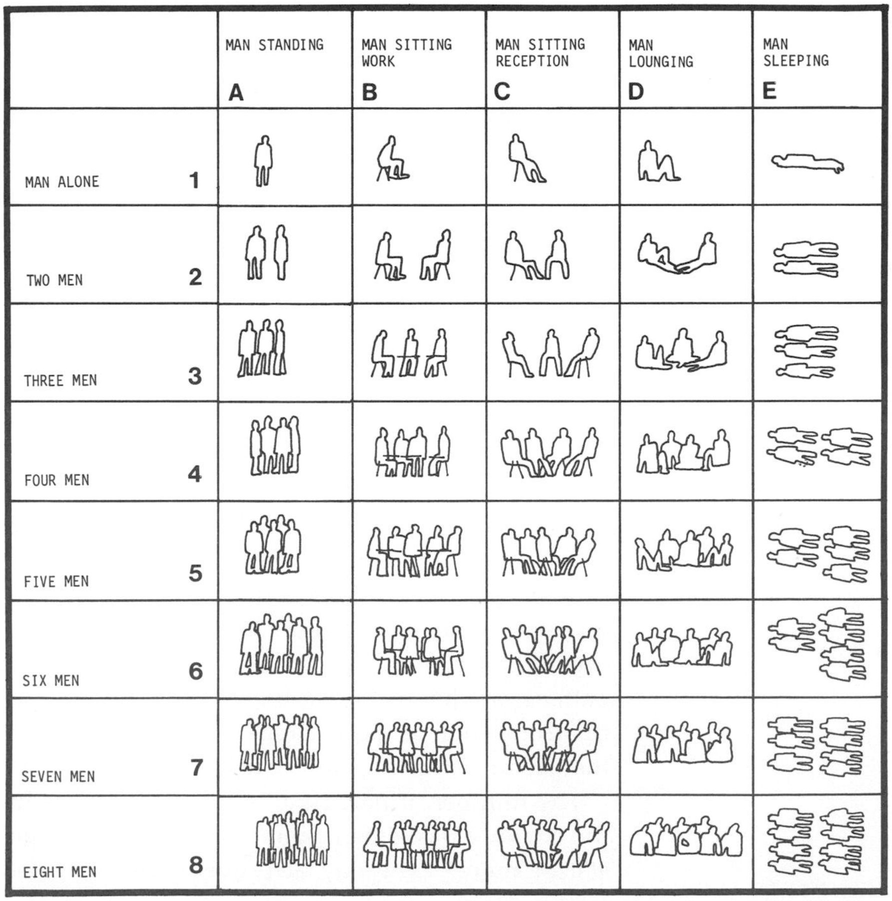

Fig. 4.3 Possible physical interactions, from one to eight people.

		MAN STANDING **A**	MAN SITTING WORK **B**	MAN SITTING RECEPTION **C**	MAN LOUNGING **D**	MAN SLEEPING **E**
MAN ALONE	1					
TWO MEN	2					
THREE MEN	3					
FOUR MEN	4					
FIVE MEN	5					
SIX MEN	6					
SEVEN MEN	7					
EIGHT MEN	8					

tions. For example, when men are lounging and another joins the group, there is a social tension of a sort. Either the host of the loungers will rise and speak to the new participant, or he will continue to lounge and speak to the participant. Putting ourselves in the position of the "intruder," we can affirm that there is meaning in the gesture of rising or not rising. It is an example of nonverbal communication. The host "tells" the new participant what his position in the group is by the act of rising or not rising.

Other social situations come to mind when considering this chart. For example, anyone who has "held forth," standing, to a company of seven others at a cocktail party will remember the difficulty of keeping everyone's attention. If the group is to be maintained very long, the conversation must be extremely interesting and forcefully presented, perhaps approaching a shout. Otherwise there will tend to be subconversations and the eight-person group disappears.

What bearing does this have on architecture? Frankly, it suggests the possibility of developing a group graphic standard, relating in some way to the number of people, the mode of their relationships, and the probable social mores implied. An attempt at this would bring to the surface the fact that certain activities have well-defined norms and others do not. Eating at a table and being served lends itself to a formalized description, as does the passing of an offering plate in church. Other situations become far more difficult to describe, as suggested by Figure 4.4, a student lounge with indeterminate furniture, and Figure 4.5, the seeming chaos of a rock festival. What becomes apparent is that some activities are formally structured, others informally. When the structure is unwritten, a common understanding of the rules is of *greater* importance.

Fig. 4.4 (below, right) Informal seating creating informal social interaction.

Fig. 4.5 (below) Crowded rock festival—a largely unstructured social activity.

Understanding an activity becomes a complex operation. One must designate the roles of the participants, one must be aware of the social mores active in the situation, and one must presuppose the background of the participants. If the participants do not know the rules, or will not follow them, the activity breaks down; for example, a fight at the dance threatens to close the dancehall. Order, that is social norms, must be preserved.

With these considerations in mind, it seems ludicrous to believe that a building will produce particular behavior. Particular behavior may occur, but it will occur because the elements of the social activity are in order. What then is the role of the building? The building should be a social servant in the broadest sense. It should anticipate behavior so that it can provide for it; it should be flexible where social activities are flexible and efficient where social activities are set. If this is so, the following elements must be considered:

1. The social activities a building houses
2. The degree of flexibility suggested by each activity
3. The "house rules" that prevail or should prevail
4. The background and goals of the participants

Background/Goals

The outline of individuals above may seem complex, but behavioral psychologists tell us that the situation is even more complex. The background of the participant may be reasonably determined by norms of education, job experience, marital status, and so forth. However, the participant's aspirations which affect how an activity is perceived relate to an indeterminate value scale. For example, a couple may have certain aspirations when first married and a different set of aspirations as their relationship grows older. The aspect of shifting goals is perplexing for it superimposes an additional variable on any interpersonal relationship. Even goals once acceptable may change for the same individual or group of individuals. In trying to determine what is acceptable behavior or what is an acceptable environment one constantly is asked to ascertain the needs of individuals, yet these needs may shift from one level of aspiration to another.

Some form of evaluation is required as a check on the success or failure of architecture considered in human terms. Many scales of ascending aspirations have been attempted, by Maslov and others. A scale by Leighton which he describes as "convenient handles" seems reasonable (see also Figure 4.8). In ascending order his goals run as follows:

- Physical security
- Sexual satisfaction
- The expression of hostility
- The expression of love

- The securing of love
- The securing of recognition
- The expression of spontaneity (called variously positive force, creativity, volition)
- Orientation in terms of one's place in society and the places of others
- The securing and maintaining of membership in a definite human group
- A sense of belonging to a moral order and being right in what one does, being in and of a system of values[1]

In other words a person cannot be defined by any one situation or activity alone; rather the person must be considered to need various kinds of fulfillment.

The question of goals and their fulfillment cannot be divorced from the environment, for the environment can create a positive support for goal seeking or it can work negatively against the individual's goals. The concept of "quality of life" suggests both the goals of the individual and the setting for those goals.

Quality of Life

The Environmental Protection Agency (EPA) was formed to deal with decisions affecting the environment; such decisions required a value scale that could establish priorities in the environment. The agency has, therefore, become deeply involved in establishing a value scale for development. It held a symposium in the early 1970s called "The Quality of Life Concept—A Potential New Tool for Decision Makers." Findings from this symposium are germane to the issue of establishing values for individual buildings. This discussion suggests that the EPA may broaden its mandate and become the governmental agency most closely involved in requiring a *human value scale.* A quotation from the book[2] published on the symposium lends credence to this view. The mandate spelled out by the National Environmental Policy Act not only relates the environment directly to the concept of quality of life but also provides for the federal government to exercise leadership "in protecting and enhancing the quality of the Nation's environment to sustain and enrich human life." In so doing, the Council on Environmental Quality was authorized to "promote the development of indices and monitoring systems . . . to determine the effectiveness of programs for protecting and enhancing environmental quality."

---

[1] Alexander H. Leighton, *My Name Is Legion: Foundation for a Theory of Man in Relation to Culture,* vol. I of the Stirling County Study of Psychiatric Disorder and Socio-cultural Environment (New York: Basic Books, 1959).

[2] U. S. Environmental Protection Agency, *The Quality of Life Concept: A Potential New Tool for Decision Makers,* pp. 10–11.

Elsewhere in the report it is stated that,

> Although the literature offers no consensus on a QOL definition, a clear consensus does exist regarding the importance of the concept. People in business, in government, and in the universities are rethinking the old tendency to equate a rising Gross National Product with national well-being.[2]

In a paper prepared for the symposium by Arnold Mitchel, Thomas J. Logothetti, and Robert E. Kantor of the Sanford Research and Development Program, a new concept was introduced.

> The basic premise underlying the approach is that what people need, value and believe (NVB) are the dominating determinants of their sense of quality of life. That is to say the QOL is highly subjective, especially in its loftier reaches. As has been pointed out, it matters more how a person feels about his situation than how his status, measured in some "objective" way, compares with others. This approach thus seeks to reflect a person's inner evaluations, his sense of the discrepancy between what is and what his needs, values and beliefs lead him to anticipate.

Later in the paper, the NVB scale is expanded as a basis for value judgment to include satisfaction, survival, security, belongingness, esteem, and self-actualization. Of particular significance is the manner in which the needs and satisfactions are considered in time.

> It is obvious, to the point of evading attention, that the lower needs must be satisfied more frequently than the higher needs. Needs for physiological survival must be satisfied at frequencies of the order of pulse rates (65/min) breathing rates (12/min), eating rates (3–4 per day), and sleeping rates (once a day). Belongingness needs are typically satisfied at lower frequencies, as exemplified by social participation rates for love making (a few times a week), church attendance (a few times a month), and voting behavior (a few times a year). Esteem needs are satisfied even less frequently; the deferred gratification pattern leads to recognition, at the rate of an education milestone every four years, or a major contribution to a profession a few times in a lifetime. Lastly, and least frequently, self-actualizing experiences are so rare that they are typically once in a life-time affairs, with the majority of individuals never having a peak experience.
>
> The hope is that satisfaction frequency data can be used to help quantify a QOL score. A minimum frequency at need level must be attained before the upward transition to a 1 plus 1 level can be made.[3]

Archetypal Activities/Archetypal Spaces

There may be disagreement about which value scale one uses, but the similarity between these scales is more significant than their differences. People must survive before they can look to other goals. Drives towards sex,

[3] Ibid., pp. 11–40.

expressions of hostility and love-seeking are the next level of aspirations. People require esteem from others and self-expression within their culture. Human activities revolve around the needs outlined. There are reasonably few activities seen from a generic point of view and these all relate to goal fulfillment of one kind or another. There are a series of activities related to survival, concentrated in farm activities in production of staples, commercial activities in distribution of staples, and home activities in the preparation and consumption of staples. There are work activities, divided broadly into physical work and more abstract work activities. Then there are a series of social activities which express civic pride, religious belief, or recreation in sports, dances, vacations, and so forth.

Activities can be categorized by the number of participants. There are (bio)physical reasons that this is so. Human beings are limited by the fact that their eyes are set looking only in one direction. Before electronic communication systems, the distance the voice could carry became the determinant in social gathering. How many people could surround a speaker and hear him?

The "presence" of a person has not been electronically reproduced successfully and breakthroughs anticipated by the picture-telephone have not materialized. With all the existing means of communications from telephone to television, businesspeople still fly thousands of miles to meet face-to-face when important nuances of negotiation are anticipated. Participants are anxious to absorb the nonverbal communication as well as to hear the verbal.

With each meeting situation go "house rules." In larger settings there are not only "house rules" to keep attention focused but well-constructed ceremonies. The problem a speaker has in holding the attention of seven others at a cocktail party must have been multiplied a thousandfold throughout history as one person attempted to hold the attention of multitudes. The solution is the ceremony; a ceremony that is learned, repeated, and at best requires individual participation.

The complex view of the individuals we have outlined, a view that places them in roles, roles which have them move through predictable and repetitive patterns as their patterns interweave with others in group activities, must be carefully carried across now into building settings. People are not automatons, nor actors on a stage. They are multidirected persons seeking a series of fulfillments, and the current activity they are in does not necessarily define them.

These complex individuals need symbolic signs of their position in society; these complex individuals need a cue to the "house rules"; these complex individuals will approach interpersonal relationships with a preconceived notion of appropriate behavior and in large groups with an expectation of ceremony. These thoughts lead naturally to a search for archetypal activities and concurrently to search for archetypal spaces. *Archetypal activities* can be defined as common, repetitive activities, which are reasonably predictable given a particular set of circumstances. *Archetypal spaces* are spaces commonly associated with the performance of these activities. When we find the activity it will be a complex one, with interweaving roles. When we find the space, we will find it a setting for the activity, with signs and symbols apparent that will communicate to individuals where they are psychologically as well as physically. Only a complex individual would need the myriad cues that buildings generate. Only a complex individual would need architecture to be at once an enclosure and a signpost. For buildings blare forth a visual language. The language is there, clear as any billboard, if only we would bother to read it.

The Visual Language

The visual language of buildings is the hidden psychological dimension of buildings, hidden at least from "modern" eyes. Buildings in other ages were supposed to broadcast and all civic buildings did so with the pomp and circumstance expected of them. For instance, churches were entered through statued porticoes.

Only "rational" persons of the modern day have overlooked the visual meaning of buildings, just as they have simplified the complexity of humanity. In seeking archetypal activities and archetypal spaces, I am not trying to perpetrate the simplification of humanity. Quite the contrary, I am trying to see again human beings in their complexity, something lost in generations that were certain people and form were not complex.

Figure 4.6 is an architectural drafting room. Where are the storage bins, the reference books, the workrooms? Does this lack cues about the "house rules"? Quite the contrary, it is clear from the photograph that the "house rules" are rigid, that the occupants are sublimating, if you will, a great many other desires in order to fit into the mold predetermined by the architectural setting. This kind of architectural setting creates an ethos about industrial order.

It was naïvely felt that by taking information off the signpost people would stop reading it. What has happened instead is that people have kept on reading, reading the blank signpost and understanding what that means. Figure 4.7 is a photograph of the vacant building at Webbe, a low-income housing project in St. Louis. Is there a connection between this building and the drafting room? I read that there is, for each one broadcasts a concept of humanity that is simplistic, and if complex, rigidly ordered by hierarchy.

Fig. 4.6   Architecture class under Mies. This drafting room suggests, by the absence of objects, that people are better served by simplicity. (Hedrich Blessing, photographer.)

Fig. 4.7   A vacant building at Webbe broadcasts abandonment.

The tragedy of the Modern Movement in architecture is that it did not ask questions about income and background and goals; it assumed a simple, rational, reasonably affluent person. The only model close at hand for such a simplistic notion was the architect himself—a sobering thought for architects.

Activities take on natural configurations when unencumbered by superimposed density. Rural life without such encumbrances is a rich source of examples. These activities fall into reasonably repetitive forms. Mayer Spivak talks of archetypal place, listing in support of that place repetitive tasks. For him there are only thirteen, from shelter tasks, through sleeping and feeding tasks, to competing and working tasks. Perceptions of these tasks vary, depending primarily on the life-cycle stage of the participant, from the child to the aged (see Figure 4.8).

Others talk of archetypal places in direct relationship to the size of the group considered. Christian Norberg-Schultz speaks of three basic village types in central Europe: the cluster village, the linear village, and the round village. Similarly Kevin Lynch has articulated repetitive forms in cities, concentrating attention on the *district*, or cluster, the *street*, basically linear, and the *square*, analogous to the circular town. Norberg-Schultz goes on to point out that the archetypal place of the street is all but destroyed in the modern planning of cities that isolates buildings and turns streets into fast-moving traffic arteries for cars not people. The logic behind making corridors work for cars and not for people can be traced to a simplistic view of humanity.

How do people interact with buildings? What real connection is there between the activities once discovered and their architectural settings, prototypical or not? There is one step missing, for me, in discussions of archetypal place. I do not feel it is possible to talk about archetypal place before one talks about archetypal geometry. The cluster, the linear, and the square were discovered as archetypal places—my question is, are they archetypal places or archetypal geometries? Too often places are "discovered" as if there were alternatives. What may be occurring is that instead of discovering places we are actually discovering the constraints of geometry. That in turn is a formalistic way of saying we are discovering the constraints of our human existence, the constraints of bodies that can only look one way without turning the head, that move at predictable pace with the horizon always at eye level, that can communicate naturally only a given distance, that live in a three-dimensional world that for planning purposes is really two-dimensional since people cannot fly without aid. Perhaps we will discover that the cluster, the linear, and the square are archetypes for humanity, but in the process we may discover that they are because there are no alternatives geometrically. In a profound sense, peo-

Fig. 4.8 (opposite) Life cycle chart. (Mayer Spivak.)

GENERALLY RELATED LIFE CYCLE STAGES

		A	B	C	D	E	F	G
		INFANCY: Reflex control; orientation; communicate with siblings and parents.	CHILDHOOD: Gain motor, social, verbal, intellectual, emotional competence.	ADOLESCENCE: Forge identity; establish peer group regulations; social/sexual exploration.	COURTING-MATING: Group with peers; pair-bond; obtain sexual privacy.	REPRODUCTION, CHILD CARE: Nesting/nurturing: symbiosis; socialization.	MIDDLE LIFE: Care of aging parents: re-emphasis on worldly affairs; redefine identity.	AGING MATURITY: Maintain identity, contact, health; accent care by others, mortality.

TASKS

THE TOTAL SET OF BEHAVIORALLY DEFINED ARCHETYPAL PLACES

1	SHELTER	Elemental protection; protection for nesting activities; retreat from stimulation, aggression, threat, social contact; emotional recuperation.
2	SLEEP	Neurophysiological processes; recuperation, rest; reduced stimulation; labor and birth, postnatal care of mother and child; death.
3	MATE	Courting rituals; pair-bonding; copulation; affectionate behavior; communication.
4	GROOM	Washing; mutual grooming.
5	FEED	Eating, slaking thirst; communication, social gathering; feeding others.
6	EXCRETE	Excreting; territorial marking.
7	STORE	Hiding of food and other property; storage; hoarding.
8	TERRITORY	Spying; contemplation; meditating; planning; waiting; territorial sentry; defending; observing.
9	PLAY	Motor satisfactions; role testing; rule breaking; fantasy, exercise; creation; discovery; dominance testing; synthesis.
10	ROUTE	Perimeter checking; territorial confirmation; motor satisfactions; social and community control.
11	MEET	Communication; dominance testing; governing; education, worship, socialization; meditation; cosmic awe; moral concerns.
12	COMPETE	Agonistic ritual; dominance testing; ecological competition; inter-species defense; intra-species defense and aggression; mating; chauvinistic conflict.
13	WORK	Hunting; gathering; earning; building; making.

A 1 Protection from elemental extremes; explore dwelling. A:2 Recognize bed; learn daily rhythms. A:3 XX A:4 Lose fear of wet face, sudden temperature change; regular grooming as primary contact ritual. A:5 Regulate feeding satisfactions. A:6 Discover excretion as separate from self; associate with setting and time. A:7 Acquire confidence in food abundance. A:8 Identify bed as primary secure place. A:9 Explore close environment; develop manipulative, cognitive skills. A:10 Route connects parts of shelter structures, provides orientation & change; motor satisfaction. A:11 XX A:12 Master frustration in competition w/siblings for attention & toys. A:13 (See A:9).

B 1 Differentiate subsettings; retreat from overstimulation, threat; emotional recuperation. B:2 Associate bed w/fatigue; learn volitional control of sleep; illness and recuperation. B:3 XX B:4 Learn to bathe, dress oneself. B:5 Coordinate feeding tools; communication; differentiate food from symbiotic source in mother. B:6 Autonomously control excretion. B:7 Learn to prepare food. B:8 Establish play "turfs"; orient to neighborhood; play protect territory from lookout; plan, wait. B:9 Role modeling; interact w/peers; fantasy, exercise, exorcism, creation, discovery, dominance testing. B:10 Enlarge route maps; differentiate settings, provide social encounters; learn safe wandering limits. B:11 Regular play/meeting rituals & places; elaborate functions; dominance testing. B:12 Games; fight; agonistic ritual; dominance testing. B:13 Acquire intellectual, motor skills.

C 1 Find alternate private shelter; auto, attic, stairwell. C:2 XX C:3 Meet w/opposite sex in private, public settings; obtain sexual privacy anywhere: autos, barns, etc. C:4 Groom for mating encounters. C:5 Communicate w/peers over food & drink. C:6 Privacy in excretion. C:7 XX C:8 Expand territory into intellectual domains, job. C:9 Learn autonomous hobbies. C:10 Provides social contact w/opposite sex. C:11 Meet w/peers, both sexes; establish new rituals. C:12 Sexual display: cars, sports, clothes (see C:3). C:13 Refine work skills.

D 1 Find new shelter. D:2 Share bed w/mate. D:3 Select mate; achieve couple privacy. D:4 XX D:5 Share food w/mate; increase food abundance. D:6 XX D:7 Enlarge larder for family. D:8 Expand territory to include mate. D:9 (see D:12). D:10 Maintain community of contacts. D:11 Meet w/couples. D:12 Personal display; ecological, mating competition. D:13 Apply skills toward life support.

E 1 Expand shelter for offspring (see E:5). E:2 Maintain sexual privacy against invasion by new young family. E:3 XX E:4 XX E:5 Increase abundance; feed family; gather, communicate w/family. E:6 XX E:7 Increase capacity & variety of food. E:8 Expand territory to include young & check frequently. E:9 XX E:10 XX E:11 Expand functions, contacts; governing, educating, mystical awe. E:12 Display in common values; conspicuous consumption. E:13 Improve capacities, performance.

F 1 Shelter contracts as young leave. F:2 through F:7 XX F:8 Territorial needs contract as young leave shelter. F:9 through F:13 XX

G 1 Maintain location or adjust to imposed change; adapt surroundings to needs. G:2 More time in bed, sleep less; possible confinement, compression of world to bedside. G:3 Adjust sexuality to changing libido; possible illness or loss of mate. G:4 Possible inability to care for self. G:5 Arrange special diet; reduction of taste, smell spectra. G:6 Possibly require aid and equipment; lowered mobility may reduce functional dependability. G:7 Possibly require assistance gathering & preparing food. G:8 Passive observation of archetypal activities performed by others. G:9 New leisure activities to fit changing capacities. G:10 Reduction in home range scale; fear of exposure to attack. G:11 Need for contact w/& support from peers. G:12 Probable withdrawal from competition/defeat by young; defensive, evasive postures. G:13 Less active roles w/in former context; fend off retirement.

ple throughout time will be forced to live with these constraints, the constraints of life itself.

In keeping with the line of development here, it is essential to discuss buildings as constraining devices before discussing the interface between people and buildings. If people are to be seen in complexity, buildings are to be seen in their constraints. It is the study of these constraints that is commonly called systems design.

5
Buildings:
A Systems
Overview

What are systems? In the discussion below, systems will be used in three contexts. First, systems will be described as logic diagrams, leading the designer to orderly and accountable design decisions. Second, systems will be discussed in the generic sense, referring to repetitive elements in the physical world that define places through patterns of corridor and form. Third, systems will refer to building systems and subsystems technology, touching briefly on the major systems programs and manufactured items that are available to date.

Logic Diagrams

A useful logic diagram is presented in Figure 5.1*a*. In this case the diagram presents steps in a fast-tracking process, that is, the process by which elements in a design procedure can be accomplished at an accelerated pace.

Beginning at the top left, the project proceeds by defining the systems components first. These components can be "fast-tracked" through preliminary design, contract documents, bidding, and construction while work on other aspects of the project are still being programmed. The foundation (Fdn) follows next through the fast-track steps and is run ahead of the systems components in construction, which is appropriate to the construction sequence. The diagram presents the elements to be considered in the design process, the steps that each must move through, and the interrelationship between these steps. In this particular chart an indication of time is implied by moving from left to right, suggesting that construction can be commenced while nonsystems components are still in the preliminary design.

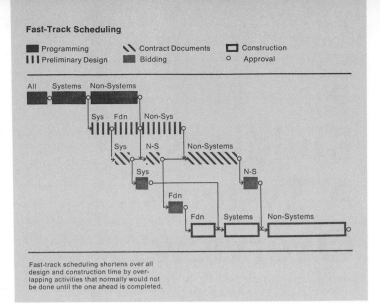

Fig. 5.1 (a) Fast-track scheduling diagram. (From Educational Facilities Laboratories, Systems.) (b) A computer program can print out room plans and furniture. The designs are created by logic diagrams stored in the computer to be recalled when needed. (Perry Dean Partners, Inc.)

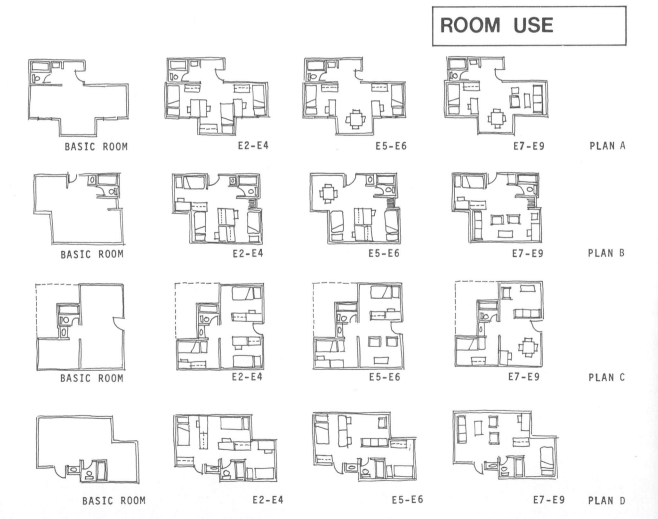

The particular diagram is of interest because of the particular information it describes, for fast-tracking is one of the advantages of using systems components. The diagram is also important as it exemplifies the amount of information that can be communicated at a glance.

Fundamental to this diagram is the concept that a design process can be predetermined. It is the predetermination of the process that links logic diagrams to the systems approach to design. As items in the diagram increase in number and the relationships increase, it becomes difficult to draw a visual diagram. Visual diagrams are constrained by the two-dimensional field: elements can only be stacked from top to bottom or from left to right. (Three-dimensional diagrams have been attempted, but they are generally difficult to follow, if for no other reason than that they communicate more information.) More often when complex procedures are communicated, logic diagrams are developed in sequence, much like a series of circuit diagrams on electronic equipment. A natural progression leads from single logic diagrams to a series of logic diagrams to a computer program. There is nothing essentially different between logic diagrams and computer programs, in fact the logic diagram is the precursor of computer applications. A computer stores logic diagrams and recalls them when a particular problem is presented to it. Figure 5.1*b* shows a computer printout of various room arrangements and various ways such rooms can be furnished. Although this printout is more complex, behind it is a series of predetermined logical steps that make each element in the printout totally accountable.

Whether the diagram is a one-line procedure diagram, a more complicated critical path diagram, or a fully developed computer program, the importance of the diagram is the same—it directs the design process in a predetermined, orderly, and accountable manner.

Geometry and Repetition

Let us look at familiar historic buildings and find repetitive "systems" in three photographs which may at first seem to be devoid of systems design, or repetitive form, as normally viewed. However, if one were to reconstruct the house of Pompeii (see Figure 5.2), or the street in Alberobello (see Figure 5.3), or the City Hall at Todi (see Figure 5.4), one would find each conforming to strict laws of geometry, however complex and interlocking. These photographs are communicating cultural data in their details; but if these cues are ignored, the configurations are definable in geometric terms. The fact is, a court design today is based on the same geometric constraints as the court design in Roman times.

Three sketches from aerial photographs illustrate the geometric form be-

Fig. 5.2 Pompeii. Subtract the cultural cues and the house is fully definable in geometric terms.

Fig. 5.3   Streetscene, Alberobello, Italy. The visual quality of
this streetscape is tied directly
to the geometry underlying the
individual houses. Repeat the
geometry exactly and the visual
impression will be repeated exactly.

Fig. 5.4   Todi, Italy. The
massing, while seeming arbitrary, is determined by the constraints of geometry.

Fig. 5.5 Drottingholm Palace, Sweden. The forms are a product of controlled geometry.

hind the compositions as well as the cultural overlay of detail and scale. Figure 5.5 is a study in symmetry; it is an example of the free-standing monument that dominates the landscape. From the garden viewers would move toward the building and have their visual world increasingly dominated by the composition. The power of symmetry to mesmerize the viewer is always surprising; it would work here without doubt. What can also be seen from the sketch is the manner in which the building was composed with domed elements at each end linked to courts and culminating in the center linear building. Strip the cultural overlay away, if you will, and the building can be categorized by its essential geometric components. Figure 5.6, the Plaza Major in Madrid, is an example of urban open space that dominates the spatial composition of European cities. From a behavioral point of view there is no question that such plazas dominated the social life of the city, and do so today, for the remaining spaces are close-packed, allowing for local activities, but not allowing space for large group activities, ceremonies, and festivals. A viewer is enclosed by architecture and is likely to meet others as they approach from four sides. The geometry is predictable because it is based on a two-dimensional grid which allows central space within an otherwise tight-packed composi-

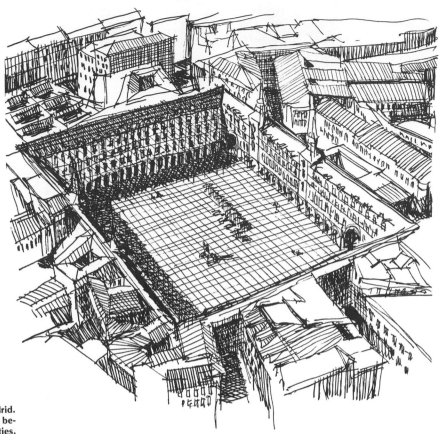

Fig. 5.6 Plaza Major, Madrid. The geometry of the square becomes the natural focus of activities.

tion. How different is the geometric configuration from that of Pot Creek Pueblo in Taos, New Mexico? (See Figure 5.7.) At first glance it would seem completely different, for the pueblo is made up of free-form elements in something of a random configuration. Yet there is a central plaza, created in the same way that the Plaza Major was created by being surrounded by building elements.

It is the nonceremonial, nonfocus areas of an ancient city that best exemplify a systems approach to building. Figure 5.8 is a detail of a nondescript element of the citizen's residence in a European city. The building seems arbitrary in its form, yet inspection would show that it is part of a pattern of buildings determined by a few fundamental variables. One variable is the five- or six-floor height, determined by the distance people would walk daily without elevators. More significant from a systems overview is the wall-like linear quality of the composition, narrow to allow for cross-ventilation, continuous to conserve space, articulated by narrow

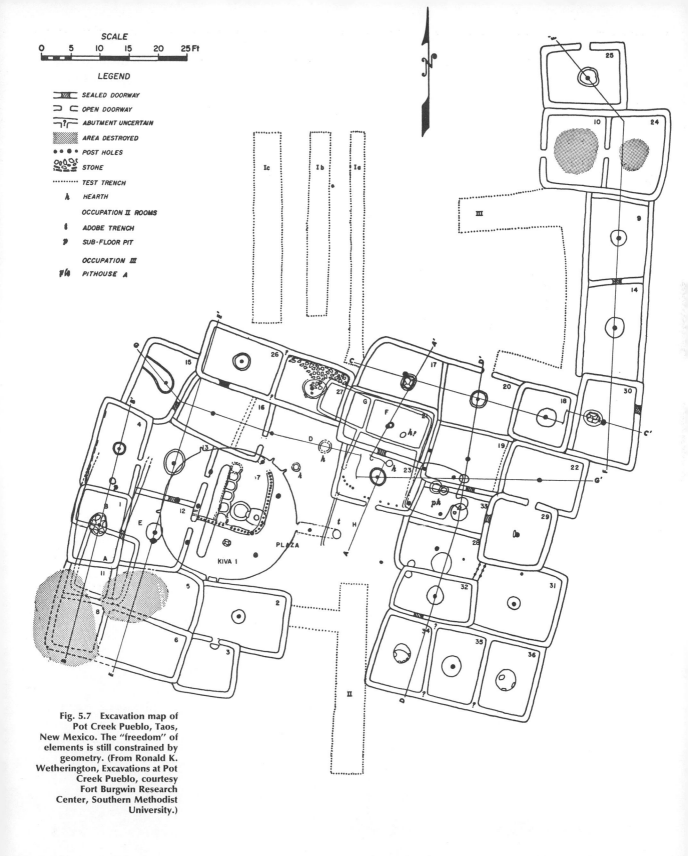

SCALE

0 5 10 15 20 25 Ft

LEGEND

◨ SEALED DOORWAY

⊐ ⊏ OPEN DOORWAY

⌐∩?⊏ ABUTMENT UNCERTAIN

▒ AREA DESTROYED

••••• POST HOLES

⊙⊙ STONE

·········· TEST TRENCH

ʜ HEARTH

OCCUPATION II ROOMS

ɪ ADOBE TRENCH

ᵱ SUB-FLOOR PIT

OCCUPATION III

ᵱʰ PITHOUSE A

Fig. 5.7 Excavation map of Pot Creek Pueblo, Taos, New Mexico. The "freedom" of elements is still constrained by geometry. (From Ronald K. Wetherington, Excavations at Pot Creek Pueblo, courtesy Fort Burgwin Research Center, Southern Methodist University.)

streets and courts. In a real sense the major living spaces in historic cities are the megastructure of block living units. Today these cities can still be experienced at pedestrian scale as they were built to be perceived.

The view of New York in Figure 5.9 demonstrates the essential grid pattern of streets that underlies the development of space. It is the essential grid behind building and cities that is the generic systems dimension under discussion here. It is simply a fact of physical space that there are only a limited number of grids that work in developing the essential two-dimensional planning of the physical environment. While historians have traditionally concentrated on the cultural statement of buildings, the repetitive grid format has gone largely unnoticed. Yet the architect and planner must deal with the constraints of this repetitive grid in every building situation.

Hidden Behavioral Assumptions   Not every grid pattern is suitable for human occupancy. For example, a honeycomb beehive is based on a close-packed hexagonal configuration, but it does not provide for corridors linking each cell. Rather, each cell is adjacent to six others but the life pattern does not require movement except into adjacent cells (see Figure 5.10). In contrast, the xx-yy axis that is the one repetitive grid underlying almost all human occupancy allows for corridors connecting every inhabited room with every other inhabited room. The necessity for such connection is the hidden dimension that makes grids based on circle derivatives difficult to use in repeated form (see Figure 5.11). From the xx-yy base grid, most

Fig. 5.8 (below)   A part of the residential megastructure of European cities—a building defined by behavior.

Fig. 5.9 (below, right)   New York City housing development. Cities are defined by underlying grids. (PFI—Charles Rotkin.)

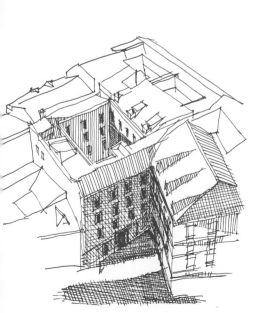

Fig. 5.10 Beehive cells and grid. Human habitation requires that each unit of space be connected with every other unit of space. Only grids with corridors will work.

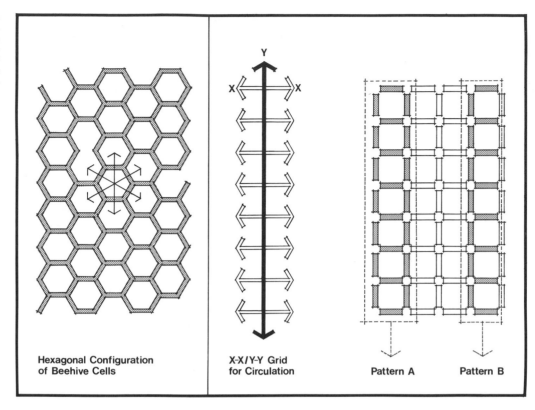

Hexagonal Configuration
of Beehive Cells

X-X/Y-Y Grid
for Circulation

Pattern A   Pattern B

Fig. 5.11 By inspection it is clear that a linear progression provides corridors easily and that a nonlinear progression provides corridors into complex intersections.

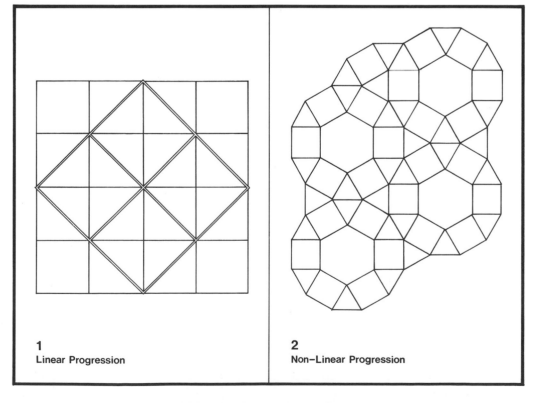

1
Linear Progression

2
Non−Linear Progression

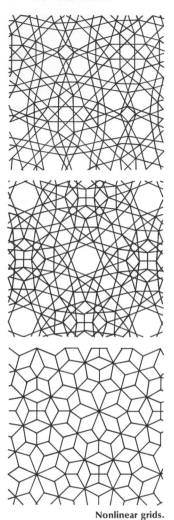

Nonlinear grids.
(Maryann Heimsath.)

building configurations evolve: from pattern A the court scheme evolves; from pattern B the repetitive wing-shaped building evolves (see Figure 5.10). The dimensions of the grid can change, creating smaller courts between elements or elongated blocks, but the fact remains that the basic configuration is derived from the single xx-yy axis.

Considering the building in the context of individual rooms rather than as a block of form points up a second hidden assumption which limits possible configurations: there is a human need for exterior light and air. Experiments in interior classrooms and laboratories have developed a rationale for alternatives to this general rule with proper forced-air ventilation, but interior rooms meet with continued, worldwide resistance. The first hidden necessity of corridors linking every inhabited room, then, is joined by a second hidden necessity—placing occupants adjacent to exterior windows. The block-like diagrams in patterns A and B of Figure 5.10 are predicated on this hidden assumption. There are a limited number of room configurations within the geometry of space, given the need for connecting corridors and the desire for exterior light and air (see Figure 5.12).

Consideration of this fact leads to repetitive human situations. For example, room adjacencies are a critical factor in defining the particular world of an individual within a building. If one must go from room A to room B and the two are not adjacent, one must physically bypass all the rooms in between. This fact is obvious, but it is too important to remain hidden in the planning of buildings. More often than not the client and architect discuss building alternatives as if there were an infinite number of possible solutions. While there may be, if one considers all the variables including symbol, status, sequence, and so forth, there are only a limited number of solutions in view of the restrictions of geometry. Geometry, because of its limitations, becomes one constant in the fields of architecture and behavior.

Adjacencies At the microscale of building there are only three formats for adjacencies. In diagram 1 of Figure 5.13, a corridor is first drawn to indicate the major ordering element to which adjacency solutions must relate. In the bypass format, area B is placed at the opposite side of area A. If area B were a bathroom and area A a bedroom, this relationship would be quite reasonable since the space is related to the occupants in area A. However, there also needs to be access through area A to get to B, since all areas in every building are connected in some manner with all other areas. An interior corridor is implied by this adjacency format.

A second adjacency relationship is shown in diagram 2. Here the adjacency is accomplished by placing area B side-by-side with area A. Connection from the corridor is direct, and A need not have an implied interior

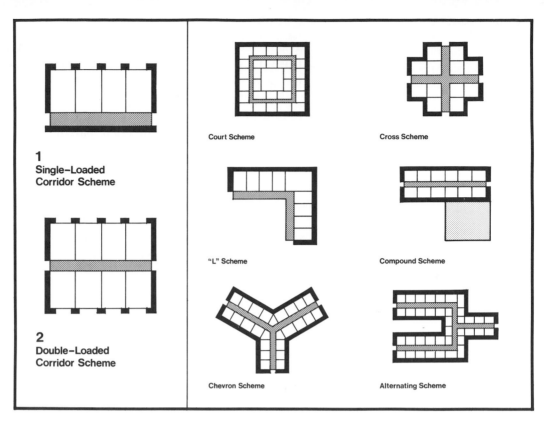

1
Single–Loaded Corridor Scheme

2
Double–Loaded Corridor Scheme

Court Scheme

Cross Scheme

"L" Scheme

Compound Scheme

Chevron Scheme

Alternating Scheme

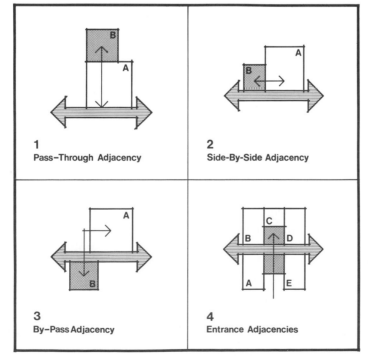

1
Pass–Through Adjacency

2
Side-By-Side Adjacency

3
By–Pass Adjacency

4
Entrance Adjacencies

Fig. 5.12 (above) Generic buildings. All buildings are the same.

Fig. 5.13 (left) Adjacency diagram. In the miniscale of buildings, there are only three formats for adjacencies.

corridor. In diagram 3 there is a bypass adjacency. Area B may be nearby, but one must use the general corridor system, bypassing other areas to reach it. It may seem simplistic to concentrate on these three examples which can be affirmed by inspection. However, it is significant that there are no other arrangements—only three. That there are three is apparent; that there are only three is not immediately apparent!

Consider a second adjacency situation which occurs over and over again in building. Areas are set adjacent to the entrance. It will be shown that entrances are of considerable social importance in a building, for there is particular social status attached to being adjacent to the entrance. Yet it becomes apparent that only five areas can be placed adjacent to an entrance and the two elements D and E require a bypass corridor or a deep entrance recess if they are to be used. Again the diagram makes this apparent. What the diagram fails to do is prove that from a generic standpoint there are no other solutions. In each case the diagrams underlie the constraints imposed on buildings, requiring that rooms have light and air, that corridors connect all spaces, and that there be adjacencies in performing human activities within a building.

What does this fact mean in practical planning terms? An example is shown from a study which involved placing an activity room adjacent to a chapel nave. There are three basic nave arrangements based on site lines and a desire for proximity to the altar area (see Figure 5.14a). When the requirement was added that the activity room must adjoin the nave for double use in overflow services, the interior configurations of nave seating became secondary to the limitations of geometry. It develops that there are only two nave/activity room arrangements, one which places the activity room on the side, and one which places the activity room to the rear, if the major circulation corridor is assumed to be at the bottom of each diagram. The third adjacency of bypass through the nave was not acceptable for obvious reasons. In no sense are there unlimited numbers of solutions. Given a limitation in entrance corridor space, a solution much like Figure 5.14b would evolve, requiring as it does that the entrance be off-center. It would be geometrically impossible to place these two spaces together in their current orientation and have a central entrance. The point is that decisions about placements are directly related to the geometry of the solution. Since placement of elements affects human use of buildings, it is clear that geometry and use cannot be separated.

Vertical Bypass/Horizontal Bypass The fundamental reason for vertical buildings is overlooked. The reason is bypass. Given the constraints of geometry described above and the need for a person to bypass areas in the horizontal plane when going from point A to point B, the advantages of

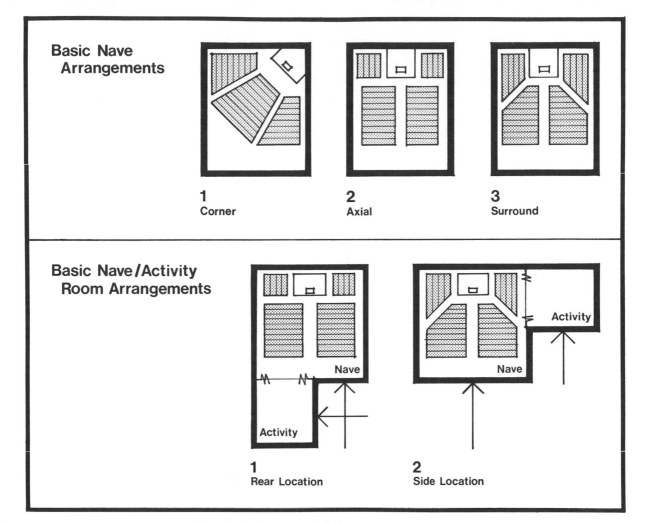

Basic Nave Arrangements

1 Corner

2 Axial

3 Surround

Basic Nave/Activity Room Arrangements

1 Rear Location

2 Side Location

Activity

Nave

Activity

Nave

Nave and Activity Room Arrangement

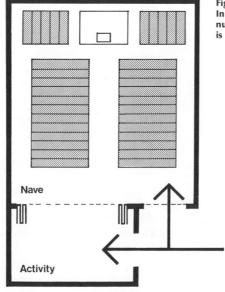

Nave

Activity

Fig. 5.14 Nave arrangements diagram. In a church there are only a limited number of arrangements; the constraint is geometric.

vertical stacking become obvious immediately. Figure 5.15 is presented to illustrate the kind of visual excitement that misses the point of vertical adjacency. Such a scheme is presented in the spirit of systems perhaps, but certainly not as a product of logical thought. Vertical relationships are fundamentally adjacency relationships. It takes only a moment to go upstairs or downstairs. In doing so one can bypass every other room on the floor! Elevator movement is rapid and, more significantly, one is not aware of the bypass. If bypassing rooms along a corridor is a problem in time, it is far more of a problem in perception. Figure 5.16a shows a corridor in a modern airport. It was designed for peak traffic and therefore is unnecessarily broad and uniformly uninteresting most of the time. But the design could be predicted. Behind the design was the decision to ask travelers to walk out to the departure lounges, in a sense bypassing all the space between. A vertical adjacency is not possible in the case of airports. It is in this context that Saarinen, faced with the horizontal geometry dilemma, conceived of Dulles Airport, where people are moved from the terminal to their plane; they are not asked to walk (see Figure 5.16b). In every sense Dulles Airport is a behavioral solution, not a physical one. Perhaps it is inevitable that architects become intimately involved with the behavior within buildings, for geometric solutions are limited unless accepted social patterns can be changed. At Dulles they were.

Vertical adjacencies, on the other hand, are effective only when the elevator is vertical. Elevators that can move at 45° angles are an interesting possibility if in this way they solve particular adjacency problems. In the meantime, until such problems are defined, buildings will be vertical for the logical reason that that is geometrically the simplest means of pro-

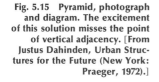

Fig. 5.15 Pyramid, photograph and diagram. The excitement of this solution misses the point of vertical adjacency. [From Justus Dahinden, Urban Structures for the Future (New York: Praeger, 1972).]

Fig. 5.16 (a) The problem of adjacency is accentuated in airports. (b) Dulles International Airport—movable lounges, a behavioral solution to horizontal adjacency. [(b) Department of Transportation, Dulles International Airport.]

viding adjacency between areas on different floors. This fact is the logic behind modern buildings such as the apartment tower illustrated in Figures 5.17 and 5.18. From one central parking area and one main entrance, a great many people can move with minimum inconvenience to their apartments. This is systems logic. Whether or not this fact should prevail over possible disadvantages in high-rise living is the matter of design evaluation. Yet, to evaluate, one must first clarify the logic to be evaluated, separating it from the emotional and cultural overlay generally associated with any building configuration.

Briefly, in describing a generic systems overview we have started with some historic buildings and the cultural messages they relate. Disregarding these messages, we have concentrated instead on the configurations behind these compositions, realizing that the limitations of geometry affect buildings at any period in history. The limitations, then, become a constant to be considered in the design process. The limitations constrain the number of possible solutions to adjacency problems and ex-

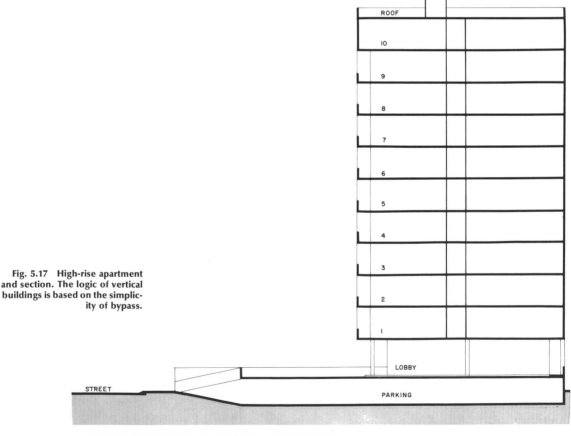

Fig. 5.17 High-rise apartment and section. The logic of vertical buildings is based on the simplicity of bypass.

SECTION THROUGH A TYPICAL APARTMENT

0   5   10   20   40

plain in a logic of adjacency the proliferation of vertical buildings, even in areas where there is not high land cost. A geometric overview is important. Reconsidering historic compositions based on their underlying geometry allows one to see them in a new dimension, the dimension of geometric constraints.

Building Systems

Buildings are geometric forms of enclosure for human occupancy. Human occupancy within buildings is based on repetitive activity; for example, interpersonal office functions are repeated endlessly in a business organization. These two facts tie systems to behavior. Today it is not necessary to begin from the beginning and construct a system of building components. A series of systems programs have been developed, and they have created products which are available nationally. Systems development began in the 1960s with schools, at a time when new techniques for teaching were being promulgated. These techniques led to team teaching and open classrooms. Concurrently the teaching techniques sponsored a new kind of flexible school container. The by-product of this systems analysis of schools is that a generation of interrelated building products is available to solve building problems in bigger increments than before.

School Construction Systems Design (SCSD)   In 1961 a conference was held to see if a market could be brought together representing a sufficient building dollar volume to interest manufacturers in producing new products. The desire was a systems building approach that would make schools more flexible, easier to build, and less costly. A number of school districts in California created such a market, $30 million of construction

Fig. 5.17 (continued)   The section of the experimental pyramid illustrated in Figure 5.15 shows the complexity of bypass in contrast to the simplicity of the vertical high-rise apartment.

1. Pedestrian walk
2. Traffic route
3. Church
4. Cinema
5. Covered garage
6. Community centre
7. Offices
8. School

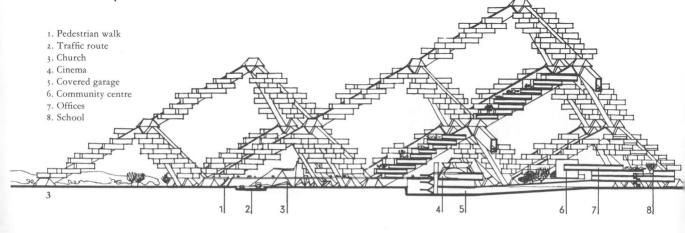

being considered the minimum, and Educational Facilities Laboratories (EFL) helped fund the initial design study. School Construction Systems Design (SCSD) designers concentrated on a series of recurring problems in schools, such as the need for relocatable partitions. They decided they needed three kinds of partitions: those that were fixed, those that could be relocated, and those that were both operable like a folding wall and relocatable. In conventional schools operable partitions generally are too expensive to move. They weigh too much to be handled easily, since to be acoustically effective they must weigh at least 3 lb/ft². The SCSD designers specified the partition need in terms of performance specifications, and

Fig. 5.18 A high-rise apartment project connects apartments to parking, with minimum bypass problems. Most important, the speed of bypass makes the other apartments pyschologically nonexistent. (From MIUS Energy Study, Johnson Space Center, Urban Systems Project Office, Clovis Heimsath A & E support contractors.)

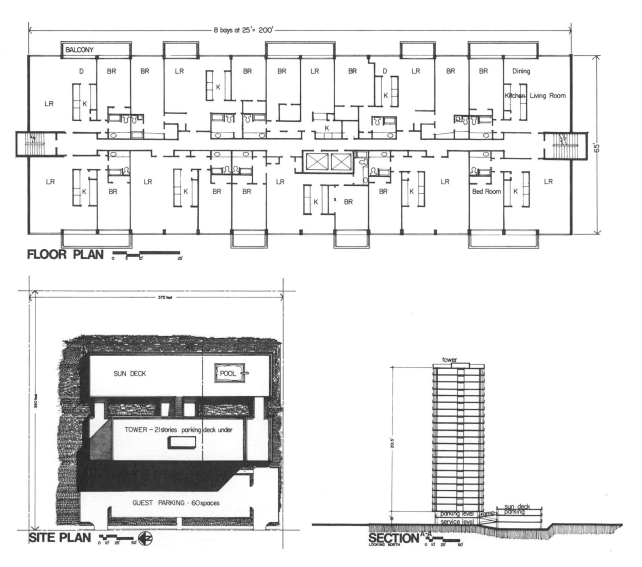

they required contractors to solve the problem they posed on a competition basis.

The partitions, however, could not be divorced from the ceiling system of lights and air conditioning, for each movement of the partitions created new rooms that would thereby have altered requirements for lighting and ventilation. SCSD required that a second set of subcontractors that dealt with ceiling systems and lighting systems integrate their designs with partition systems (see Figure 5.19).

The partitions, air-conditioning ductwork, and lighting all affected the structure of the building, for the ducts had to pass through the structure and the degree of changeability had to conform with the configuration of structural members. SCSD developed an open specification format; that is, each manufacturer had to show that its subsystem component was compatible with those of at least three other manufacturers. The responsibility for proving compatibility rested with the manufacturer. Figure 5.20 shows a subsystem compatibility matrix relating the major elements of structure, heating, ventilating, and cooling, and the ceiling-lighting system. The ceiling-lighting system had to be compatible in turn with proposed partition systems.

Design of subsystems developed through four stages:

1. Establishing user requirements
2. Establishing performance standards based on these requirements
3. Integrating the components into a coordinated building system
4. Testing the components to be certain they satisfied performance specifications

Subsystem Compatibility

		Lighting–Ceiling															
		Armstrong C-60/30	Armstrong C-60/60	Butler L/C20, 30 GRID	Clg.Dyn. LAMBDA,OMEGA V	Clg.Dyn. MOD II-V,MOD V	Celotex VARITEC 800	Conwed FIVE PLUS FIVE	Donn Coordinator	Keene SPEC 10-SPEC 90	Lok VCR, CUSTOM	Lum. Clg. TEC VI	Nat. Clg. 1000-3000	O-C DIMENSIONAIRE	Soundlock SOUNDLUME	Sunbeam IS1000-IS6000	Syncon
Heating, Ventilating, Cooling	Acme SERIES "E"	○	◓	○		○		○		○			○		○		
	AAF MZRM	◐	●	○	◓	●	○	○		○	○	○	○		○	○	
	Carrier 37K, 42 H, MOD.	○	◓	◓	○	○	○	○	○	○	○	○	○	○	◓	○	○
	Carrier 48MA	◐	●	◐	●	●	◐	◐	●	◐	◐	◐	◐	◐	◐	◐	◐
	Chrysler CMS	○	◓	◓	○	○	○	○	○	○	○	○	○	○	○	○	○
	Dunham-Bush RTMZ	○	◓	○	○	○		○	○	○			○		○		○
	ITT RMA 100, 400, 600	●	◓	●	◓	◓		◓	●	●		◐	○	○	○	◐	●
	Lennox DMS-1	●	●	●	●	●		○	○	●	●	◐	○	○	○	◐	●
	Lennox DMS-2	●	●	●	●	●		○	○	●	●	◐	○	○	○	◐	◐
	Lennox DMS-3	●	●	●	●	●		○	○	●	●	◐	○	○	○	◐	●
	Mammoth ADAPT-AIRE	○	◓	◓	○	○	○	○	○	○	○	○	○	○	○	○	○
	Mammoth ADAPTA-ZONE	○	◓	◓	○	○		○	○	○	○		○		○		
	McQuay ROOFPAK	○	○	○	○	○	○	○	○	○	○	○	○	○	○	○	○
	Schemenauer MULTIZONE	○	◓	○				○		○			○	○	○		
	Trane CLIMATE CHANGER	○	◓					○		○			○	○	◓		
	York MULTIZONE	○	◓	○				○		○			○	○	○		
Structure	Butler SPACE GRID	●	●	●				◓	○	○			○		○		
	Butler LANDMARK	○	○	◐	○	○	○	○	●	○		○	○		○		
	COMPONOFORM	○						○		○			○		○		
	Dominion Bridge	○	◐					○		○			○		○		
	DYNA-FRAME	○	◓		◓	◓		○		○	○	○	○		○	○	
	Francon RAS	○	◓					○		○			○		○		
	Haven-Busch JOISTRUSS	◐	●	○	●	●	○	○	○	◐	◐	○	○	◐	○	◐	○
	Macomber V-LOK	●	●	◐	●	●	◐	●	●	●	◐	◐	◐	◐	◐	◐	◐
	PCA DUOTEK-S	○	○	○	○	○	○	○	○	○	○	○	○	○	○	○	○
	Romac MODULOC	●	●		●	●	○	●	●	●	○	◐	○	○	○	○	○
	Steel Fab. FAB-LOK	○	○	○	○	○	○	○	○	○	○	○	○	○	○	○	○
	Syncon	○	○					○		○			○	○	○		●
	TrusJoist TJC	◐	●	○	○	○	○	○	○	○	○	○	○	○	○	○	○
	Unistrut 5' Module	◓	◓					○	○	○		○	○		○		

		Structure													
		Butler SPACE GRID	Butler LANDMARK	COMPONOFORM	Dominion Bridge	DYNA-FRAME	Francon RAS	Haven-Busch JOISTRUSS	Macomber V-LOK	PCA DUOTEC-S	Romac MODULOC	Steel Fab. FAB-LOK	Syncon	TrusJoist TJC	Unistrut 5' Module
Heating, Ventilating, Cooling	Acme SERIES "E"	○				○		○	◓	○	○	○	○		
	AAF MZRM	○	○			○		○	●	○	○	○	○		
	Carrier 37K, 42 H, MOD.	◓	○	○	◓	○	○	○	◓	○	○	○	○	○	○
	Carrier 48MA	◐	◐	◐	◐	◐	◐	◐	●	◐	●	◐	◐	◐	◐
	Chrysler CMS	○	○	○	◓	○	○	◓	◓	○	○	○	○	○	
	Dunham-Bush RTMZ	○				○		◓	◓	○	○	○	○		
	ITT RMA 100, 400, 600	●	○		◓	○	○	◓	●	●	●	○	●		○
	Lennox DMS-1	●	◐	○	○	◐	◐	●	●	●	●	○	●	○	○
	Lennox DMS-2	●	◐	◐	●	◐	●	●	●	●	●	◐	●	◐	◐
	Lennox DMS-3	●	◐	○	○	◐	◐	●	●	●	●	○	●	○	○
	Mammoth ADAPT-AIRE	◓	○	○	○	○	○	○	◓	○	◓	○	○	○	○
	Mammoth ADAPTA-ZONE	◓						○	◓	○	○	○	○		
	McQuay ROOFPAK	○	○	○	○	○	○	○	○	○	○	○	○	○	○
	Schemenauer MULTIZONE					○		○	◓	○		○	○		
	Trane CLIMATE CHANGER	○				○		○	◓	○	○	○		○	
	York MULTIZONE	○				○		○	◓	○	○	○			

○ Probable compatibility claimed by one or both manufacturers, and/or probable or full compatibility claimed in previous edition of this report and not revised by manufacturer(s).

◐ Full compatibility claimed by manufacturer of product listed at side of chart, but not at top of chart.

◓ Full compatibility claimed by manufacturer listed at top of chart, but not at side of chart.

● Full compatibility claimed by both.

Fig. 5.20 Compatibility matrix, lighting-ceiling systems. (EFL/West, 3000 Sand Hill Road, Menlo Park, California.)

Awards to particular manufacturers were made, and other manufacturers who did not win in the initial award could produce compatible products for later bidding. The success of the process is best seen in its influence within the building community. In the first 10 years, over 1,300 schools with a construction volume of over $1 billion had used one or more subsystems developed by the SCSD program, and the components were even as widely used in nonschool construction.

The systems process was affirmed by federal agencies, including the General Services Administration, which has prime responsibility for general government construction. They in turn developed major systems building programs aggregating markets large enough to require additional subsystem development and coordination. Finally, a number of additional school design programs have been developed; the major ones

Fig. 5.21 In the SEF system design, a pole is developed for flexible conduit positioning. (From Educational Facilities Laboratories, Systems; George Zimbel, photographer.)

are Toronto's Study of Education Facilities (SEF), Montreal's Research in School Facilities (RAS), and the University Residential Building System (URBS). Each of these programs added items to the required compatibility matrix, while correcting shortcomings of the earlier programs. For example, the SEF program required that there be an integrated electronic network for intercom systems, telephones, and so forth. It also required an integrated roofing system, plumbing system, and another subsystem combining carpets, gym floors, and hardware. SEF disallowed the use of subfloor conduits, so a pole device was developed for use where partitions were not available to carry conduits (see Figure 5.21).

The RAS program was for multistory schools and required concrete construction for fire codes. Integration of subsystems required the structure be designed to receive ductwork, as shown in Figure 5.22. Also required was a partition that was only 2¼ in. thick, rather than the standard 4-in. partition commonly in use. By using the narrower partition, 7 ft² of floor area was added to each 25 × 30 ft classroom, or nearly 1 percent.

The problem of ducts running in both directions in the constricted area of the ceiling chase was addressed in the URBS construction specification. The solution was a combined mechanical and structural ceiling—a solu-

Fig. 5.22 In the RAS program, the fireproof concrete structure is designed to receive ductwork. (From Educational Facilities Laboratories, Systems.)

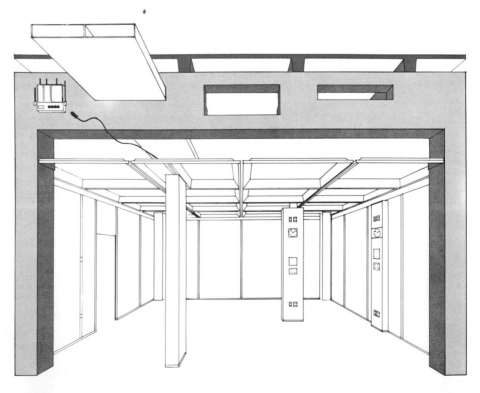

tion possible only because the requirement for coordination was specified from the beginning.

Breakthrough, a major systems design and construction program sponsored by HUD in the late 1960s produced responses from over 500 companies and awards to 22 which led to building developments in eight cities. While I believe much of the residential prefabrication industry can be traced to the Breakthrough impetus, the impact was far less important than the SCSD program. The construction of private homes is a process unlike general building construction and has traditionally been highly fragmented so that large developers control less than 2 percent of the market. In the area of general building, however, a handful of major manufacturers control whole subcontract areas (such as ceiling systems or gypsum partitions) and a hundred contractors dominate the dollar volume of construction.

Building subsystems are available today to coordinate the areas of structure, partitions, mechanical equipment, and ceiling-lighting systems. As indicated in Figure 5.23, use of systems components can lead to fast-track construction, speed, and related economies. More important from a behavioral point of view is the fact that there is in the systems approach a built-in predesign for flexibility and change over time. The implications of these built-in characteristics will be developed in more detail in considering the interface between buildings and behavior.

Fig. 5.23 The URBS solution shows ducts running in either direction within the constricted area of the ceiling chase. (From Educational Facilities Laboratories, Systems; Rondal Partridge, photographer.)

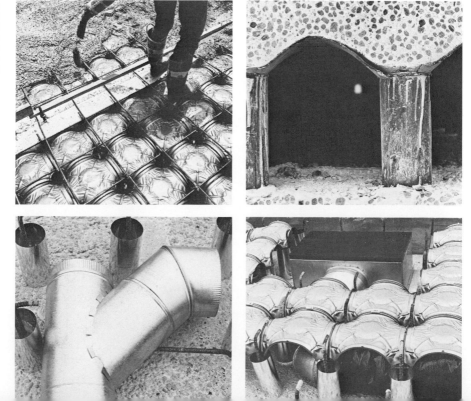

6
The Building/Behavior Interface

An individual left alone builds shelter against the elements and against animals. An individual "locks himself in" at night and when threatened. When an individual is with others, shelter is used as protection from others as well as from the elements and animals. The feeling of "security" in this basic sense requires an enclosure of walls and a roof to exclude all else. This person is "safe." From early ages this fundamental need for personal protection is woven into myths, folklore, and fairy tales. "The Three Pigs" is an expression of this desire to be invulnerable against the wolf. The reverse of protection is servitude, where someone cannot escape, where one person is under the domination of another person. Again, this alternative anxiety is expressed in fairy tales. The castle of defense is breached by the wolf in "Little Red Riding Hood," and when Red Riding Hood arrives she is held captive within the house, formerly grandmother's castle. Fortunately, the woodsman comes and restores social order, and once again the life within is normalized.

Sharp terror is the natural response when the contrast between protection and servitude is abrupt and the person recognizes, at once, that walls of protection have turned into walls of servitude. This is a classic format of mystery thrillers. The heroine typically awakes in an awesome castle, hears the rain, sees the fire in the hearth, and feels warm and protected from the elements without. A crash of lightning, the banging of a window, and the heroine is shown in terror as she sees a dark figure enter to enslave her. The fortress is now a dungeon, for she cannot escape from the very walls that protected her before!

The full implications of these basic feelings, the warmth of security and the terror of servitude, are beyond the scope of this discussion. It is the castle itself, in its dual role of protector and enslaver that is important here. The enclosure in either case remains the same. What is different in the two situations is how one uses that enclosure. Certainly it must be acknowledged that the heroine has strong reactions to her physical situation according to whether she is free or enslaved.

Corridors and Rooms

Mystery thrillers that want to build suspense often use another technique that deserves mentioning. There are twenty rooms in the mansion and the antagonist does not know which one to enter, so he enters one down the row from the heroine, thus awakening her with a start. An opening and closing door or footsteps in the hall tell her that he is getting closer. Finally, the doorknob turns and the audience is braced for the lightning flash that will herald his entrance.

Everyone in the movie house, whether a child or a college graduate, knows about the terror and knows about the hallways. It is no surprise to anyone that the bang of a window in a nearby room will mean a turn of the doorknob in a few minutes. It would be surrealistic to have the mystery man plunge to his death as he stepped out of the first room and found, instead of a corridor, a void between the bedrooms. Just as the lightning flashes, there will be a corridor to walk down.

How does this discussion of corridors enter into building design? When architects are asked to design an elementary school, they will be given a program of rooms. These rooms will have to be arranged in some order so that people can move from one to the next easily. The architect is also given a site on which to place the school, and it is bounded by a rectangular grid of streets or by adjoining property. A high percentage of the time the checkerboard (or xx-yy grid of 90° intersections) is used for site and building design because the lot is rectangular or nearly so, and because the client will seldom accept nonrectangular rooms without special justification. The grid pattern of the city underlies the site planning; the grid pattern of rectilinear rooms underlies the building planning. A building must be connected to sewer lines, electrical lines, telephone lines, water lines, and often gas lines. These utilities are essential to the site plan. Cars must be parked on the site and, of course, they must be parked in closely packed ways to avoid using more space than necessary.

One might see each part of the design process as independent of the other. The point of view that sees all physical planning as a part of a web of systems, however, sees all the above interconnected. The utilities and streets of the city (often termed the infrastructure of a city) are both part of citywide grids. Each constitutes a system of distributing persons and goods. The parking, which must be accommodated off the street, is a system of space ordering which can be determined from parking charts. The building itself will develop as the rooms are positioned along corridors, within a finite number of possibilities.

As the architect gets into the building design itself, the rooms will be grouped into hierarchies. Not everyone needs to walk past the storage closet for the kitchen or the bathroom for the principal. Preparation of a series of flow diagrams becomes the natural first step in building design. Since there are only a finite number of decisions that can be made (generically speaking), the diagrammatic process will soon resolve itself into a few basic solutions. In the case of the elementary school there are many conventions that come into play, including good school plans that the client likes and good school plans found in architectural publications. It is a convention to place the administration offices together; it is a convention to place classrooms across from one another in double-loaded corridor configurations. It is a convention to use formats that provide exterior light in each room. These are some typical rules of thumb for school design. Like the rules of thumb for general design listed in Chapter 2, the reader will note that they do not take particular modes of behavior into account although there are unspecified behavioral assumptions implicit in them.

Given the geometric limitations, the checkerboard grid and the conventions of elementary school arrangements, a plan at this stage is similar to stringing beads on a latticework of strings.

Double-Tracking, Simultaneous Use, and Symbols

The example of the elementary school stated thus far in systems terms seems simple, but in terms of social organization it becomes much more complex. In order to understand what *really* is implied in the design, it is necessary to go beyond strict physical discussion and introduce three concepts not normally used in discussing buildings: double-tracking, simultaneous use, and symbols. The discussion that follows will introduce these three concepts through examples.

Architecture does a very effective job of establishing alternate circulation systems within a building. On the larger scale, planning does an effective job of continuing this alternate circulation system into the fabric of the urban community. Alternate circulation systems will be called here *double-tracking.* (Although there may be more than two circulation systems in a building, generally only two are compared at one time.) Double-tracking is an essential physical tool providing social and job distinctions between people. The full implications of double-tracking do not become apparent, however, until buildings and cities are seen as being used simultaneously, that is, by all the occupants at once! It is of interest that a methodology of simultaneous use has never been developed by architects, yet it is only when one considers all the occupants of a building at any given hour that one is conceiving of the building as it really works. A simultaneous use view of a building points up double-tracking, for it locates various groups of people within the same building, perhaps doing similar things, and it shows them to be separated by corridors and different room divisions. Obviously, it is a physical impossibility for each person to be next to every other person in a building or in a city at the same time. This physical fact requires physical separations, and the physical separations have significant social implications.

Simultaneity is an important concept in understanding the double-tracking of buildings and cities, for the physical division of the world into corridors and places allows time as well as space to separate. For example, it is acceptable for maids to be present in upper-income suburbs during the day, when the children of the suburban families are at school, the housewife often visiting, and the father at work. It is acceptable for a custodian to be in the president's office to clean after hours. It is acceptable for kitchen help to eat in the dining room before or after the guests are to be served. Separation of groups is still maintained, but one prime group is elsewhere when the space in question is occupied by a member of a second group.

A third concept related to double-tracking and simultaneity of building may seem unlikely when first introduced, but it will be shown to be an essential third fact in understanding how architecture and planning influence people. The concept is the symbolism associated with aspects of building, specifically the size of spaces, the relative location of spaces one to the next, and the maintenance of the building or neighborhood.

People live by symbol as a ready-reference of fact. For instance, the custodian in our elementary school, who is in a lower income bracket and therefore "forced" to live in a lower income neighborhood with all its implications, will often drive an old automobile without hubcaps. In the school parking lot, therefore, the custodian deposits his car, turned symbol, as an announcement of his social position. The viewer invariably reads into automobiles the social and economic position of the owner, particularly at extremes in the symbol scale, the Rolls-Royce at the top, the rusted and hubcapless car at the bottom. Again, the custodian in a building will be given to understand that the janitor's closet is his resting place when not actively working. Invariably the janitor's closet scarcely will have room for a chair, and that chair will not be provided. The custodian will in all likelihood find a used chair, perhaps install a hotplate, and relax in a space that, rigged for use, becomes a symbol. The overstuffed chair, the hotplate, the bare electric bulb say minimal service and, somehow, slovenly life-style as well. In the same school, the teachers are provided a lounge which says a great deal about the role the teachers play in the school. When not working, the teachers can relax comfortably, but the significance of being in one place or another goes beyond the comfort of the chairs. The location and its accouterments are given a symbolic significance well beyond their function.

Maintenance is a symbol—one of the most pervasive. Uncollected garbage, broken windows, derelict cars are visual indices of poverty and neglect, suggesting hopelessness. Clean lawns, painted homes, new construction are indices of affluence and health. These are obvious examples. Closer investigation of the visual environment will indicate the subtlety and pervasiveness of symbols, each broadcasting to uneducated and educated alike considerable knowledge of the behavior patterns to be expected of the people involved in that space. Symbols are self-reinforcing; that is, symbols are created by the behavior of individuals and, having been created, they operate to reinforce the behavior of individuals. The custodian, in the janitor's closet, will have his self-image reinforced by the surroundings. If the custodian looked in a mirror each day, it would show an interior room, an overstuffed chair, and lunch on the hotplate. Conversely, the teachers will have their self-images reinforced by the good magazines on the coffee table, the pleasant view, or the reflection of acceptance in the attitude of a visitor who is obviously pleased to be associated with these pleasant surroundings.

Social Organization of Buildings

The social organization of buildings can be classified broadly into four groups, reflecting the social complexity and the role that architecture plays in supporting this complexity (Figure 6.1). Without exception the more complex social functions that hold people in time require more complex architectural environments.

Group 1 Buildings   Group 1 buildings are most often office buildings, where a group of businesses are brought together largely intact, operating largely independently of one another. The group 1 buildings have these three characteristics:

1. They operate as a location and exterior symbol within the community.

2. They operate as an interior symbol between occupants, placing major tenants on upper floors and at corners.

Fig. 6.1 Social organization of buildings.

Group 1	Group 2	Group 3	Group 4
Office buildings	Schools	Long-term hospitals	Lighthouse
Public spaces	Hotels	Psychiatric centers	Remote post
	Motels	Geriatric centers	Monastery
	Restaurants	Orphanages	Superport
	Stores	Homes for retarded	Ship at sea
	Factories	Homes for the blind	Spacecraft
	Airports	Ships in port	Space station
	Churches/temples	Prep schools	
	Clinics	Detention homes	
	Short-term hos-	Jails	
	pitals	Prisons	
		Characteristics	
Symbols	Symbols	Symbols	Symbols
	Double-tracking	Double-tracking	Double-tracking
	Situation produc-	Situation produc-	Situation producing
	ing	ing	Hold service and
		Holds served on a	served on a 24-
		24-hour basis	hour basis

3. They allow for variable subdivision of interior spaces so that various businesses can freely subdivide for their needs.

Group 1 buildings have a relatively minor effect on the social organization within them unless as a symbol they take on strong positive or negative overtones quite aside from space divisions within. (For example, a new building is a positive symbol for all occupants.)

Group 2 Buildings Group 2 buildings are those which have well-defined double-track circulation and activity patterns but do not operate on a 24-hour basis. We have noted that the double-track interior patterns of a building have a significant effect on individuals and serve to institutionalize the status quo in time. Group 2 buildings are those where there is a direct contact between people in two roles: the role of served occupant, and the role of service occupant. The modern supermarket, a group 2 building, uses fewer people than a traditional market, for it is largely self-service, but it still maintains a large staff of service occupants to check and replenish the stock. Moving up the scale of complexity in group 2, we find department stores, restaurants, and hotels. While the hotel operates on a 24-hour basis for service occupants, it does not for served occupants and as such is related more to other short-term social functions than to the third category of institutions that operate for the served occupant on a 24-hour basis. The major functional characteristics of the group 2 building, aside from its location and exterior symbol, are the double-track circulation and activity substructure. The building separates occupants so that the service and served occupants meet only where it is socially acceptable to do so. Furthermore, the spaces provided for meeting are calculated to symbolize the separations between the two (and sometimes more) occupant classifications. Finally, the spaces for private use of the service or served group are designed to continue in size, location, and symbol the differentiation of occupant status.

While group 2 buildings are integrally involved in supporting the social functions the buildings were designed to produce, occupants, both service and served, are free to leave on a daily basis. The influence of the building is a strong but not necessarily an overriding influence on the lives of either group.

Group 3 Buildings Group 3 buildings, like the group 2 buildings, have well-established double-track circulation and activity spaces, but more fundamentally they operate on a 24-hour basis for the served and on a daily basis for the service role. Architecture in these instances has considerable influence in supporting the social organization of the institution and thereby influencing the lives of the occupants served; in particular, it is in institutions, group 3 closed environments, that the influence of buildings on the lives of people is most graphically exemplified. The institution must be equipped to handle all of the occupants' needs: eating, sleeping, sanitation, recreation, health, and purchases. The institution becomes a microworld for the occupant, particularly the served occupant, and the intricacies of the social organization require elaborate architectural support. The group 3 buildings require kitchens, dining rooms, bedrooms, bathrooms, lounges, laundries, stores, recreation areas, and service spaces. Owing to double-tracking of occupants to separate service and served, a group 3 building will more often than not have nearly duplicate facilities for all activities, from dining rooms to separate bedrooms and bathrooms. Clearly the architectural format of a group 3 building is critical to the smooth operation of the social world within.

What is seldom realized is the extent to which architecture is used to support the explicit and implicit goals of the group 3 closed environment. By controlling the total day of the served occupant, the administration can manipulate the life pattern of the occupant. For example, in an intensive care wing of a hospital, the nursing station is immediately adjacent to the critically ill patients so that the nurses can serve these patients with minimum delay. These patients may be giving up all their personal freedom to be situated there, but it is medically required that they be there.

In other closed environments the placement of service and served occupants is also critical to the life pattern of each. A child entering a prep school, a group 3 building complex, is assigned to a dormitory and a close physical companion is at once determined. Whether or not the child is assigned a single room or a room in a dormitory will influence the child's life in the school.

Group 4 Buildings   Group 4 buildings are buildings where the service and served members of the group are both isolated from the rest of society for extended lengths of time. Historically, cities or forts under siege were such building categories; today, the remote post may be a radar station in Antarctica, a superport, or a drilling rig. But the current situation of greatest interest is man traveling in space.

What has been noted in literature is the subtle change that occurs when people must exist together, as in shipwrecks. "Gilligan's Island," the television serial of the mid-1960s, developed endless variations on this common isolation situation. A current article deploring the widespread isolation of jurors for important cases suggests that judges would be far less likely to prolong trials if they were required to be isolated nightly in a hotel room with the jurors, away from family and public communications. The roles of service and served change when people must exist together without freedom to leave except periodically. Yet, the roles do not disappear; quite the contrary, they may be more explicit. The double-tracking apparent on a large ship, with separate officers' quarters for sleeping, dining, recreation, and even work areas, is carried through into small ships as well. A destroyer escort has the differentiations of a larger ship, although some are no more than symbolic, like the ward room for officers which serves other functions as well because of the lack of other available spaces.

At some point, when physical surroundings are constrained sufficiently, additional changes in the social pattern occur. In the Tektite II studies, missions from 14 to 20 days were carried on and monitored in an underwater habitat of considerable constraint. The participants' attitudes toward their surroundings were documented during the period of time, and likewise their attitudes toward others in the group. Privacy, variety, and leisure time were shown to be valued more than had been expected, in physical terms. One reason that privacy was valued so highly was that it became a vehicle for "escaping" from the constant presence of others. (See Figure 6.2 for a list of activities on board.)

But the newness of the methodology in evaluating concise relationships between the physical and social dimensions is exemplified in the design of the space station. Allen J. Louviere in "Engineering Aspects of Habitability" points to this lack of significant data.

> The proper apportionment of volume in a spacecraft best exemplifies the dilemma caused by the unavailability of data needed to make firm decisions in an area greatly influenced by psychosocial factors. Volume will be a major

**Fig. 6.2 Leisure time categori-
zation chart.**

Item	Crew Members Involved	Duration of Leisure Activity	Location of Leisure Activity
Nonmission relevant conversation between crew			
Listening to audio cassettes			
Watching television films			
Snacking			
Reading a leisure book			
Leafing through a book or reading a magazine			
Writing a letter			
Napping			
Looking out windows or viewports			
Resting quietly			
Spontaneous interpersonal actions			
Taking camera pictures			
Watching closed-circuit television			
Tinkering with personal gear			
Nonmission relevant conversation with noncrew			
Quietly watching or listening to other crew			
Playing musical instrument			
Wandering			
Fixing audio or television tapes			
Physical exercise for fun or personal development			
Reading letters			
Looking through leisure facilities for something to do			
Games			
Waiting			
Reading newspaper			
Sketching			
Listening to radio			

issue in the next generation of spacecraft design. The established precedent of volume primarily for systems and experiments will be difficult to overcome. Some generalized data for various volumes have been compiled and plotted against time for quarters and against time correlated to crew size for total spacecraft volume.[1]

A most telling concept, perhaps the first of its kind widely discussed, increases the physical size of the bunk room as the duration of time in-

[1] Allen J. Louviere, "Engineering Aspects of Habitability," presented at the First National Symposium on Habitability, a research report (71-7873-2).

Fig. 6.3 (opposite, above)
Situation chart—small group. The
chart shows situation and
building types. It suggests
the role players in each
situation. It points out the
similarity of activities within
buildings.

Fig. 6.4 (opposite, below)   Situation chart—large group.

creases. While the material claims to be developed pragmatically (not unlike the LUI scale data criticized earlier), the important point is that it acknowledges that acceptable space is a function of time and the number of people involved in a given space.

Situation Charts

Classifying buildings according to the degree of social complexity stresses the real differences between them. What becomes apparent is that the more complex buildings have more numerous social activities. In this sense the more complex buildings are closed; that is, they are replicating a larger and larger number of the normal activity patterns of the participants. In a sense they replicate the open society. A second realization is that activities are clustered, as mentioned earlier, into basic sizes with the largest cluster involving between one and eight participants. The major difference in the activity of counseling, say, in a prep school and in a psychiatric hospital is the role each participant plays. There is nothing unique about the setting, or should not be, for both situations require a person-to-person discussion in a pleasant conversational environment.

Figures 6.3 and 6.4 develop this thesis by presenting prototypical activity areas present in buildings of varying social complexity. Because there will be double-tracking in institutions, sleeping, rest rooms, and food service have been presented for more than one role player, on the assumption that the service and served roles are separated in these areas. The charts are presented to make explicit that buildings really are activity groupings.

Building Size

One final realization about buildings needs airing. There is an assumption, like so many other false ones, that if an institution is large it is performing adequate social functions. This often is not the case. At the Darst-Webbe-Peabody complex in St. Louis, involving 2,500 families and two-score buildings, it might be assumed that a wide variety of activities was available; in fact, this was not the case. The size of the complex was developed by replicating only one facility over and over again—the housing unit.

How many units should make up a building? Perhaps this is the fundamental question that should be asked. Should there be a new building at all? Perhaps the use of existing space which is already tied into the fabric of the community is a far better solution. These questions must be asked and answered. For a building is not better because it is bigger; more often it is socially less effective, particularly when its size is created by duplicating one facility endlessly, be it a living unit or an office.

BUILDING TYPE	GROUP	REST ROOMS 1	REST ROOMS 2	REST ROOMS 3	SLEEP 1	SLEEP 2	HOUSEKEEPING	FOOD PREPARATION	LAUNDRY	BEAUTY BARBER	YARD PROJECTS	CONSULTING
OFFICE BLDG.	1	Lessee					Clean					
PUBLIC BLDG.	1	Visitor					Clean					
STORE	2	Customer	Others (5)(6)(7)(8)				Clean					
CHURCH	2	Worshipper	Minister	Teaching			Clean					
RESTAURANT	2	Guest	Others (5)(6)(7)(8)				Clean/Service Manager	Kitchen Help Service/Mgr.				
GRADE SCHOOL	2	Student	Teachers and Principal	Kitchen and Clean			Clean Principal	Kitchen Help Principal				Student Teacher
MANUFACTURER	2	Worker	Manager				Clean					
GEN. HOSPITAL	3	Patient	Medical and Administrative	Other Staff	Patient Nurses	Interns	Clean and Nursing	Kitchen Help Hosp. Admin.	Nursing Helpers Hosp. Admin.	Patient Special Staff	Special Staff	Patient Doctor
RESORT HOTEL	3	Guest	Staff (5)(6)(7)	Recreation Help	Guest	Staff	Clean and Service	Kitchen Help Manager	Kitchen/Service Manager	Guest Special Staff	Special Staff	
UNIVERSITY	3	Student	Faculty	Administration	Student		Clean and Students	Kitchen Help Business Staff	Student	Student	Special Staff	Student Teacher
JUVENILE HOME	4	Ward	Teacher and Admin. (6)(7)	Other Staff	Ward Foster Family	Foster Family	Ward/Clean Foster Family	Kitchen/Fos. Fam. Supervisor	Kitchen/Fos. Fam.	Ward Special Staff	Ward Foster Family	Student/Family Teacher/Admin.
HOME FOR RETARDED	4	Ward	Teacher and Admin. (6)(7)	Other Staff	Ward Foster Family	Foster Family	Clean/Ward Foster Family	Kitchen/Fos. Fam. Supervisor	Kitchen/Fos. Fam.	Ward Special Staff	Ward Foster Family	Student/Family Teacher/Admin.
PREP SCHOOL	4	Student	Teacher and Admin. (6)(7)	Other Staff	Student Faculty Family	Faculty Family	Student/Clean	Kitchen Help Headmaster Staff	Kitchen/Fos. Fam.	Student	Student Maintenance	Student Teacher
PSYCHIATRIC HOSPITAL	4	Patient/Visitor Nursing Helper	Medical Staff	Other (6)(7)	Patient Medical Staff	Interns/Staff	Patient/Clean Medical Staff	Kitchen Help Hosp. Admin.	Nursing Helpers	Patient Self/Nursing	Patient Nursing Helper	Patient Medical
REMOTE POST	4	Worker			Worker		Worker	Worker/Kitchen	Worker		Worker	
SPACE SHOP	4	Astronaut			Astronaut		Astronaut	Astronaut	Astronaut			
JAIL/PRISON	4	Inmate	Guards/Admin.	Other (4)(5)(6)	Inmate Guard		Inmate/Clean Guard	Kitchen Help Warden Staff	Inmate Guard	Inmate	Inmate Guard	Inmate Lawyer/Family

BUILDING TYPE	GROUP	SMALL SOCIAL	SMALL RECREATION	HOBBIES	TEACHING	FOOD SERVICE 1	FOOD SERVICE 2	LARGE SOCIAL	LARGE RECREATION	WORSHIP	ATHLETICS	EMPLOYMENT
OFFICE BLDG.	1	Lessee / Lessee										
PUBLIC BLDG.	1											
STORE	2	Customer / Friends										
CHURCH	2	Worshipper / Worshipper	Worshipper / Worshipper		Parishioner / Volunteer	Parishioner / Volunteer Help		Parishioner / Minister	Parishioner / Parishioner	Parishioner / Minister	Parishioner / Special Volunteer	
RESTAURANT	2					Guest / Service Help	Service Help / Kitchen Help					
GRADE SCHOOL	2	Student / Student	Student/Teacher / Student/Teacher	Student / Teacher	Student / Teacher	Student / Kitchen Help	Teachers / Kitchen Help	Student/Family / Teachers	Student / Student/Teacher		Student / Special Teacher	
MANUFACTURER	2	Worker / Worker	Worker / Worker			Worker / Worker						
GEN. HOSPITAL	3	Patient/Staff / Patient/Staff	Patient/Staff / Patient/Staff	Outpatient / Special Staff	Staff / Special Staff	Patient / Nursing Helper	Staff / Kitchen Help			Patient / Minister		
RESORT HOTEL	3	Guest/Staff / Guest/Staff	Guest/Staff / Guest/Staff	Guest / Special Staff	Convention Format	Guest / Service Help	Service Help / Kitchen Help	Guest / Guest/Staff	Guest / Guest/Staff		Guest / Recreation Staff	
UNIVERSITY	3	Student / Student	Student / Student	Student / Faculty	Student / Faculty	Student / Kitchen Help		Student / Student	Student / Student	Student / Chaplains	Student / Special Teachers	
JUVENILE HOME	4	Ward / Foster Family	Ward / Ward/Foster Fam.	Ward / Teacher	Ward / Teacher	Ward / Foster Family			Ward / Family and Staff	Ward / Minister	Ward / Foster Family	
HOME FOR RETARDED	4	Ward / Foster Family	Ward / Ward/Foster Fam.	Ward / Teacher	Ward / Special Teacher	Ward / Foster Family			Ward / Family and Staff	Ward / Minister	Ward / Special Teacher	
PREP. SCHOOL	4	Student / Faculty Family	Student/Staff / Student/Staff	Student / Teacher	Student / Teacher	Student / Student/Kitchen		Student / Student/Faculty	Student / Student/Faculty	Student / Minister	Student / Special Faculty	
PSYCHIATRIC HOSPITAL	4	Patient/Staff / Patient/Staff	Patient / Patient/Staff	Patient / Special Staff	Patient/Staff / Special Teacher	Patient / Nursing Helper	Staff / Kitchen Help	Patients/Family / Patients/Staff	Patient / Patient/Staff	Patient / Chaplain	Patient / Special Faculty	Patient / Patient/Staff
REMOTE POST	4	Worker / Worker	Worker / Worker	Worker		Worker / Kitchen Help						Worker / Worker
SPACE STATION	4	Astronaut / Astronaut	Astronaut / Astronaut	Astronaut		Astronaut / Astronaut						Astronaut / Astronaut
JAIL/PRISON	4	Inmate/Staff / Inmate/Staff	Inmate / Inmate	Inmate	Inmate / Special Teacher	Inmate / Kitchen Help	Staff / Kitchen Help	Inmate / Family	Inmate / Family	Inmate / Chaplain	Inmate / Special Staff	Inmate / Inmate/Guard

A quick estimate of any building or building complex is possible by merely designating three areas: the entrances (points of control), the special rooms for diverse activities, and the repetitive areas regardless of function. When it is remembered that bypass is built into any circulation pattern within a building, a focus on repetition is also a focus on the visual life of the environment.

Up to this point in discussing issues, the emphasis has been on buildings and closed environments. City areas also become closed environments because although residents may have the theoretical freedom to leave, they may have neither the ability nor the motivation to do so. Speaking earlier of the "trickle-down" theory of city change, it was pointed out that the constant changing of our cities is a process that concentrates the poor. On the other hand, in Toronto, where the middle class remained downtown, in 1976 two major department stores began rebuilding downtown, with one investing in a structure of 1 million ft^2. The stores are tied into subway connections and elevated sidewalks. The inner city of Toronto is being designed to last at a time when American cities are losing the white middle class, the tax base, the quality of schools, and the quality of their city life. The problem is too simple to see; we design American cities piecemeal, a process which assures failure. Technological advances require comprehensive planning, and in the United States we do not even have a national land-use policy!

Tomorrow it must change, and tomorrow has a new urgency with the energy crisis. We will be able to build duplicate cities for only a few more years.

New Towns—a New Chance

For many today, the concept of new towns is related to the proposals for utopian tomorrows. What is understood in the planning and construction fields to be a major new format for urban development is relatively unknown to the general public, although Columbia and Reston may be recognizable names. Brown Miller[2] suggests that the next 30 years in the United States will witness the construction of as many dwelling units, and the associated city facilities attendant on dwelling units, as have been built in the last 300 years. The National Committee on Urban Growth Policy recommended that 100 new towns of at least 100,000 population and 10 new cities of over 1 million be undertaken between now and the year 2000.

Impetus for these new communities is underway through Title VII of the Housing and Urban Development Act of 1970, which guarantees the ob-

[2] Brown Miller, *Innovation in New Communities* (Cambridge, Mass.: M.I.T. Press, 1972).

ligations of community developers up to $500 million. In 1974, there were fifty-one new towns designated by Housing and Urban Development, and while many have not qualified for government subsidy as yet and many that have qualified are having financial difficulties, this is an indication of the number already past the first planning phase. One reason for the enthusiasm for new towns is suggested in the 1968 Gallup poll which showed that 56 percent of the American public would choose rural life if they had the choice. Only 18 percent would choose a city and 25 percent a suburb.

Two factors categorize the major impetus toward the new town solution. First, there has been a recognized decrease in the quality of life in existing cities. Second, major changes in existing cities are extremely expensive; in 1976, both Washington, D.C., and New York City were extending subways which involved untold cost and disruption, a process which required among other things underpinning existing buildings adjacent to the subway route, and rebuilding buildings that would serve as subway stations. The great expense and limited value of urban renewal schemes can be traced directly to the unplanned, largely speculative growth pattern of all major cities in the United States. While extraordinary efforts are being taken in some urban areas, notably New York City, to rebuild within the existing city fabric, most cities lack the funds or the effective city government to incur the incredible cost of first unbuilding a section of a city and then rebuilding it. Second-generation urban renewal thinking is developing strategies that will involve the whole city fabric; notable examples are community-based programs of the New York City Planning Commission and the Centennial Plan for Philadelphia, Pennsylvania, which links significant areas throughout the city and strengthens their pedestrian ties. While the approach is more constructive, involving the rehabilitation of existing neighborhoods rather than the uprooting of "crisis ghettos," the complexity, and endless necessity of dealing with citizens already inhabiting land surely makes the alternative of pre-planned communities look attractive.

In 1973, I visited new towns in Israel, Sweden, and England. Not only are new towns advanced, so that in England the currently developing new towns are called "third-generation," implying two generations of feedback from the first projects, but many new towns are of considerable size, pointing again to the length of time they have been developing. In the United States at the time of the trip, Columbia had the largest population of any American new town, with 26,000 inhabitants. In contrast, the new town of Ashdod, Israel, at the same date had 48,000 inhabitants, Vallingby, Sweden, had 61,000 inhabitants, and Stevenage, England, had 67,000 inhabitants.

New Town Behavioral Assumptions   What are the assumptions behind new towns in Western Europe? How similar are those towns to new towns being developed in the United States? First of all, the new town movement, whether in this country or in Europe, is surprisingly similar in the format of design, designating parts of cities and then building the structure from these subelements. The differences between the new towns in Israel, Sweden, and England are not as great as might be expected although the motivation to build new towns differed in each country. In Sweden the new town movement predated World War II, with the first legislation being passed in 1933, following an even earlier movement for "sun, light, and air."

Sweden, neutral in World War II, was under continued population growth all during the war and developed new towns to disperse population from the center of existing metropolitan areas, particularly Stockholm. The new towns in Sweden, therefore, are tied closely by public transportation with the existing city center. England, heavily damaged in World War II, had two main goals in developing its new towns: one was the urgent need for housing brought on by the war, and the second was a decentralization plan that would find the population in England less concentrated in the future. Israel, implementing new town legislation in 1948, immediately upon receiving independence, needed to build cities for immigrants and, like England, needed population dispersal.

These differences, and the differences of climate, while pronounced, have little influence on the arrangement of the subunits of design that most intimately deal with people. The most telling indication that all new towns, including all those in the United States, develop physical design on the basis of anticipated social behavior can be seen in the recurrence of almost identical elements, regardless of which country or which climate is considered.

The format of new towns can be characterized as follows:

1. Large-acreage developments
2. Development of arterial roadway connections with adjoining cities
3. Separation of industrial from residential and commercial areas
4. Development of neighborhoods and greenbelt pedestrian paths
5. Village centers to serve one or more neighborhoods
6. Town centers of higher density to serve one or more neighborhoods
7. Public transportation connecting the neighborhood center with the town center, either by bus or, in the case of Sweden, by subway. (See Figures 6.5 and 6.6.)

While it is necessary to see the community scale for some things (for schools, shopping, job opportunities, social, political, and worship activities), it is not necessary to think in communitywide terms when analyzing

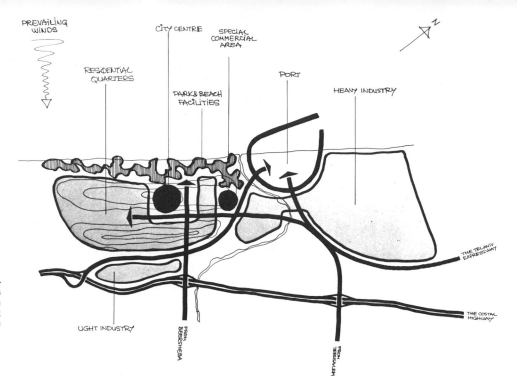

PREVAILING WINDS

RESIDENTIAL QUARTERS

CITY CENTRE

SPECIAL COMMERCIAL AREA

PARK & BEACH FACILITIES

PORT

HEAVY INDUSTRY

THE TELAVIV EXPRESSWAY

THE COSTAL HIGHWAY

LIGHT INDUSTRY

FROM BEERSHEBA

FROM JERUSALEM

Fig. 6.5 (right) Ashdod, Israel— schematic analysis. Master plans of new towns are based on behavioral assumptions. (Yitzhak Perlstein.)

Fig. 6.6 (below) Ashdod, Israel—master plan. (Yitzhak Perlstein.)

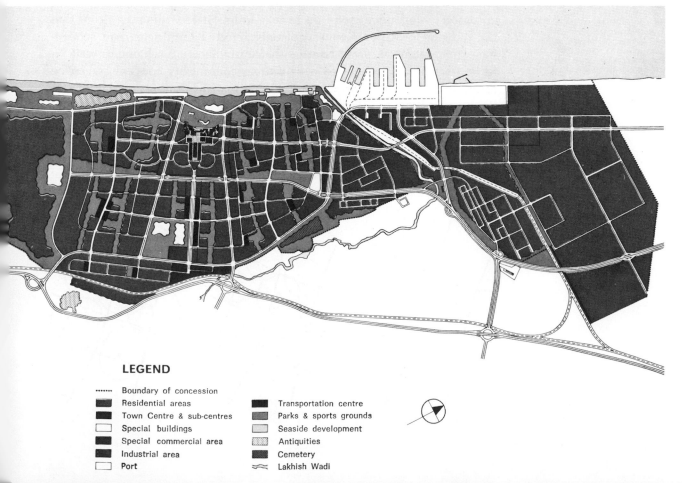

LEGEND

.... Boundary of concession

Residential areas

Town Centre & sub-centres

Special buildings

Special commercial area

Industrial area

Port

Transportation centre

Parks & sports grounds

Seaside development

Antiquities

Cemetery

Lakhish Wadi

the daily life pattern of a family with children. It should be reassuring to those concerned with the quality of life that new towns return to a pedestrian scale found before the industrial revolution in communities around the world. What new towns do is integrate the service pattern of roads and services that are products of modern technology with pedestrian-scaled subunits based on the family with children.

The three prototype design formats are: (1) the ring radial, (2) the linear, and (3) the grid. Since there are a limited number of grids, it is not surprising that all new towns represent one overall form of organization or another. While the grids representing major streets are set, the location of elements within the grids has significant influence on the lives of people living within the towns. For example, Milton Keynes is laid out using a grid pattern with the major intersections encompassing approximately 220 acres (see Figure 6.7). Placement of a school or a shopping area within the center of this supergrid would make the school or shopping area central to all families living within the block, but it would isolate the school or shopping area from other such centers in adjacent blocks.

This problem could be "solved" at least for shopping as it has been in the existing cities of the United States by placing all shopping along the feeder streets themselves. Without arguing about the disadvantages of the automobile-dependent solution in the United States, it is significant that the planner of Milton Keynes not only rejected the linear road scheme based on automobiles but rejected the central location scheme as well. In Milton Keynes, as advanced a new town community concept as can be found in Europe, the planners argued that to make double circulation safe they would have to introduce underpasses for pedestrians at each block, not at the traffic corners but at the midpoint of the blocks. These crossing points become the acceptable location for commerce and education rather than the midpoint of any one superblock. The edge ties two blocks of the community together, developing richness in social contact and variety at

Fig. 6.7 Milton Keynes neighborhood diagrams. (Milton Keynes Development Corporation; Llewelyn–Davies Weeks Forestier–Walker and Bor.)

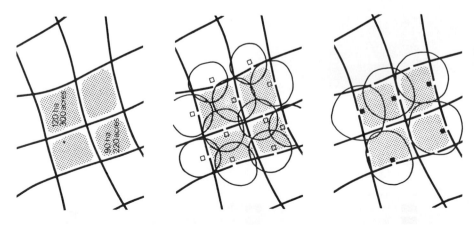

each intersection. Two superblocks support the activities. (One could argue that the corners of supergrids would be better for neighborhoods; however, this would concentrate both pedestrian and vehicular traffic at the same intersection. The designers chose *not* to do this.)

Once the logic of the subunits is accepted, the patterns of new towns unfold almost by themselves. There is no question that the decisions underlying new towns are based on human behavior; yet seldom questioned are the premises used. For example, it is a proven fact that it takes approximately 5 minutes to walk ¼ mile, 10 minutes to walk ½ mile, and so on. What is less assured are the design decisions that stem from this biophysical fact, that is, that people will walk ¼ mile instead of using a car and, therefore, certain elements should be within this distance, such as elementary school, convenience shopping, and open-space recreation. The 220-acre supergrid at Milton Keynes is developed to accommodate slightly under 20,000 people in each neighborhood, figuring densities of fifteen to twenty units an acre and reasonably small families. Social modeling from this first decision places first schools for children 5 to 8 in schools ranging from 160 to 240 pupils and middle schools for children 8 to 12 at school environments of twice the size. Children in secondary school will presumably be old enough to ride their bikes, and, therefore, middle schools will serve more than one neighborhood.

In the 10-minute walking distance, or ½ mile, are placed a middle school, a health clinic, a religious institution, a day-care center, and an indoor public entertainment center. In the 20-minute, or 1-mile, area are placed a high school, major cultural activities, a mental health center, and community television. In the 30-minute, 1½-mile distance from citizens are placed a regional college, regional shopping, regional recreation, and employment.

To round out the scheme, two additional decisions are made at Milton Keynes and at almost all new towns here and in Europe. First, the subshopping and activity center, called a neighborhood center, is located, and it is linked by free or almost-free public transportation to other neighborhood centers and to the larger town center. Second, in every case an early planning decision is made which separates the industrial and heavy commercial area of the town from its residential areas.

In visiting new towns in three countries, I came away with a strange, almost subversive thought that something was still wrong, that new towns outside of London have none of the festive quality of London itself; Ashdod has none of the charm of Tel Aviv; Vallingby and Farsta, except for the town centers, have none of the vitality of Stockholm. Presumably, the new towns recognize behavior, the needs of children to be within walking distance of school, the needs of families to have places in which to walk that are green and natural, the needs for recreation, entertainment, and informal social life. Why then are the buildings so drab? Why then is the whole plan so simplistic? From a balcony in a new apartment complex in Ashdod overlooking a grid of parking lot and play yard, I thought of neighborhood communities that have meant a lot to me: Brooklyn Heights, New York, the Parioli section of Rome, Italy, the downtown Montrose area in Houston, Texas, and more recently the central Texas Czechoslovakian town of Fayetteville, Texas.

Each of these communities has something I felt was missing in the new towns; perhaps it was the fact that I was a stranger in the new towns and a resident for a part of my life in each of the other communities. Yet, the excitement I feel about these various communities I know I also feel when visiting communities where I am also a stranger, for example, many neighborhoods in Rome, Georgetown in Washington, D.C., the Back Bay in Boston, neighborhoods in San Francisco, and so on. Perhaps the element missing is the community input to a communitywide environment.

Traditionally, there have been three staples for social cohesiveness, and they are still largely present in the communities I admire most: the family, the national heritage, and commonly held religious beliefs. If these three are under attack, as evidenced by a high divorce rate and experiments in unmarried relationships, in the distrust of elected officials, in callousness toward public worship, it could well be said that this is a bad time to design cities based on aspirations that are in doubt or on new patterns that have not emerged.

Jane Jacobs, for example, would question the first premise to new towns, that of separating the industrial and heavy commercial area from the living area. Such separation assures a segregation of families into work days with father gone and mother tending children, and evening days when families are at home but there is no bustle of city life. Take a closer behavioral look at the historic city space so admired by sensitive planners and the public as a whole, and it can be seen that commerce and living units were almost always together, with shops below and living above as in the Roman imperial town of Pompeii and much Roman city life of 1974.

Developers of a new town outside of Dallas, Texas, question strongly whether the neighborhood subunit has any meaning today, since almost everyone is relatively mobile and the neighborhood has expanded culturally well beyond neat groupings for systems ordering. But the questions posed by Jane Jacobs, or planners, or any critics will have a basis for analysis since the assumptions behind these towns have been explicitly stated, and time will tell how effective the assumptions are. New town planners, particularly those who design for the possibility of change, as at Milton Keynes, are to be commended for setting the stage for meaningful feedback in years to come.

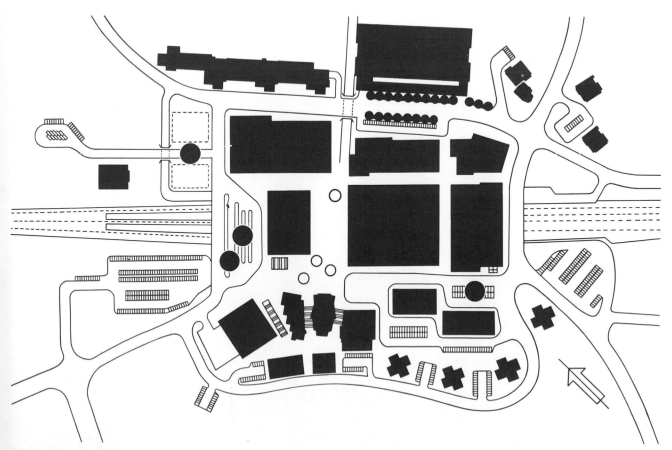

offices

garden

offices

offices

parking and storage

pedestrians

short-duration parking

Fig. 6.8 Borrowed space—sectional.

Fig. 6.9 Plan of Vallingby center.

Summary

In three chapters of Section 2, the issues suggested by behavioral design have been discussed. Complexity is clearly one conclusion, both in viewing humanity and in viewing building. The possibility of ordering is suggested by the repetitive nature of activities based on the basic goals of people, however fluctuating these goals may be for any one person at any one time. Ordering is also suggested when buildings and planning are seen in the generic overview, constrained by the limitations of geometry.

Tying behavior and building together in a comprehensive design approach is clearly a pressing need, for the lack of planning has proven to be counterproductive. Section 3 presents techniques that can be used now to effect a behavioral design process.

In many ways, we, as Americans, are very far behind in recognizing the need for comprehensive design. Figure 6.8 discusses "borrowed space," a concept of integrating people and facilities for built-in activity. Figure 6.9 is the plan of Vallingby center, a plan not unlike a regional shopping center, except that it is built above the rapid transit stop to Stockholm bringing 30,000 people through the shopping plaza daily. Vallingby was planned a decade or more ago. We in America continue to develop duplicate cities, both urban and suburban, with each element separated by traffic and parking. Time is running out—our energy advantage is over.

section three

Behavioral Design

7
Techniques

Design Guides

A major theme of this book is accountability and how it can be achieved. What is apparent to any architect working with a federal or state agency is that accountability at one level is achieved under the current design system. Some agencies have developed a "definitive" plan for each building type with which they are concerned. This plan is given to the architect for guidance and to the administrator for monitoring the designs once completed. Definitive plans are the design equivalent to definitive specifications; in both cases the architect is told what to do in specific terms. That such heavy-handed accountability has led to thoughtless, inflexible, and needlessly repetitive design is apparent to design professionals and the government alike. To offer an alternative to the simplistic design standards, the U.S. Corps of Engineers developed in the 1970s a Design Guide approach to achieving both accountability and adaptability to local conditions. If successful in achieving its ends, the guide approach may find favor with other major government agencies like the Veterans Administration and the General Services Administration, as well as with state agencies and private clients that have repetitive building programs. It is hoped that by avoiding the needless overbuilding which is a consequence of using definitive plans the Design Guide approach can be shown to produce better, that is, more responsive architecture, and actually cost less money.

The Design Guide approach will have impact however widely it is adopted by government agencies, for it has allowed architects to concentrate attention on the problems of design process and communications. In the process, a methodology has been documented that is essentially behavioral. It became apparent to those working on developing the guide approach that the user's needs, determined at various context levels from the individual work station area to the building itself, must be the basis for the design. A major breakthrough in the guide format was the recognition of the area, the area clusters, and the building itself as three distinct contexts for design. By establishing these contexts it was possible to make explicit the particular design elements that support activity at each level of social interaction.

The guide format becomes a behavioral design logic diagram, a technique of particular value where accountability requires prespecified data that are usable for many buildings of varying size and needs (see Figure 7.1). The Chapel and Religious Education Facility Guide is used here to demonstrate the technique. Section I, Introduction, covers general information concerning purpose, policy, and responsibilities. Section II, General Design Consideration, begins the multilevel technique for relating information to design context. In this section general information is developed that has bearing on the project as a whole, more specifically, on the building context and its relationship to the service community.

In Section III, Individual Space Criteria, information about each distinct activity area is presented by describing the activities and participants, the character, adjacency, accessibility, spatial definition, size variation, visual and acoustic considerations (see Figure 7.2). What is apparent from this guide is the development from user's need to architectural enclosure. Each heading relates to this development. Each heading relates to the user's perception of the space. Prior to developing individual areas, the guide describes the activities in some detail in a separate discussion, as well as the general background of the participants. The illustration ties the specific area to a general area diagram, with the area under consideration darkened. The use of a pictogram to recall activities will be discussed below.

In Section IV, Space Organization Criteria, area clusters are developed, making it possible to present information pertaining to this building context. Recognition of area clusters implicitly recognizes that an individual in action utilizes more than one work station in moving through the pattern of a particular activity. For example, a sergeant arriving for work at the Religious Education facility illustrated here will hang up his coat, talk with associates, move to work files, use the coffee bar or rest room, perform routine chores, and in general be active in a number of adjacent areas during the working day. The sergeant's pattern of activity involves various areas, and a building description is more precise when it acknowledges this. The sergeant's associates, as well, interact with him and each other in a cluster of areas. Information presented within the cluster context relates information to group needs rather than to individual needs. Activities considered at the cluster level are group activities, suggesting strongly that group dynamics must be studied to understand utility of the space.

Affinity Matrices   A technique which is used in developing area clusters in the Design Guide is the development of affinity matrices. A matrix, quite simply, places each area in a graphic juxtaposition with every other area in the building. By no means a new technique, it takes on new sig-

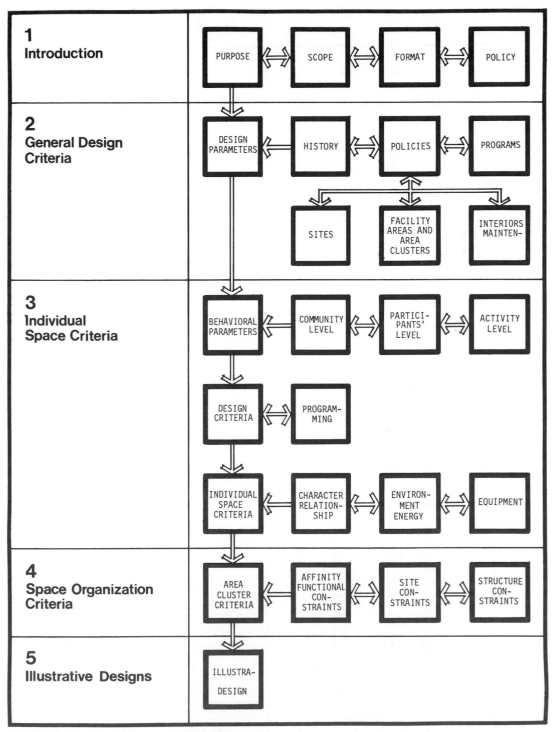

1 Introduction
PURPOSE — SCOPE — FORMAT — POLICY

2 General Design Criteria
DESIGN PARAMETERS — HISTORY — POLICIES — PROGRAMS
SITES — FACILITY AREAS AND AREA CLUSTERS — INTERIORS MAINTEN-

3 Individual Space Criteria
BEHAVIORAL PARAMETERS — COMMUNITY LEVEL — PARTICI-PANTS' LEVEL — ACTIVITY LEVEL
DESIGN CRITERIA — PROGRAM-MING
INDIVIDUAL SPACE CRITERIA — CHARACTER RELATION-SHIP — ENVIRON-MENT ENERGY — EQUIPMENT

4 Space Organization Criteria
AREA CLUSTER CRITERIA — AFFINITY FUNCTIONAL CON-STRAINTS — SITE CON-STRAINTS — STRUCTURE CON-STRAINTS

5 Illustrative Designs
ILLUSTRA-DESIGN

Fig. 7.1 Process organization chart, Design Guide.

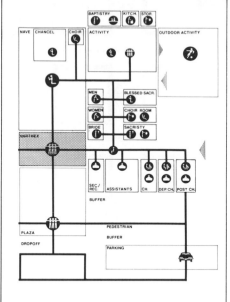

ASSEMBLY
SECTION
2-2.3.10

NAVE 3-4.2.2,
CIRCULATION
3-4.5.6,
SECRETARY/
RECEPTIONIST
3-4.3.3

REFER TO
WORSHIP AND
ACTIVITY
CLUSTER
SECTION 4-3.2

REFER TO
AFFINITY
MATRICES
SECTION 4-2

SPACE TABULA-
TIONS SECTION
2-3.3

STRUCTURAL
SYSTEM
SECTION 2-5.2

SECTION 5-2
200 SEAT CHAPEL

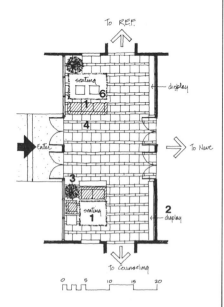

A) Activities / Participants:

The narthex is the major entry for all Chapel Center visitors. The narthex provides for socializing and informal gathering or waiting before and after services. Display areas and information areas should be provided including building register, pamphlet display, artwork, and access to information desk or window. The narthex must allow the congregation to exit quickly and easily after services or in case of emergency.

B) Character:

The narthex should prepare persons psychologically to enter into the sanctified atmosphere of the chapel interior. The narthex should lend an air of welcome and provide a positive first impression for the Chapel Center. The narthex should be easily located from the exterior and provide exterior and interior orientation.

C) Adjacency:

The narthex must be directly adjacent to the nave, circulation and secretary / receptionist's area. Convenient access should be provided to the bride's room, chaplain's offices, choir room, religious education facilities, nave / activity area, and assembly / classroom. The narthex should not be adjacent to kitchens, or private spaces. Coat and hat storage areas and restrooms should be provided nearby.

D) Accessibility:

The narthex must remain unlocked for access to the nave for private worship. A direct fire exit to outdoors is required with panic hardware.

E) Spatial Definition:

The floor area should be 8%—12% of the gross area of the Chapel. A clear circulation path equal to occupant load divided by 50 feet must be maintained for fire exit. (UBC) The narthex must be oriented to provide easy circulation to all major plan elements. A 10'-0'' minimum ceiling height should be maintained. The building entry should be on axis with entry to the nave.

F) Size Variation:

Refer to spatial definition.

G) View:

Approaching visitors should have a view into the narthex for orientation. The secretary / receptionist or assistants, and optionally, REF administration office or director of religious education offices, nificance when communication of information in a visual format becomes important, as it does in transmitting concisely the additional burden of information behavioral design implies. The guide develops a series of matrices: adjacencies related to activity, adjacencies related to accessibility, and adjacencies based on acoustic, visual, and mechanical criteria. As furniture makes accountable the volumetric enclosures for a particular area, so adjacency matrices make accountable area clusters. (Often a series of matrices are combined, forming a combined-use matrix.) Accountability suggests that a change in the criteria as documented in the matrix diagram would develop a different cluster arrangement. For example, in the Chapel and Religious Education facility, the activity room is presented as being adjacent to the nave so that it can provide double service as an overflow worship area, while functioning primarily as a general meeting room. Were the affinity relationship to change, then additional freedom would be possible in locating the major areas in the composition. This affinity relationship suggests a predetermined activity, that is, large services at special but infrequent intervals. Were the architect to place the activity room in a position not adjacent to the nave, the issue of activity would immediately surface. Matrix diagrams effectively communicate considerable information in graphic terms and "store" relationships to be considered only when they vary from the preprogrammed norm.

Pictograms   Architects have traditionally used bubble diagrams to relate areas. One preprogramming technique in common use develops an area diagram in which areas correspond to the rule-of-thumb size generally accepted for that activity. In Figure 7.2 such an area diagram is presented, and superimposed on it are pictograms used for ready recall of the activity presupposed to take place in that area. In developing the pictogram it was assumed that designers working on a project seldom have time or inclination to read data descriptions when actively involved in the visual language of drawing. Recalling the activities through pictograms is a technique of placing the image of behavior directly before designers each time they refer to the base area diagram. The pictograms were developed for the particular building and are introduced adjacent to a general description of the activity to cross-reference the material.

The Design Guide develops illustrative plans through areas and area clusters. Relationship of elements produces myriad solutions, as illustrated earlier (Chapter 3), a by-product of a systems approach to variation and accountability.

Discussed later are computer applications using as illustration a project based directly on the context format of the guide and sponsored also by the U.S. Corps of Engineers to test the versatility of the guide approach.

Fig. 7.2 Narthex diagram. A typical page from a Design Guide.

Behavioral Design Process Model

The concepts presented under the Design Guide format apply to a general design technique rather than the general direction of the design process. A general Behavioral Design Process Model will now be presented, based to a large extent on the approach developed above but including additional material.

In keeping with a major thrust of this book that graphic communication is essential to a behavioral design approach, the material describing the general process model will be presented in both verbal and graphic form. The charts (Figures 7.7 to 7.10) serve three purposes: (1) they act as a checklist reference to elements that need to be considered, (2) they suggest by adjacencies of elements the process itself, and (3) they are available for actual use in performing the suggested step. The illustrative charts are filled out for the Library–Study Center at St. Stephen's Episcopal School in Austin, Texas (see Figure 7.3).

Fig. 7.3 Library–Study Center, St. Stephen's Episcopal School, Austin, Tex. Above, right: Exterior view. Use of the entrance was perceived quite differently by students and staff: for students it should be a place to congregate; for staff it should be unencumbered. Right: Interior view. Openness and variety led to a split-level system of floors around a central sky-lit atrium. (Architects: Clovis Heimsath Associates; photographs: Armstrong Company.)

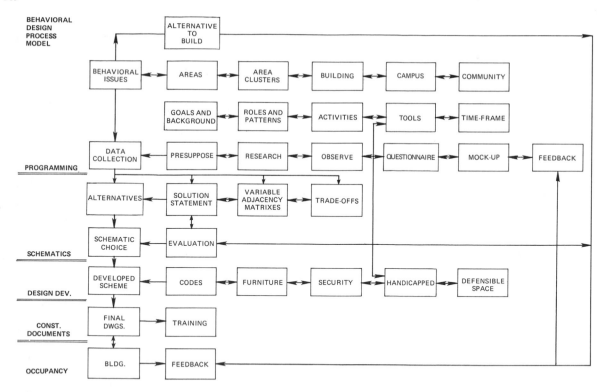

Fig. 7.4 Behavioral Design Process Model.

Figure 7.4 diagrams the process model in some detail and introduces the major parts of the model and their relationships. The emphasis here is on a means of collecting and quantifying behavioral information. Expanding the scope of the Design Guide, five contexts are presented as fundamental control points in establishing and quantifying data. Besides the three areas the guides stress, a campus and community context are included. The logic is simply that these five steps in building scale must be considered whenever someone designs a building. The room scale considers one or more people in defined activities; room clusters consider people working in groups in particular areas of a building; the building scale considers the complete social organization within a building, and so forth, to the campus scale and the community itself. Each scale becomes a context for design; each scale relates the natural archetypal activity patterns. In this regard, the superblock of Milton Keynes (discussed earlier) relates to the distance one can walk in 5 minutes, that is, ¼ mile; it becomes, naturally (or behaviorally if you will), the dimensions of a community. Whether merely convenient or even profound, the five contexts set a reasonable fix in the wilderness of information (see Figure 7.5).

Five Contexts for Design

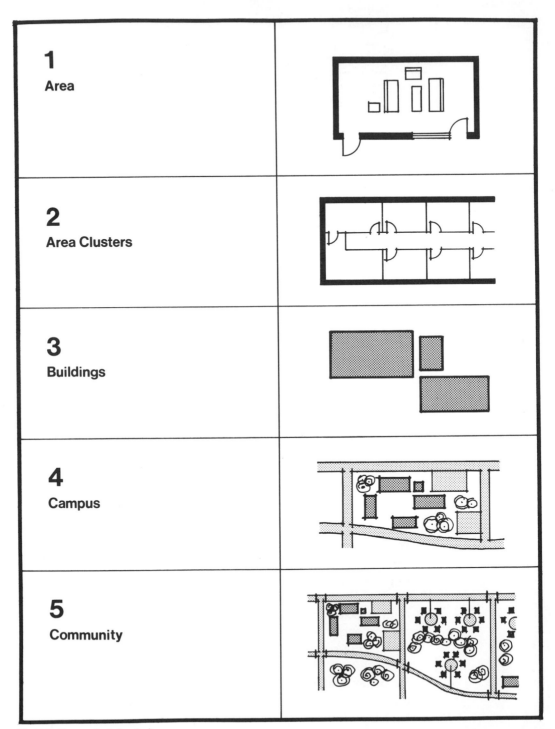

1 Area	
2 Area Clusters	
3 Buildings	
4 Campus	
5 Community	

Fig. 7.5   Five contexts for design.

Design Contexts

Behavioral Issues: **Available Information:**

	Behavioral Issues	Available Information	
1	Roles Activities Tools User Requirements Flexibility	Human Engineering Standards Subsystem Data Furniture Systems Mock-Up	
2	Roles & Patterns Activities Adjacencies Circulation Control Time-Frame Flexibility	Research Observation Questionnaires Adjacency Matrices Management	
3	Expansion/Change Activities Social Dynamics Hierarchy Circulation Control/Freedom Security/Surveillance	Research Observation Questionnaires Systems Data Simultaneous-Use Diagrams Feedback	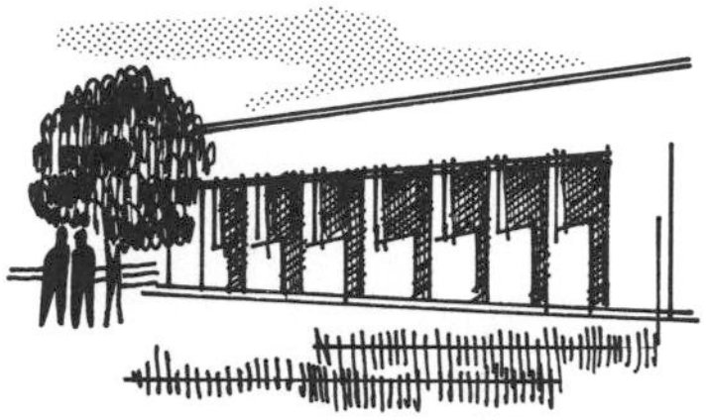
4	Ecology Social Dynamics Hierarchy/Symbol Circulation Control/Freedom Defensible Space	Zoning Data Transportation Data Research-Planning Observation Questionnaires Simultaneous-Use Diagrams	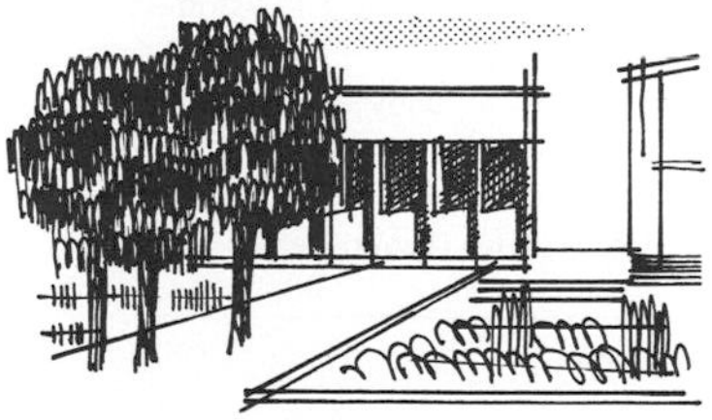
5	Ecology Community Norms Diversity of Activity Circulation Size Change	Zoning Data Research-Planning Transportation Data Service Data New Town Data Planned Unit Development Data Questionnaires	

Fig. 7.6   What are the behavioral issues? What information is available?

Figure 7.6 lists a series of issues that must be considered at each scale of design, from the area to the community. Across from the issues are sources of information available to clarify these issues. Considerable information is available, for instance, at the area level, that documents the size of furniture and proposed spacing. At the community scale, considerable data are available justifying the grid spacing of streets in new towns. The chart is presented here as a ready-reference to the scope of issues and sources.

Chart 1   Chart 1 (Figure 7.7) is developed to document in succinct terms the major aspects of the goals and background of the role participants. It is generally easy to determine in any particular building situation what the service and served roles will be. At St. Stephen's the roles fall into administration, faculty, and students. What is clear is the difference of goals and background perception of the participants in the project depending on the role each participant plays. It is also apparent, therefore, that to be successful the building must be successful for at least three role players.

Fig. 7.7 Chart 1, Goals and background—St. Stephen's Study Center.

CHART: 1	GOALS AND BACKGROUND	ST. STEPHENS STUDY CENTER

FILLED OUT BY ROLE 1 ☐ ADMINISTRATION (SERVANT)
ROLE 2 ☐ FACULTY
(SERVED)
ROLE 3 ☐ STUDENTS
ARCHITECT ☐ (PRESUPPOSE)

ADMINISTRATION GOALS	BACKGROUND
(List administration goals and assumed user goals)	Full-time librarian - master's degree
Admin. Central focus of activity at school Orderly operation	Help by part-time teacher's aides - master's degree
User-creative learning experience	

FACULTY	
Centrally located offices Student and resource availability Quiet, privacy, group cordiality, and identity	All faculty use library, have offices there Younger members master's degrees Established few

STUDENTS	
Social interaction Pleasant study areas Interest and change	Pre-high school Some discipline problems High school Generally white middle-class values

Chart 2 Chart 2 (Figure 7.8) is developed to bring behavioral information one step closer to a design impact. This form is designed to be filled out for each major area in a building, recognizing that the participants, the implications of the role player, and the activity all may vary. For example, consideration of the open stacks, reading areas, and faculty offices involves all the participants. Consideration of the librarian's work area if it were used in an example would more likely involve only the staff and students.

Recognition of a time frame for activities is essential if the life of the building in a 24-hour time frame is to be ascertained. It is also essential if time-use diagrams and simultaneous-use diagrams are to be developed, each a study tool described below.

Fig. 7.8 Chart 2, Area-role-activity chart—St. Stephen's Study Center.

CHART: 2	AREA-ROLE-ACTIVITY CHART			ST. STEPHENS STUDY CENTER	
FILLED OUT BY ROLE 1 ☐ ADMINISTRATOR (SERVANT) ROLE 2 ☐ FACULTY ROLE 3 ☐ STUDENTS ARCHITECT ☐ (PRESUPPOSE)					
AREA(S)	ROLES	ROLE IMPLICATIONS	ACTIVITY	TOOLS	TIME-FRAME
Open stacks Reading areas Faculty offices (open)	1. Library staff	Req. control/order needs work space adjacent. Sets rules	Library functions as required study hall for slow students, resource center for all ages	Audiovisual carrels. Movie area (adjacent) Reference books and catalogs. Informal seating areas	Daytime. During dinner closed Evenings to 10:30 P.M.*
	2. Faculty	Office hours flexible supervisors required during office hours Have studies at home therefore this is second, more public space		Variety for various size study groups and times Conference room for private conversations	*Staffing problem for long day
	3. Pre-high school	Short time frame need supervision lack of library training			
	4. High school	Used to various size work groups. Good study habits inquisitive			

Chart 3 Chart 3 (Figure 7.9) relates material gathered on Charts 1 and 2. Here the intent is to make succinct the possible conflicts of point of view between participants. Each space in the building is listed, and the point of view each participant has toward that space is listed.

Chart 4 Chart 4 (Figure 7.10) is a vehicle for making design solutions explicit. It is the key chart for feedback because it lists the particular decision and relates it to both the building context and the issue to be solved in that context. For example, exterior lockers were provided at St. Stephen's in an attempt to keep day students and their friends away from the main entrance. The main entrance was designed for families and visitors. A number of questions were raised when this solution was proposed, particularly concerning the distance of lockers from rest rooms. A major behavioral assumption behind this solution was that use of the rest rooms was not integral but only incidental to the day student's routine in arriving and stowing gear in the morning or waiting for the bus in the evening. By analyzing the building a few years from now it will be possible to test this assumption.

Fig. 7.9 Chart 3, Area–role–point of view chart—St. Stephen's Study Center.

CHART: 3	AREA–ROLE–POINT OF VIEW CHART	ST. STEPHENS STUDY CENTER
POINT OF VIEW	FILLED OUT BY ROLE 1 ☐ ADMINISTRATION (SERVANT) ROLE 2 ☐ STUDENTS ARCHITECT ☐ (PRESUPPOSE)	POINT OF VIEW
ROLE 1 Administration (Servant)	BUILDING SETTING AREA	ROLE 2 (All ages) (Served)
Central location important to parent arriving	Exterior	Place for student meeting Place to wait for day student's bus
Checkout required suggests manning problems. Possibly display area	Entrance foyer	Lounge furniture ideal for reading Where can I stash books between classes?
For children and parents	Librarians-checkout	
Must be adjacent to work area or visually controlled. Lockable	Work area	Best equipment is in work area Want access to it without supervision
Use by faculty or students, requiring scheduling	Conference	Want free use for student meetings
Open plan difficult for status/quiet	Faculty offices	Good access, don't like implied supervision
Problem of misfiling material	Open stacks	Best use of library is open stacks, need clear identification of sections
Difficult student supervision	Study areas desk, carrel, lounge	A carrel gives privacy, is personal, desire variety in group seating
Breakage, control problem	Audiovisual	Filing and returning equipment a drag
Requires trained students, storage	Movie	Need good access in and out
Not separate, privacy. Problem	Rest rooms	Never know if faculty is in there

CHART: 4	SPECIFIC DESIGN SOLUTIONS EXPLICIT CONTEXT AND ISSUE		ST. STEPHENS STUDY CENTER

IMPORTANCE TO   BY: ADMIN. ☐
PARTICIPANT
WEIGHED 1-10 (MAX)   USER   ☐
                               ARCH. ☐ PRESUPPOSE

BY ARCHITECT

CONTEXT	SOLUTION	BEHAVIORAL ISSUE	
Entrance area in front of building—building scale	Provide for exterior lockers for day students apart from main entrance stairs (two entrances for students and visitors)	Students want place to meet, day students need place to wait for bus. Must discourage belongings left in foyer *See 1, Chart 3 Also need clear entrance for parents adjacent to control desk *See 2, Chart 3	
			6
Student seating area—cluster scale	Provide seating landscape of plywood (carpeted) for low cost and change-ability	Students want variety of seating seemingly unsupervised, informal size in group *See 3, Chart 3	
			8
Separation of floors—building scale	Each floor is half level above or below, adjacent central skylight links floors and provides seating on lower level	How to relate feeling of freedom for student with informal faculty supervision: Also allow for maximum flexible change in time	
			8
Conference room—area scale	Located adjacent to faculty offices also for easy student access, glass to ceiling for acoustic privacy	Both students and faculty need place for structured meetings and acoustic privacy	
			6

Fig. 7.10 Chart 4, Specific design solutions; explicit context and issue—St. Stephen's Study Center.

Techniques for Information Gathering

Six techniques are presented for information gathering, beginning with the most commonly used technique, described here as "presuppose."

Presuppose In reading material developed by behavioral psychologists in the last few years, I have been struck by the degree of success they achieve in presupposing behavioral patterns and verifying them in observation of one kind or another. On reflection it does not seem surprising, for they are trained to anticipate behavior, have broad knowledge of behavior in other related settings, and are attempting to be not seers but expert verifiers. Many of the conflicts they presuppose are obvious ones. However, it is also true, on reflection, that architects generally are not asked to presuppose even those presuppositions of point of view which are apparent to the ordinary person, for example, the conflict between the desire for play on the part of students and the desire for order on the part of faculty.

To make myself an honest man in approaching behavioral design, perhaps even to make some behavioral psychologists honest, I present the presuppose technique for gathering behavioral data as the first and perhaps most useful one. Architects, in their capacity as thinking adults, have a wide range of knowledge about people and how they interact. They know more than the average person because their profession offers access to a wide variety of situations, in a wide variety of building types. It has been suggested by critics that many architects project their middle-class mores onto their designs. I feel that criticism is inaccurate only because it assumes that architects within the current design situation spend much time projecting mores into the designs at all. Intuitively, of course, a good designer is considering myriad influences in arriving at a decision, but the current design process does not encourage the architect to presuppose very much. (There are dramatic exceptions of course, and there are firms that pride themselves on problem finding as well as problem solving. It must be acknowledged, I fear, that such firms today are in the minority largely because clients that sponsor such creative thought are in the minority.)

Presupposing can be accomplished by the architect alone, but more usefully it can be a tool for communicating with the owner and participants in a building. The architect by presupposing gets the ball rolling, so to speak. By suggesting logical positions and asking responses to them, the architect combines this technique with direct observation. It will be apparent later in discussing the chart for evaluating designs that the decisions can be no better than the individual weighing the items and scoring them. Here again, I suggest, the team member who scores the evaluation sheet is making judgments which rely to a large extent on that individual's ability to presuppose.

The process model presented here is a general one, considering building projects of varying social complexity. For simple building projects I suggest that the architect is quite capable of articulating the user's conflicts and problems. For more complex social projects the architect must utilize additional data collection techniques, and as the need for precision in data collection increases, the desirability of working with behavioral psychologists increases. The question of teamwork is discussed in Chapter 8.

Research Considerable data are available that bear on behavioral issues. As the technique of presupposition must be affirmed, so must the design data generically considered under the term *graphic standards* be affirmed. *Graphic Standards* is also the name of a much-used reference book, but it is a term more broadly used to describe material presented in *Time-Saver Standards* and other data reference volumes. These volumes give significant data on room arrangement, rule-of-thumb area per person for various activities, and repetitive room clusters for precise activities, such as operating suites in hospitals (in a group 3 institution).

A cursory glance at such data indicates a shortcoming of such a ready-reference approach; that is, it is presented without people. The data developed from such sources are valuable as pragmatic beginning points. Presupposing activities and movement on these diagrams can expand their value; techniques for juxtaposing motion and plans are discussed below under the heading "Simultaneous Use."

For any building type there are buildings which have been recognized as significant by architectural editors and award juries. The standard for judgment is often as vague as the motivations behind the solutions; however, these plans offer a second source of relevant data when interpolated for probable use patterns. Working with a consultant specializing in the particular building type or with a behavioral psychologist, the architect can become conversant with a series of related buildings merely from studying plans; the process suggests issues to be followed in making visitations. For example, in the Marin County Community Mental Health Center, reviewed in a feedback document by the architects some years after construction, the central lounge area was designed with a low, rather than a high, ceiling, and this idea which supposedly sponsors intimacy received good marks by the participants.[1] See Figure 7.11.

Research of behavioral literature is a third major source of information, although it must be interpolated. Here it is imperative to use a trained

[1] "An Evaluation, Marin County Community Mental Health Center," Kaplan & McLaughlin Architects, San Francisco.

Fig. 7.11 (below and below, right) Marin County Community Mental Health Lounge. (Kaplan & McLaughlin; Ernest Braun, photographer.)

behavioral psychologist as a team member, for the interpolation of relevancy needs to be made by someone within the field. The following quotation is from a study of bedroom size made during the development of a dormitory project:

> In this context, the pattern of activities in the bedrooms would suggest that the functional meaning of privacy is not being alone but rather having the widest range of personal choice. The small room provides this range of options, of which being alone is only one. Furthermore, being alone in a small room does not necessarily lead to withdrawal. Our data indicated that patients assigned to small rooms showed less withdrawal behavior than those in larger rooms.[2]

This item needs interpretation, yet it suggests a line of questioning that may bear fruit through other data-collecting vehicles.

Observe; Feedback   Architects traditionally visit buildings of a similar nature during any building project. Visitation, however, is distinct from behavioral observation. Often visitation will take place as a tour with the administrator as guide. More valuable is an unobtrusive evaluation of behavior within a building by deciding to spend the day there, arriving with the first users and leaving with the last.

Feedback is a term used to describe an organized system of reevaluation of a building after it has been in operation for a number of years. Three years is a reasonable period of time to wait before making a feedback evaluation, for the normal patterns of activity are a year or more removed from the traumatic first year of operation which for every building tends to be unique in both positive and negative ways. But feedback is not different from visitation and behavioral observation in any operating building, except that feedback presupposes that explicit lists of design decisions have been kept for the three-year period and are available for comparison with actual observation. Recognizing the infancy of behavioral design, it is unlikely that many buildings comprehensively evaluated today have such explicit design statements (see Figure 7.10, Chart 4). However, it is probable that the major design decisions could be reconstructed by the members of the design team. What is essential is that a methodology be developed within an office so that comparable questions are asked and recorded in each building reviewed. When one recognizes that there is nothing generically different between a feedback procedure and observation of existing buildings, a technique of evaluation should be used which correlates both visitations and feedback on completed buildings. The basic items described for each of the five contexts can be used to formulate such a research document.

---

[2] William H. Ittleson, Leanne G. Rivlin, and Harold M. Proshansky, "Bedroom Size: Social Interaction in a Psychiatric Ward," *Environment & Social Sciences,* American Psychological Association, 1972.

Many architects working in behavioral design feel a national clearing-house is needed to correlate feedback data and make it widely available to the profession. At this writing no such agency exists, and informal groups that are working in the field, such as Environmental Design Research Association (EDRA), have not filled this role.

Questionnaires Questionnaires are the most reliable source of data gathering, and their development is an advanced art practiced by firms operating in the human resources field. Architects can commission such firms to prepare questionnaires for a particular project using the professionals to prepare, administer, and evaluate the findings. Questionnaires are basically structured in two formats, standardized interview questionnaires and open-ended questionnaires. The most common is the standardized questionnaire that uses "fixed-alternative" questions. The respondents are asked to check the one answer that most closely approximates the situation they know. In the "open-ended" questionnaire the respondents are asked to finish the sentence or describe how they feel about a particular subject. These questionnaires are designed to elicit free response from the respondents. Each format has particular advantages and disadvantages. The standardized-format questionnaire assures that the answers will be given in a particular frame of reference. Further, when questionnaires are tied to computer compilation programs, the alternative answer is an essential element. However, the weakness of this kind of questionnaire is that respondents may be forced to make a statement of opinion about which they do not have any particular conviction, and omission of alternative responses may lead to a bias.

Figure 7.12 is a diagram for the organization of a questionnaire and the flow of information expected from it. This questionnaire model was prepared to test the desirability of developing a neighborhood shopping center. Figure 7.13 is the result of a questionnaire to determine local residents' interest in various types of housing. The questionnaire, cross-referenced by computer analysis, pointed out a fundamental fact, that none of the groups interviewed wanted either high-rise or multiuse high-rise accommodations. Only the single age group 35 to 64 wanted medium-high-rise living. In this case the questionnaire was prepared to advise a developer whether or not to build high-rise apartments adjacent to existing office towers. Seldom are the results of questionnaires more conclusive. Needless to say, the developer refrained from embarking on such a program.

Mock-up Particularly at the context 1 area level, mock-ups can be valuable tools. They are often used to test partition and work station arrange-

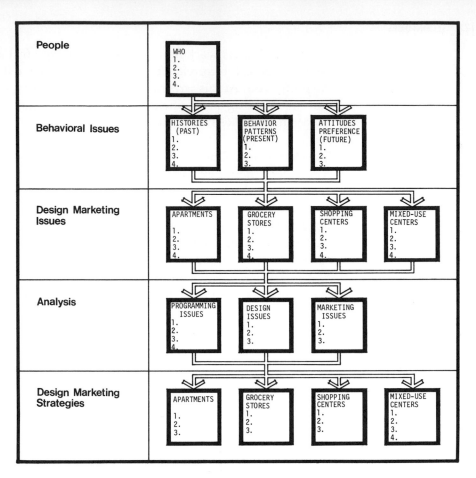

Fig. 7.12 The chart is a logic diagram behind a questionnaire developed to ascertain preferences in neighborhood shopping. (Rice Design Center.)

Fig. 7.13 The results of a questionnaire on housing preferences. No group wanted multiuse high-rise living.

◐ Suitable
● Very Suitable

	Town Houses	Patio Houses	Row Houses	Terraced Houses	Stepped Houses	Garden Apts	Patio Apts	Med Rise Apts	High Rise Apts	Multi Use HR	Composite
Young Single	●	●	◐	●	●	◐	●	◐	◐	◐	◐
Young Couple	●	●	◐	●	◐	●	●	◐	◐	◐	●
2 Parents −35	●	●	◐	●	●	◐	◐	●	◐	◐	●
2 Parents 35+	●	●	◐	●	●	●	◐	●	◐	◐	●
1 Parent	●	●	◐	●	●	●	●	◐	●	◐	●
Empty Nester 35−64	◐	●	◐	●	●	◐	●	◐	◐	◐	◐
No Kids 35−64	●	◐	◐	●	●	◐	●	◐	◐	◐	◐
Single 35−64			◐						◐	◐	

ments. Work stations suggest a repetitive pattern of activity, partitions, desk arrangements, and storage units, all available commercially or custom-designed by the architect for a particular building. We purchased a commercially available work station system for our own offices just as a number of other architects have with the advent of open planning. After using the system for a few years, which incidentally placed draftsmen at desk height, we felt sufficiently comfortable with this "mock-up" to design a custom system which could be built by the general contractor at some savings. The modified system sponsored by a grant from Educational Facilities Laboratories (EFL) has been included in the St. Stephen's Library–Study Center for faculty offices. In the same building we experimented with a variable seating pattern for students on the lower level. In this case we felt that student use of the area could be the only test of the configuration; so it was designed inexpensively in carpet-covered plywood so that it can be evaluated by the students during the next few years and, if found lacking, inexpensively replaced (see Figure 7.3). The mock-up/use concept has opened up the idea of providing low-cost, disposable furniture in particular locations. Imaginative, changeable furniture systems are also available commercially and have been used with enthusiasm particularly in dealing with young children where the activity is unstructured.

None of these methods of data collecting are unique or unknown to the general practitioner. They are presented here in outline to emphasize their use as an integral part of a structured system of data collection and design. Referring again to Figure 7.3, the Behavioral Design Process Model, it will be noted that these methods are all available and can be used in whatever mixture seems appropriate to collect data and thereby construct a view of a building based on probable users' needs, activities, and attitudes.

In continuing the behavioral design technique (see Figure 7.3), an additional chart is presented (see Figure 7.14) which suggests three adjacency characteristics of basic areas in an institution. In column A the areas are related to corridor bypass. In column B the areas are related to the desirability of an exterior window. These two adjacencies, to corridors and to exterior light, are the hidden behavioral indices of most spaces. Table C suggests a third level of adjacencies based on a presupposed analysis of appropriate clustering. The chart is presented in a graphic format to provide a summation of adjacencies. For a particular building the adjacencies may vary. If a chart such as this is prepared for a building, the designer has made the decisions explicit in the act of filling out the chart. The chart suggests changes based on a realignment of adjacencies and additional matrix charts drawn to cover particular aspects, as illustrated in the Design Guide discussed above.

A Circulation Bypass
B Window
C Interrelationships

○ Undesirable
◐ Desirable
● Required

	A	B	Sleep 1 (served)	Sleep 2 (service)	Rest room (1-8)	Rest room (40+)	Housekeeping	Food Preparation 1	Laundry	Beauty/Barber	Yard Activities	Consulting (offices)	Small Hobbies	Learning	Food Service 1	Food Service 2	Large Social	Large Recreation	Worship	Athletics	Employment
Sleep (served)	●	●		○		●		◐		◐	◐			◐					◐	◐	◐
Sleep (service)	●	●	○			●		◐		◐		◐	◐	◐					◐	◐	◐
Rest room (1-8)	○	●	●	●			◐		●	◐		◐	●	●	●	●	●	◐	◐	◐	◐
Rest room (40)		◐				◐		●			●		●	●	●	●	●	●	●	●	●
Housekeeping	●		◐	◐				◐	◐	◐		○	◐	○	◐	○	◐	○	○	○	○
Food Preparation 1	●	◐			●	●	◐		◐	◐		○	◐	○	●	●	◐	◐	○		◐
Laundry	●	◐	◐	◐	◐	◐		◐	◐		◐	◐	○		○	◐	○	○	○		◐
Beauty/Barber	●	○	◐			●	◐	◐	◐		◐										
Yard Activities				◐				◐													
Consulting offices)	●	●		◐	●		○	○	○										●		●
Small Hobbies	●	◐	◐	◐	◐		◐	◐				◐	○	○	◐		○				
Learning	●	◐		◐	◐	●	○	○	○		◐		◐	◐	◐	◐	◐	◐			◐
Food Service 1	◐	◐		●	●	●	●	◐		○	◐	◐			◐	◐	◐	◐			
Food Service 2	◐	◐		●	●	●	●	◐		○	◐	◐			◐	◐	◐	◐			
Large Social	◐	◐		◐	●	○	◐	○		◐	◐	◐	◐			◐	◐				
Large Recreation	◐	◐		◐	●	○	◐	○		◐	◐	◐	◐			◐	◐				
Worship	●	●	◐	◐	◐	●	○	○	○		●	○	◐	◐	◐	◐	◐				
Athletics	○		◐	◐		●	○			◐											
Employment	●	◐	◐	◐	◐	◐	●	○	◐		●		◐								

Fig. 7.14 General activity/adjacency relationships. (Assume a Group of Buildings.)

Trade-offs House rules control actions within a building. As the social organization of a building becomes more complex, as in group 3 closed environments, the house rules proliferate. Shipboard life, requiring high-density living of a most extreme type, is buttressed by the rank of participants. Distinctions between participants can be maintained by physical separations as well (discussed earlier as double-tracking). Activities can be performed in various ways, substantial changes in the character of an activity can be made in various ways, and the character of an activity can be achieved merely by varying the size of the group participating in it. For example, group therapy sessions take on a particular form, quite unlike individual counseling, and individual bedrooms affect the occupant in significantly different ways from dormitory accommodations. Again, cafeteria service functions as a very different activity from served dining. In a proper evaluation of a building, both the physical and social alternatives come to the surface. Variations are not only in plan arrangements but in trade-offs between space and personnel. The procedure of trade-offs is understandable in general terms but difficult to discuss in generalities since each building situation is complex. Returning to the prototype areas again, a series of trade-offs are suggested by way of illustration. Sleeping accommodations can be grouped in singles, doubles, triples, or larger elements. The trade-off here suggests greater personal privacy on one hand and lack of surveillance on the other. If the same degree of surveillance were to be accomplished in smaller bedrooms, then additional personnel would be required. The trade-off involves (1) room divisions, (2) privacy, (3) surveillance, and (4) personnel.

In Villa Maria, a home for unwed mothers, we faced a trade-off between individual bathrooms for each bedroom for two girls and central bathrooms that would leave space for an adjacent lounge, beauty preparation, and sewing area. Each plan would cost the same amount; each would require identical supervisory personnel. The trade-off was between personal privacy and extra activity space; we opted for the latter.

Solution statements, variable matrices, and trade-off evaluations all lead to alternatives at each context. Accountability suggests that there be alternatives and a process for evaluating them. It is in the evaluation chart that the attempt is made to quantify behavioral indices.

Evaluation Chart Six areas of evaluation are listed in this chart (see Figure 7.15). Section 1, Accountability, directs attention to four main elements of importance to the owner building the facility. The individual rating a particular design would be required to judge to what extent the design fulfilled each of the four elements listed. It is assumed that data covering these items are available. In a similar way the individual rates elements under Section 2, Activities. Sections 3 and 4 both involve elements under Comfort and Use, one column directed to the service (role 1), the other to the served (role 2).

Sections 5 and 6 relate to differences in point of view. In developing these sections, it is assumed that the building is an institution of some type where the service role is also an administrative role and some degree of surveillance is required.

A word about the use of these forms. It is assumed in preparing the form shown in Figure 7.15 that the six sections are reasonably identical in value, which means that if any section gets a perfect score, it would affect the total grade on the design by one-sixth. If a section needs more or less weight, such weighting of sections is possible prior to evaluating alternative plans. In a similar way each item under each section can be weighted. It is clear that this form could be weighted in such a way that the preconceived ideas of the architects and administrators would always win. How-

Evaluation Chart

Filled Out By: Role 1, Role 2, Architect

W Weight
R Rate
S Score

☐ Simple Score
○ Weighing
▭ Weighted Score
✱ Change Flexibility Expansion

1 Accountability

W		R	S
	Purpose		
	Systems		
	First Cost		
	30 Year Cost		

☐ ✖ ○ = ▭

2 Activity

W		R	S
	Adminstrative Goals		
	User Aspirations		
	Frequency		
	Comprehensiveness		

☐ ✖ ○ = ▭

3 Comfort & Use

W	Role 1	R	S
	Dimensions		
	MEP		
	Tools		
	Modularity		

☐ ✖ ○ = ▭

4 Comfort & Use

W	Role 2	R	S
	Dimensions		
	MEP		
	Tools		
	Modularity		

☐ ✖ ○ = ▭

5 Point of View

W	Role 1	R	S
	Security		
	Surveillance/Control		
	Maintenance		
	Quality of Life		

☐ ✖ ○ = ▭

6 Point of View

W	Role 2	R	S
	Variety		
	Privacy/Freedom		
	Personal Expression		
	Quality of Life		

☐ ✖ ○ = ▭

Fig. 7.15 Evaluation chart.

ever, the form was not developed to be misused; rather, it becomes a tool in the difficult task of quantifying behavioral input. Subjective judgment is essential here as in intuitive design; the intent of behavioral design is to make design more responsive to human needs and more accountable, not to replace the subjective decision-making activity of architecture. The evaluation chart then should be a useful tool, requiring two evaluations: the first takes place when the chart is weighted, and the second evaluation takes place when various designs are rated. It is suggested that rating be done by a team representing the architects, the owners, and a consultant behavioral psychologist.

Computer Analysis In discussing computer analysis an example is essential, for computer processing is difficult to discuss in the abstract but easy to follow in the concrete. There are many computer programs and a growing number of firms offering computer-related services. A major shortcoming of such services is the extraordinary cost for the production of information seemingly done now by the architect's intuition. In the years to come a substantial reduction in these costs is predicted as procedures become more routine and architects realize more precisely how to use the computer. However, relatively few architects are aware of the extraordinary value of a computer; the illustration below will help make this value clear.

As an adjunct to the Design Guide program, the U.S. Corps of Engineers commissioned the architectural firm of Perry Dean Partners Inc. to develop a computer analysis program for a systems BOQ project that would involve millions of dollars. Shown in Figures 7.16 to 7.19 are some examples from their report showing the variety of solutions possible with computer storage and printout capabilities. A concept diagram is shown as the basis for the organization of the area clusters into buildings, based largely on circulation and building size. The computer printed out the outline of the building configuration, and the perspective rendering was finished by a draftsman. The computer was programmed to search out alternatives at the building scale based on data developed at the area and area cluster scale. Figure 7.20 demonstrates the information possible based on a room cluster alternative. The clusters are based on a variety of bedroom arrangements (illustrated earlier in Figure 5.16), and the computer is programmed to estimate the cost of each configuration.

A number of behavioral variables were considered in developing the areas, area clusters, and the configuration of buildings (see Chapter 5). These variables helped produce particular plans, and an evaluation technique was used to check the value of each alternative in fulfilling the goals. Figure 7.21 is a page from one evaluation report.

PLAN

CONCEPT DIAGRAM

The site concept utilizes perimeter vehicular circulation feeding into cluster-oriented parking areas. Interior site circulation is totally pedestrian oriented with a major loop or company street connecting all of the clusters.

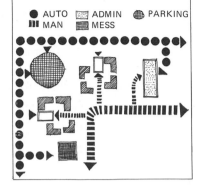

● AUTO   ▨ ADMIN   ⊕ PARKING
▥ MAN   ▦ MESS

▶ ENTRANCE
★ OPTIONAL CONTROL POINT

ENTRANCE FLOOR

ROOM TYPE B

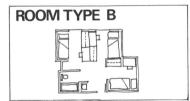

RENDERED PERSPECTIVE

RENDERED
PERSPECTIVE

Fig. 7.17 Alternative 3. Rendered perspective. (Perry Dean Partners Inc.; Robert G. Shibley, Project Architect, Office of the Chief of Engineers, Corps of Engineers, Washington, D.C.)

Fig. 7.16 Alternative 1. An example of computer-aided design. Opposite, above: Plan—concept diagram. Opposite: Rendered perspective. (Perry Dean Partners Inc.; Robert G. Shibley, Project Architect, Office of the Chief of Engineers, Corps of Engineers, Washington, D.C.)

Fig. 7.18 Alternative 3. Right: Plan—concept diagram, entrance floor. Right, below: Plan—summary. (Perry Dean Partners Inc.; Robert G. Shibley, Project Architect, Office of the Chief of Engineers, Corps of Engineers, Washington, D.C.)

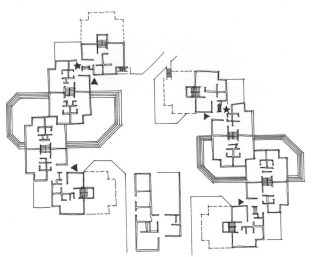

▶ ENTRANCE
★ OPTIONAL CONTROL POINT

ENTRANCE FLOOR

PLAN

CONCEPT DIAGRAM

Vehicular traffic is allowed to penetrate the site, along a centrally located spine which feeds cluster-orientated parking areas. The pedestrian spines connect all of the site with the cluster.

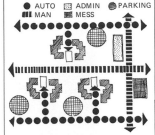

● AUTO   ▦ ADMIN   ◉ PARKING
▦ MAN   ▦ MESS

ROOM TYPE D

PLAN SUMMARY

STATISTICS

MEN/BUILDING	180
MEN/CLUSTER	90
MEN/LOUNGE	15
SQ. FT./MAN	160

REFERENCES
  PROCESS
    BOOK 2 - SECTION 2
    BOOK 2 - SECTION 3
  COST & PROGRAM
    BOOK 5 - SECTION 2

COST PER MAN

CONSTRUCTION COST/SQ.FT.	$24.88
CONSTRUCTION COST/MAN	$3981
PROJECT COST/SQ.FT.	$28.74
PROJECT COST/MAN 14% OH&P	$4135
PROJECT COST/MAN 21% OH&P	$4598
PROJECT COST/BUILDING	$716,561

*SEE BOOK NO. 5

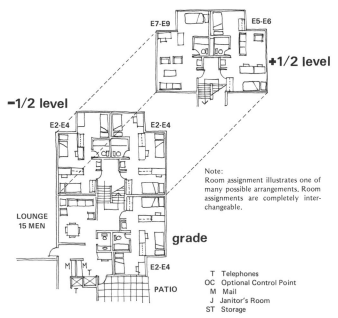

E7-E9   E5-E6

+1/2 level

−1/2 level

E2-E4   E2-E4

Note:
Room assignment illustrates one of many possible arrangements. Room assignments are completely interchangeable.

LOUNGE
15 MEN

grade

E2-E4

PATIO

T   Telephones
OC Optional Control Point
M   Mail
J   Janitor's Room
ST Storage

ALTERNATIVE 3

In order to minimize interior circulation, alternative 3 utilizes the concept of direct access to the rooms off a centrally located, interior stair tower. In addition, the entries to these rooms are located at each landing, thus creating a half level massing configuration. The lounge services 15 men, and is located either a half levels above or below the adjacent bedrooms. The 90-man clusters are to be arranged around a centrally located but detached service module. Optional control points are provided at every entry.

Fig. 7.19 Alternative 2. Right: Rendered perspective. Below: Plan—concept diagram. Next page: Plan—summary. (Perry Dean Partners Inc.; Robert G. Shibley, Project Architect, Office of the Chief of Engineers, Corps of Engineers, Washington, D.C.)

RENDERED PERSPECTIVE

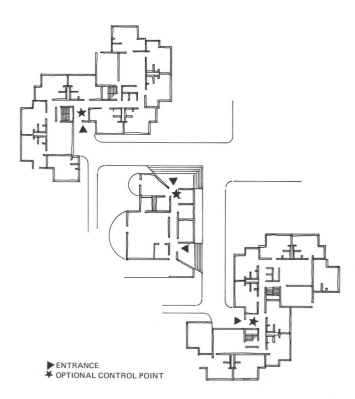

▶ ENTRANCE
✶ OPTIONAL CONTROL POINT

ENTRANCE FLOOR

PLAN

CONCEPT DIAGRAM

Auto circulation is on the perimeter of the site feeding directly into large consolidated parking areas. The pedestrian circulation system is organized on a continuous "diagrid" pattern.

● AUTO   ▦ ADMIN   ◉ PARKING
⫿⫿ MAN   ▦ MESS

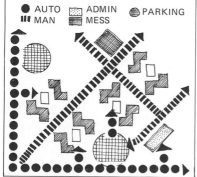

ROOM TYPE D

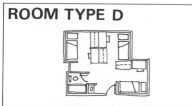

PLAN SUMMARY

STATISTICS

MEN/BUILDING	180
MEN/CLUSTER	90
MEN/LOUNGE	15
SQ. FT./MAN	157

REFERENCES
  PROCESS
    BOOK 2 - SECTION 2
    BOOK 2 - SECTION 3
  COST & PROGRAM
    BOOK 5 - SECTION 2

COST PER MAN

CONSTRUCTION COST/SQ. FT.	$24.43
CONSTRUCTION COST/MAN	$3836
PROJECT COST/SQ. FT.	$28.22
PROJECT COST/MAN 14% OH&P	$3983
PROJECT COST/MAN 21% OH&P	$4430
PROJECT COST/BUILDING	$690,393

*SEE BOOK NO. 5

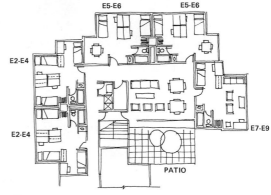

Note:
Room assignment illustrates one of many possible arrangements. Room assignments are completely interchangeable.

ALTERNATIVE 2

A very short corridor connected by two vertical stair towers constitute the circulation pattern, and thus the major concept generator, of this scheme. The rooms are arranged around an integrated 15-man lounge which is situated adjacent to the stair towers. A detached service module provides the option for a central entry control point. In addition, space is provided for optional control points at every entry.

Fig. 7.20 Alternative 1. Plan—summary. (Perry Dean Partners Inc.; Robert G. Shibley, Project Architect, Office of the Chief of Engineers, Corps of Engineers, Washington, D.C.)

PLAN SUMMARY

STATISTICS

MEN/BUILDING	288
MEN/CLUSTER	72
MEN/LOUNGE	24
SQ. FT./MAN	155

REFERENCES
  PROCESS
    BOOK 2 - SECTION 2
    BOOK 2 - SECTION 3
  COST & PROGRAM
    BOOK 5 - SECTION 2

COST PER MAN

CONSTRUCTION COST/SQ. FT.	$22.51
CONSTRUCTION COST/MAN	$3497
PROJECT COST/SQ. FT.	$26.00
PROJECT COST/MAN 14% OH&P	$3632
PROJECT COST/MAN 21% OH&P	$4039
PROJECT COST/BUILDING	$1,007,128

*SEE BOOK NO. 5

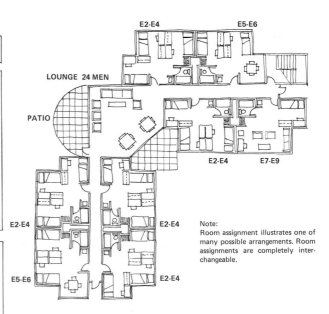

Note:
Room assignment illustrates one of many possible arrangements. Room assignments are completely interchangeable.

ALTERNATIVE 1

A double loaded interior circulation pattern was the major concept generator of this alternative. The rooms are arranged around a centrally located 24 man lounge. Centrally located to provide maximum convenience as well as the option for a central control point. The service module is integrated into the building configuration. The massing configuration of building is highly flexible.

Selection Process

Criteria	Points of View		

22460 = Total Score

	Individual	Social Groups	Military Service

Personal

Criteria		Individual	W/R/S	Social Groups	W/R/S	Military Service	W/R/S
Demography		Dimensions	2 / 3 / 6	Distances	5 / 5 / 25	Densities	5 / 5 / 25
Facilities		Living/Hygiene	6 / 4 / 24	Clusters	4 / 4 / 16	Modularities	3 / 4 / 12
Adaptability		Variety	3 / 4 / 12	Utilization	3 / 3 / 9	Purpose	3 / 3 / 9
Social Structure		Territoriality	7 / 3 / 21	Community	7 / 4 / 28	Structure Sys.	4 / 4 / 16

Personal: **4636** = (4) ✖ 1159

Individual: **567** = (9) ✖ 63   Social Groups: **468** = (6) ✖ 78   Military Service: **124** = (2) ✖ 62

Impersonal

Criteria		Individual	W/R/S	Social Groups	W/R/S	Military Service	W/R/S
Function		Organization	6 / 2 / 12	Clarity	5 / 3 / 15	Predictable	3 / 4 / 12
Flexibility		Arrangement	3 / 3 / 9	Activities	6 / 3 / 18	Assignments	3 / 4 / 12
Economy		Energy	4 / 3 / 12	Upkeep	7 / 3 / 21	Maintenance	8 / 2 / 16
Control		Security	8 / 5 / 40	Supervision	4 / 5 / 20	Accountable	5 / 5 / 25

Impersonal: **7987** = (7) ✖ 1141

Individual: **511** = (7) ✖ 73   Social Groups: **370** = (5) ✖ 74   Military Service: **260** = (4) ✖ 65

Intangible

Criteria		Individual	W/R/S	Social Groups	W/R/S	Military Service	W/R/S
Scale		Proportions	3 / 5 / 15	Interspaces	4 / 5 / 20	Identity	5 / 5 / 25
Sense of Place		Being	6 / 5 / 30	Belonging	5 / 3 / 15	Including	3 / 3 / 9
Latent Organization		Kinetic	5 / 5 / 25	Clarity	3 / 2 / 6	Acceptable	7 / 4 / 28
Life Style		Vitality	8 / 4 / 32	Satisfaction	6 / 4 / 24	Evolutionary	9 / 4 / 36

Intangible: **9837** = (9) ✖ 1093

Individual: **408** = (4) ✖ 102   Social Groups: **195** = (3) ✖ 65   Military Service: **490** = (5) ✖ 98

Project: BEQ
Ratings By: Dean, Cooper, & Everdell

Date
Weighting By: Dean, Wilterding, Cooper, Everdell, & Stewart
Alt. No.: Five

Fig. 7.21 A typical evaluation form used to compare variable printout solutions. (Perry Dean Partners Inc.)

Simultaneous Use—Use in Time

Techniques for documenting time are in short supply, yet it is the dynamics of the interpersonal life of a building that needs expression. Figure 7.22 is an example of how to plot activities against time and block out the times a space is actually used. Such a diagram would seem to be an essential check on space allocations in a building program. However, such docu-

Fig. 7.22 Area use frequency program.

AREA USE FREQUENCY PROGRAM

Space	S 7-9A	S 9-11A	S 11-1P	S 1-3P	S 3-5P	S 5-7P	S 7-9P	S 9-11P	M 7-9A	M 9-11A	M 11-1P	M 1-3P	M 3-5P	M 5-7P	M 7-9P	M 9-11P	T 7-9A	T 9-11A	T 11-1P	T 1-3P	T 3-5P	T 5-7P	T 7-9P	T 9-11P	W 7-9A	W 9-11A	W 11-1P	W 1-3P	W 3-5P	W 5-7P	W 7-9P	W 9-11P
SANCTUARY SPACES																																
NARTHEX (600sf)	W1	W1	W1	W18														W20														
CHOIR (300sf)	W4,6 W1	W1 W7																W20														
NAVE, CHANCEL (4,400sf)	W1	W1	W1															W20														
PRIEST'S VESTING (225sf)	W1	W1	W1														W1	W20														
ACOLYTES VESTING (170sf)	W1	W1	W1														W1	W20														
WORKING SACRISTY (180sf)	W1	W1	W1														W1	W20														
ORGAN	W1	W1	W1																													
CHOIR DIRECTOR'S OFFICE (150sf)		W1	W1		W5																	W6								W4	W7	
CHOIR PRACTICE ROOM (300sf)		W1	W1		W5																	W6								W4	W7	
BAPTISTY (150sf)		W1	W1																													
BRIDE'S ROOM (200sf)																																
GROOM'S ROOM (100sf)																																
CHAPEL (400sf)				W	W18	W	W	W	W	W	W	W	W	W	W	W	W	W	W	W	W	W	W	W	W	W	W	W	W	W	W	W
EDUCATIONAL SPACES																																
NURSERY (550sf)		E1	E1														F16	F16														
2 YRS. (325sf)		E2	E2														F16	F16														
3&4 YRS. (475sf)		E3	E3																													
KINDERGARTEN (325sf)		E4	E4																													
1st GRADE (325sf)		E5	E5																													
2nd GRADE (450sf)		E6	E6																													
3rd GRADE (425sf)		E7	E7																													
4th GRADE (350sf)		E8	E8																													
5th GRADE (400sf)		E9	E9																													
6th GRADE (525sf)		E10	E10 W9							W12																						
JR. E.Y.C. (875sf)				E11																												
SR. E.Y.C. (875sf)				E12															F12													
LIBRARY (625sf)		W16																	E13												W8	
AUDIO/VISUAL (800sf)																																
CHILDREN'S CHAPEL (100sf)																																
FELLOWSHIP SPACES																																
FELLOWSHIP HALL (3,600sf)														F7 F8	F2						F9	F6								F10	F5	
PARLOR (300sf)						W2														W13		W11									W15	
KITCHEN (900sf)																				F2												
STORAGE (600sf)																																
TOILETS (250sf)																																
CRAFT GUILD ROOM (600sf)																			F1													
ADMINISTRATION SPACES																																
RECTOR'S OFFICE (250sf)	A	A	A	A	A	A	A	A	A	A	A	A	A	A	A	A	A	A	A	A	A	A	A	A	A	A	A	A	A	A	A	A
ASS'T. RECTOR'S OFFICE (200sf)	A	A	A	A	A	A	A	A	A	A	A	A	A	A	A	A	A	A	A	A	A	A	A	A	A	A	A	A	A	A	A	A
RECEPTION (250sf)	A	A	A						A	A	A	A	A				A	A	A	A	A				A	A	A	A				
CLERICAL OFFICE (160sf)									A	A	A	A	A				A	A	A	A	A				A	A	A	A				
CLERICAL OFFICE (160sf)									A	A	A	A	A				A	A	A	A	A				A	A	A	A				
REPRODUCTION ROOM (125sf)									A	A	A	A	A				A	A	A	A	A				A	A	A	A				
SUPPLIES (50sf)									A	A	A	A	A				A	A	A	A	A				A	A	A	A				

mentation is seldom asked for by the client and seldom accomplished by the architect. In the example the chart was prepared for the Church of the Epiphany in an early stage when the aspirations of the building committee greatly outscaled any budget expectations. The committee insisted that the architect prepare plans for an overly large program and would not hear of any discussion of double use of facilities. The chart was developed to

Schedule chart

	THURSDAY								FRIDAY								SATURDAY							
	7–9AM	9–11AM	11–1PM	1–3PM	3–5PM	5–7PM	7–9PM	9–11PM	7–9AM	9–11AM	11–1PM	1–3PM	3–5PM	5–7PM	7–9PM	9–11PM	7–9AM	9–11AM	11–1PM	1–3PM	3–5PM	5–7PM	7–9PM	9–11PM
																				W19				
																				W19				
											W1									W19				
											W1									W19				
											W1									W19				
																				W19				
																				W19				
																				W19				
	W	W	W	W	W	W	W1	W	W	W	W	W	W	W	W	W	W	W	W	W	W	W	W	W
					W15			W14																
		F4	F4	F11 F13	F15					F14						W10		W19					
		F4	F4															W19					
		F4	F4															W19					
	A	A	A	A	A	A	A	A	A	A	A	A	A	A	A	A	A	A	A	A	A	A	A
	A	A	A	A	A	A	A	A	A	A	A	A	A	A	A	A	A	A	A	A	A	A	A
	A	A	A	A	A				A	A	A	A												
	A	A	A	A	A				A	A	A	A												
	A	A	A	A	A				A	A	A	A												
	A	A	A	A					A	A	A	A												

ACTIVITY AND GROUP KEY

WORSHIP AND WORSHIP RELATED ACTIVITIES AND GROUPS

W-1 WORSHIP SERVICES
W-2 VESTRY (MONTHLY)
W-3 ALTAR BUILD (MONTHLY)
W-4 CHOIR JR (WEEKLY)
W-5 CHOIR SR HIGH (WEEKLY)
W-6 CHOIR CANTEBURY (WEEKLY)
W-7 CHOIR SR. ADULTS (WEEKLY)
W-8 ADULT CONFIRMATION CLASS (WEEKLY 6-8 WKS)
W-9 CHILD CONFIRMATION CLASS (WEEKLY-COMBINED WITH SUNDAY SCHOOL)
W-10 ACOLYTES
W-11 WORSHIP COMMISSION (YEARLY)
W-12 MON. EXPERIMENT IN FAITH
W-13 TUES. BIBLE STUDY (WEEKLY)
W-14 THURS. NIGHT BIBLE STUDY (MEN'S) (WEEKLY)
W-15 WITNESS COMMUNITY (MONTHLY)
W-16 SUNDAY 10:AM BIBLE STUDY (WEEKLY)
W-17 LISTENING MISSION
W PRIVATE WORSHIP

FELLOWSHIP ACTIVITIES AND GROUPS

F-1 CRAFT GUILD (WEEKLY)
F-2 MEN'S CLUB (MONTHLY)
F-3 COUPLES CLUB (MEET OUTSIDE CHURCH
F-4 WOMEN OF THE EPIPHANY (MONTHLY)
F-5 BOY SCOUT TROOP 734 (WEEKLY)
F-6 BOY SCOUT TROOP 488 (WEEKLY)
F-7 GIRL SCOUT TROOP 1746 (WEEKLY)
F-8 JR. TROOP 1693 (WEEKLY)
F-9 JR. TROOP 188 (WEEKLY)
F-10 JR. TROOP 411 (WEEKLY)
F-11 CADETS 1693 (WEEKLY)
F-12 CADETS 1697 (WEEKLY)
F-13 BROWNIE TROOP 1208 (WEEKLY)
F-14 BROWNIE TROOP 575 (WEEKLY)
F-15 TOPS CLUB (WEEKLY)
F-16 MOTHER'S DAY OUT (WEEKLY)
F-17 SUMMER SEX SCHOOL

EDUCATION ACTIVITIES AND GROUPS

E-1 NURSERY
E-2 2 YRS. (WEEKLY)
E-3 3&4 YRS. (WEEKLY)
E-4 KINDERGARTEN (WEEKLY)
E-5 1ST GRADE
E-6 2ND GRADE
E-7 3RD GRADE
E-8 4TH GRADE
E-9 5TH GRADE
E-10 6TH GRADE
E-11 JR. E.Y.C.
E-12 MON. NIGHT SUN SCHOOL (WEEKLY)

ADMINISTRATIVE ACTIVITIES

A ADMINISTRATION

show that the spaces it proposed were underutilized. We took its data, which had been prepared laboriously during the period of a year or so, and projected it against seven days of the week. It became apparent that the spaces were overstressed on Sunday but underutilized during the rest of the week. After the chart was presented, there was no more talk of the extravagant plan; rather discussion centered around how activities could be shifted to better balance occupancy during the week. The chart sparked a classic example of trade-off; activity shifts became an acceptable alternative to underutilized space.

Simultaneous use suggests more than seeing the building in use on a 24-hour basis. Simultaneous use tackles the difficult task of modeling the social dynamics of use of the space.

Figure 7.23 is a movement pattern developed by D. C. Wrotz, of the Garret Corporation, to demonstrate graphically how a person moves about a chamber, in this case a mock-up of a space capsule. Figure 7.24 shows examples of simultaneous-use diagrams that indicate individual movement patterns as well as furniture. These diagrams, prepared by Lorraine Snyder, of the New York State College of Human Ecology, Cornell University, demonstrate the space needs for patients in wheelchairs in a dining room situation. The intent of the mock-up photograph and the use diagrams is the same: to shift the evaluation of space from generalized notions to an intimate evaluation of how the space interacts with the user. The major advantage of such diagrams is not that they will show anything dramatically different dimensionally from charts available without people and movement patterns, but that the diagrams become a communication vehicle to refocus the designer's attention on the people and to verify through simulated movement patterns the space and the tools.

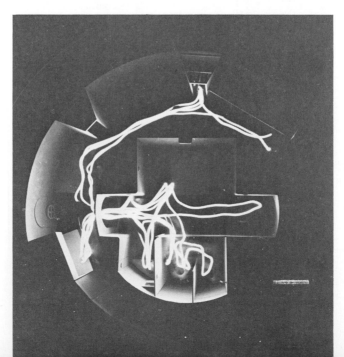

Fig. 7.23 Time-lapse photograph. A graphic representation of movement in a mock-up of a space capsule. (C. E. Righter.)

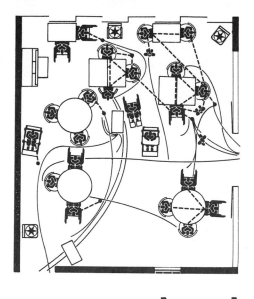

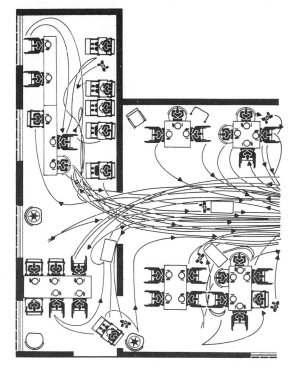

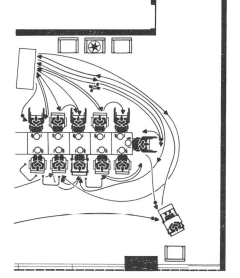

Fig. 7.24 Dining room plans. Diagrams of movement patterns. (From Lorraine Hiatt Snyder, A New Nursing Home, New York State College of Human Ecology, Cornell University, 1973.)

A major simultaneous-use project was undertaken by my office in conjunction with two firms in St. Louis.[3] The problem, simply stated, was to develop a rehabilitation scheme for a vacant building abandoned by tenants because the building was uninhabitable. It is clear from Figure 7.25 that the building could not be isolated from a density of other low-income housing units. The three-winged building in the center of the sketch is the vacant building. Although no one occupied this building, it was possible to interview tenants living in identical or nearly identical

[3] Architect Charles Fleming (Carey Jenkins and Charles Fleming Inc) and engineer Donald K. Ross (Ross and Baruzzini).

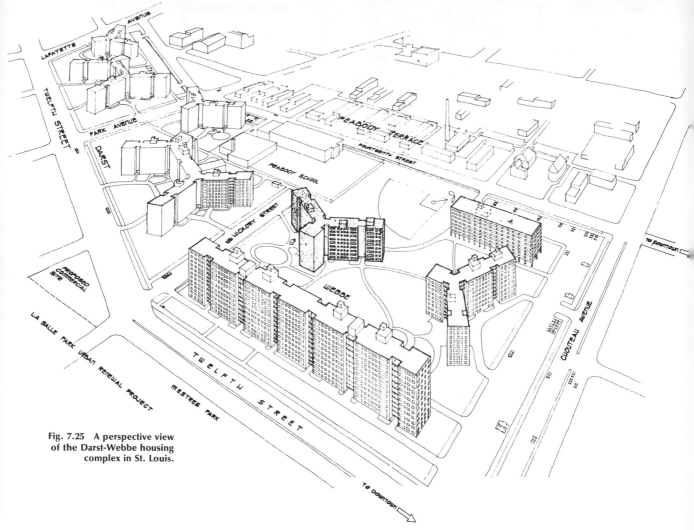

Fig. 7.25 A perspective view of the Darst-Webbe housing complex in St. Louis.

units. A description of the project will be presented now in order to place the concept of simultaneous use in a concrete context.

The problem at Webbe in St. Louis was expressing the interpersonal characteristics of a built project on three scales: the community scale, the building scale, and the room scale. Since we were interested in getting tenants' input to our renovation concepts, we began with the building scale and attempted to express the building in the perceptual terms they would recognize. The vacant building under study was similar to one occupied nearby. In talking to tenants who lived in the occupied building, it became apparent that the actual configuration of the structure, a tri-winged design, was not significant. What was significant were the circulation patterns. The apartments were objects along the circulation paths; they had no perception of rooms inside since one could not see inside in passing.

We reconstructed the building (Figure 7.26), flattening it out since the angles were not important and turning apartments into blocks along circulation paths. To our pleasant surprise the tenants immediately accepted our reconstructed building (that is, reconstructed from the norms of architectural presentation). When we analyzed the plan with them, the problems in surveillance became immediately apparent; that is, the skip-floor elevator format required occupants to use the unprotected fire exits to go up or down from the elevator stop. When we superimposed various times of day or night, we were able to focus on the 24-hour use of the building. Finally, we discussed a renovation scheme that would create duplexes rather than single-floor apartments, and this diagram likewise became a working tool for hours of conferences.

A more ambitious plan was then attempted to show on an area plan the places of use on a 24-hour basis. Our idea was straightforward enough: show each social agency surrounding the project (and there were a

Fig. 7.26 Simultaneous-use diagram.

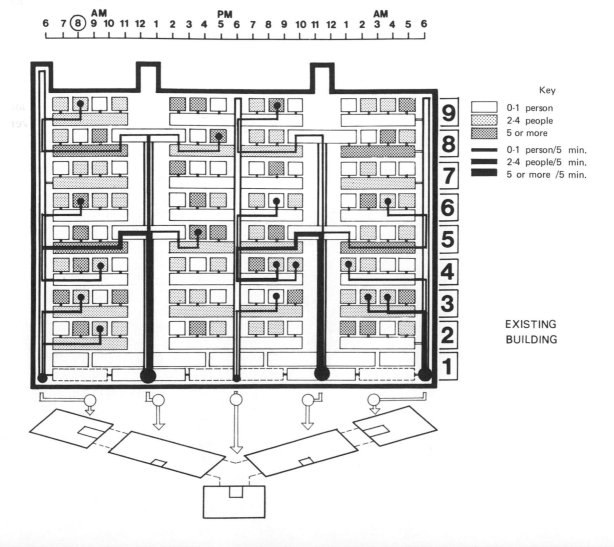

Key

☐ 0-1 person
▨ 2-4 people
▩ 5 or more

━ 0-1 person/5 min.
━━ 2-4 people/5 min.
━━━ 5 or more /5 min.

EXISTING
BUILDING

number), each school, each church, and each recreational activity (see Figure 7.27). By estimating the number of people occupied in these activity centers at various hours of the day and at various periods throughout the year, it would be possible to roughly represent the community activity patterns surrounding the housing area. The undertaking was far more ambitious than we had anticipated, and the cooperation of the social agencies was quite varied. While some agencies saw immediately that such a diagram could be of value in planning additional activities with greater precision than before, others felt nothing short of hostility for the plan. As incredible as it seemed, the consensus of some was that such a chart would become a disruptive tool. Some truth surfaced to support their anxieties, for it became apparent that there was no comprehensive plan for social activities surrounding Webbe or the neighboring housing projects, nor was there an overriding desire for one. Some agencies dedicated to helping the poor kept regular 9 to 5 office hours, while anyone familiar with Webbe realized the working members of the community could never attend any activity scheduled during these hours.

The social aspects of the problem became too complex to diagram, but the technique did turn up an interesting fact. By shifting the technique we had originally developed for social activities to test economic buying power, we were able to determine with some precision the size grocery store the project could support.

Fig. 7.27 Community utilization map.

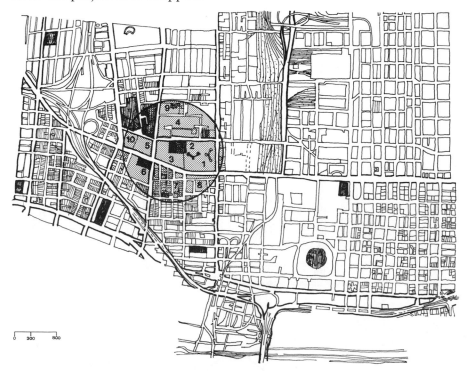

The room scale required a visual graph as well (see Figure 7.28), particularly when we presented the duplex plan in contrast to the existing single-floor plan. Talking about spaces to nonarchitects was theoretical at best; talking about possible interpersonal conflicts within spaces made far more sense. The plans for the proposed rehabilitation were drawn and possible areas of conflict plotted, contrasting the new 2-story plans against the existing 1-story plan. While the plans were less clear than the building scale diagram, the tenants grasped their intent and used them to discuss how they lived and how they might live in different surroundings.

The project became a bureaucratic boondoggle, for after we had raised the expectations of the tenants during 3 months of meetings, changing their attitude from cynicism to enthusiasm, the funds were withdrawn and the project delayed, if not canceled. The government thinks in bureaucratic time, not human time.

Fig. 7.28 Simultaneous-use diagram—family description

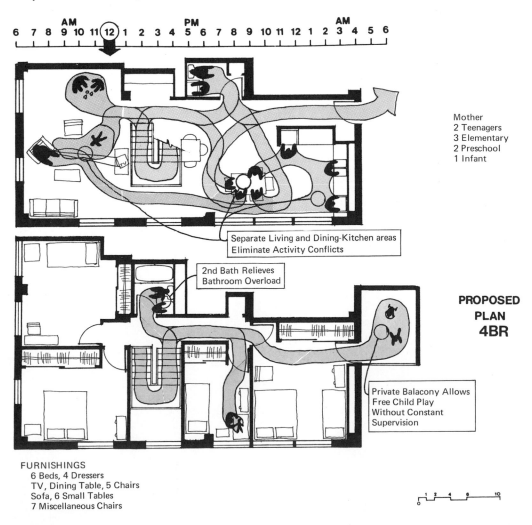

AM — 6 7 8 9 10 11 12 1 2 3 4   PM — 5 6 7 8 9 10 11 12 1 2   AM — 3 4 5 6

Mother
2 Teenagers
3 Elementary
2 Preschool
1 Infant

Separate Living and Dining-Kitchen areas
Eliminate Activity Conflicts

2nd Bath Relieves
Bathroom Overload

PROPOSED
PLAN
4BR

Private Balacony Allows
Free Child Play
Without Constant
Supervision

FURNISHINGS
6 Beds, 4 Dressers
TV, Dining Table, 5 Chairs
Sofa, 6 Small Tables
7 Miscellaneous Chairs

Techniques—Summary

Techniques for quantifying behavioral data are available and can be utilized now as additional clarification of issues continues in the research community. It should be clear that these techniques in no way replace the subjective evaluation step essential to design. What these techniques do accomplish is precisely what this book purports to affirm: (1) increased behavioral data collecting prior to decision making, (2) communicating the behavioral data in a visual format compatible with the graphic language of architecture, and (3) making the designer and evaluator accountable for their decisions in an organized and recountable manner.

The techniques discussed above are part of a total design process which concentrates attention at the beginning phase of design, the Programming Phase. In Chapter 8 the Behavioral Design Process Model will be completed within the context of a comprehensive design process from programming through feedback.

8
The
Behavioral Design
Process

The current design process was discussed in Chapter 2 and found lacking because there is no recognized programming phase; the architect is not often party to fundamental planning decisions concerning alternatives to building; the user is not a participant in design discussions. There is no behavioral design methodology, nor are there statements of accountability for decisions made, and there is no feedback mechanism or information clearinghouse. The need for a more comprehensive design process is immediate. The Behavioral Design Process is presented below in some detail as a guide to implementation of a user-oriented design methodology, expanding the methodology for data collection presented in Chapter 7. Fortunately it would seem that a major reorientation of design can be effected by reasonably minor, but specific, changes to the current process. (When I speak of minor, I am not underestimating the problems of implementation, but I am suggesting that this expanded procedure involves only a small increase or redirection of time and cost when the total commitment of effort directed to producing buildings is considered.)

A summary of the items that are not currently part of the design process but need to be included is listed below.

1. Establishment of a distinct Programming Phase in the design procedure. The Programming Phase will develop the Behavioral Design Process Model (Figure 7.3) as outlined in Chapter 7. It will also produce systems information to be coordinated with behavioral data in producing viable alternatives. The Building Systems Process Model for implementing systems material is discussed below. Finally, an Alternative to Build Document will be prepared during programming as a base line for the project. A discussion of this document is also included below.

2. Development of a training program and user document at the time of building occupancy.

3. Establishment of a Feedback Phase in the design process and a clearinghouse for dissemination of behavioral information.

The Programming Phase—General

The product at the end of the Programming Phase is a definition of the project in behavioral and systems terms considered against a base line. It is primarily a data collection procedure, but the material is collected and correlated in such a way that all major issues suggested by the project have been made explicit. Behavioral information is collected as detailed in Chapter 7; systems information is collected as discussed below. The purpose of preparing an Alternative to Build Document is to provide a base line for the project as it proceeds. Because this is a new element in design and affects all that follows, it will be discussed first.

Alternative to Build Document   During programming there is much discussion of the purpose and goals of a building. The purpose is to solve a particular social problem needing solution in physical form. The goals are more than physical; they represent the long-range goals of the building organization and involve not only the building under consideration but the aims of the institution considered in its total operation.

Statements of purpose and goals are often confused in developing a preamble to a project. Most often the wording of the preamble is not taken very seriously, for it is assumed that the purpose is viable and the goals worthy, or there would not have been a project in the first place. Architects can be excused if they are not overly critical of their clients concerning these first primary issues, for there is something of a conflict of interest in questioning the commission they have just received. However, the damage to clarity throughout the project is considerable when the issues of purpose and goals are not critically established as a first step in programming. There are three ways of establishing justification for a project. The first is to state the purpose of the project by describing what the new facility will provide. The goals of the organization can then be summarized to demonstrate that the project is in keeping with the main aspirations of the organization.

A more comprehensive justification for a project will concentrate on the needs of the users, demonstrate that the users are inappropriately served by present facilities, and indicate how the new facility will solve some or all of the needs outlined. Again, the goals are stated to show that the project is appropriate. In these first two approaches the burden of proof is on the administration preparing the statements, and it is difficult to determine what alternatives there might be to the building project as presented. The third method, developing an Alternative to Build Document, requires the administration to establish a base line for the project by explicitly stating the best alternative. What the Alternative to Build Document accomplishes is the separation of purpose and goals from actions. The purpose of a building may be desirable and the goals worthwhile; however, the project proposed may not be the only solution. In fact, it may not be the best solution.

What are the alternatives to building? One alternative is continuing in the existing location and renovating. A second alternative is to seek space in an existing building and renovating it if necessary. Other alternatives are to build in a different time frame, in different increments, or in a different location. A final alternative is not to build at all. The Alternative to Build Document requires that these issues be discussed openly and balanced one against another before beginning the designs. The product of such discussion is a specific statement of the best alternative, rather than a reaffirmation that all alternatives have been exhausted and discarded. Stating what the best alternative is immediately establishes a base line for the project in rather concrete terms.

For example, in developing Villa Maria Home for Unwed Mothers no alternative document was formally developed, although there was considerable discussion of alternatives. Had such a document been formally prepared, it would have made the project accountable. What were the alternatives? Villa Maria was designed to be built in place of two existing houses which had been used for years on a site adjacent to the sponsoring social agency. These buildings did not meet the health standards required for licensing, and if some action had not been taken, the license would have been withdrawn. The alternatives were simply four:

1. Discontinue maternity services.
2. Renovate the existing buildings.
3. Find space in an existing building that would meet the health standards or could be renovated to do so.
4. Build a new facility either on the existing site or on a new site.

Remembering the discussions clearly, I can reconstruct the priorities. The proximity to the social agency was primary since many of the social workers were to keep their offices in the main agency building. The alternatives then, if service was to continue, were two: renovate the existing houses or build a new facility on that site. There was some discussion of disbanding maternity services for various reasons, but it was resolved that the facility would be usable to house problem teen-agers if in the future the major need diminished, and the agency was committed to the goal of working in the general teen-age problem area. In a real sense, therefore, the alternative to building a new facility was designated as the cost and efficacy of renovating the existing houses. In the case of either renovation or new construction, the program had to be discontinued during the construction or the occupants temporarily located elsewhere. The alternative to build was renovating the existing buildings.

This illustration is presented to show that informally the steps suggested in this document were actually covered but in a time-consuming, somewhat piecemeal, and undocumented way. Had the alternative to building been concretely drawn, it would have been a useful document over the long period of design and construction. Today it would be a useful document in implementing a feedback procedure because it would clarify, perhaps quite favorably, the efficacy of the decision to build.

Elements of Programming   There are four elements to be developed in the Programming Phase. These elements lead to a programming document, which in turn becomes the basis for schematic concepts. The four elements are:

1. A clarification of goals for the project and the background of the organization and the participants.

2. A definition of the area requirement in terms of physical space, tools, participants, and activities, including anticipated flexibility.

3. Development of adjacency matrices based on the adjacency of social activities, environmental criteria, and servicing proximities.

4. Establishing alternatives in terms of activities, personnel, size of units, and relationship to site and community.

A Behavioral Design Process Model (Figure 7.3) was presented in detail in Chapter 7 in order to make clear how behavioral data can be developed and quantified in the same context with physical data. Much of this process is developed in the Programming Phase, and because of the considerable information to be gathered it becomes essential that the Programming Phase be separate and distinct. The material developed in programming should become the basis for the development of the alternative schemes in schematics. As developed in Chapter 7, alternatives are an essential step in behavioral design, for alternatives require an evaluation step, and the evaluation step places behavioral data on an even footing with physical data. By creating an Alternative to Build Document a first alternative has already been discussed. It is not anticipated that this document would be developed prior to working on the other parts of the Programming Phase; rather it would be developed along with the other information and be included as part of the data collected on documents at the end of programming.

Building Systems Process Model In Chapter 5 the availability of systems was discussed. Although developed for school construction, subsystems are used for all types of buildings. Figure 8.1 is a process model for selecting systems components. As has been suggested in Chapter 5 in discussing systems, one advantage in systems design is the opportunity to fast-track elements of the project, thus speeding construction and achieving the savings related to speed (see Figure 5.1). Just as important is the designation early in the Programming Phase of those areas that are susceptible to systems (and the implied flexibility systems offer) and those areas that are not. In this regard it is significant that subsystems in the School Construction Systems Design (SCSD) covered only 50 percent of the design items in the building. A later and more comprehensive systems program,

Fig. 8.1 Building systems process model. Although box diagrams are hard to read out of context, they show the interaction of the logic. In this case, user requirements are covered in programming and technical considerations in schematics.

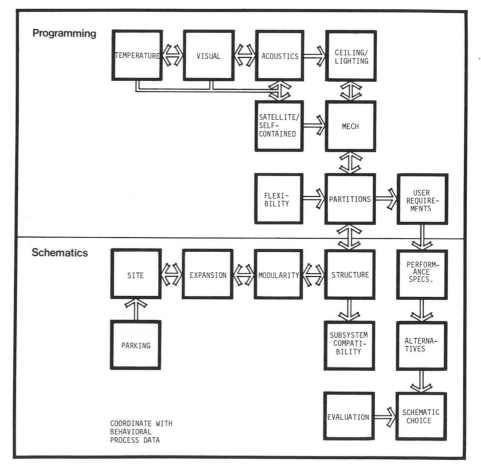

Toronto's Study of Educational Facilities (SEF), added a good many systems items to be integrated, and achieved 75 percent of the design items in subsystems. In general building projects other than schools, it is unlikely that the systems areas would approach 50 percent, but these areas are the critical ones from a behavioral point of view since they are the areas that are designed with built-in flexibility. Therefore, concurrently with the development of the behavioral model, a second study should be made to designate the magnitude of systems in the program.

Nonsystems components are stairs, elevators, kitchens, bathrooms, laundries, mechanical rooms, special storage areas, sleeping accommodations (although these may have component furniture and storage dividers), most corridors, auditoriums with special sight-line seating, and specific recreation spaces (such as handball courts, swimming pools, and most gyms). Areas of questionable inclusion depending on other factors are foyers, corridors, food service areas, and special project rooms (such as hobby shops).

Systems areas include offices, conference rooms, consulting rooms, libraries, general meeting rooms, classrooms, lounges, and entertainment areas for large and small groups. These areas need to be designated either low-bay (low-ceiling) or high-bay (high-ceiling) areas. The general rule in beginning a project is to designate areas for large-group activities as high-bay areas; included here would be food service rooms, activity rooms, and the library. Perhaps the ceiling height in the high-bay areas may be as low as 12 ft and as high as a design may indicate. Low-bay areas are standardized at 8 ft in residential construction, generally 9 to 10 ft in commercial construction. Clustering rooms by bay height develops physical clustering, creating volumetric rationale between spaces.

Prior to developing behavioral data it is possible to anticipate the various kinds of activities that are to be involved in the building by using rule-of-thumb approximations. For each type of occupancy there are characteristics that will determine the design requirements for the integrated ceiling and lighting system. These criteria will differ depending on whether or not the space is a high- or low-bay area and whether or not the partitions extend to the ceiling. The mechanical subsystem will be defined, as well, by the criteria developed for the two situations, one concerning high-bay space, the other low-bay space. Flexibility is the major issue determining the type of partition system to be specified; and each of the components of partition system, mechanical subsystem, and ceiling system must allow for the degree of flexibility desired.

Determination in rough approximations of areas leads to a statement of user characteristics. It is anticipated that the steps outlined above would be accomplished simultaneously with development of behavioral data from other sources. When a rough analysis of user requirements has been developed, it can be coordinated with the data collected in the behavioral design model.

Programming develops a document and necessary drawings to bring the project to life in both its physical and social dimensions. As each stage in the development procedure brings a project closer to completion, so each phase has a particular emphasis. The Programming Phase emphasizes alternatives as a means of defining the potential of the project.

An Example of the Process   The material which follows is an example from my experience that shows how the process just described works in practice.

My firm was commissioned to do a branch Postal Service building in the Houston area. In receiving the commission we were given a prototype plan, developed by the Postal Service as a guide for a 20,000-ft^2 Postal Service facility (Figure 8.2).

In discussions with the client it became clear that the Postal Service was interested in energy conservation; we suggested that the techniques of

Fig. 8.2 Prototype plan.

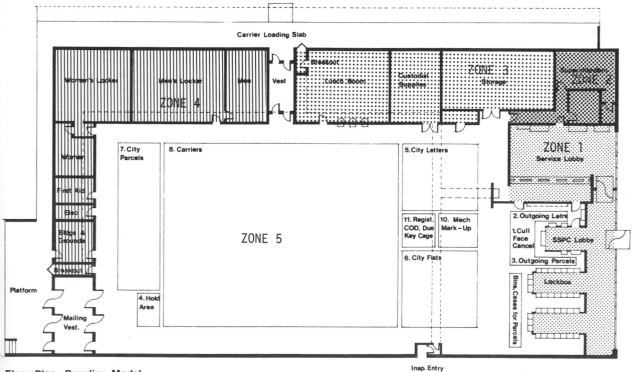

Floor Plan: Baseline Model

behavioral architecture would lead to energy savings. Traditionally, zones in buildings are related to either high-bay or low-bay areas. An evaluation of the prototype showed that the low-bay areas were interspersed between high-activity areas (such as the men's and women's lockers) and low-activity areas (such as storage rooms). We suggested that a study directed toward energy conservation needed to be keyed to an evaluation of activity patterns within the building, leading to rezoning of areas by activity level rather than by bay height. Such a study was approved. Our design of the prototype was more efficient and allowed for energy savings of 44.4 percent (Figure 8.3).

Our first effort designated service and served personnel in the facility. The served group was easily identified since the general public use the Postal Service for mail pickup and mail and package delivery. Through a series of meetings with Postal Service personnel we established five levels of service personnel. These levels were plotted against time. It became apparent that mail carriers, the major users of the facility, were only in the facility intermittently. In fact, after 10 A.M. most mail carriers had sorted their mail and were out on their delivery routes. They returned at 2 P.M. to sort incoming mail. In discussions concerning use of the building we learned that union negotiations were currently underway to balance the route loads of individual carriers and thereby eliminate the need for carriers to return to the station (Figure 8.4).

Fig. 8.3 Energy consumption diagram.

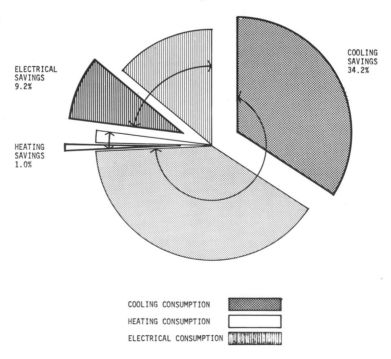

ELECTRICAL SAVINGS 9.2%

HEATING SAVINGS 1.0%

COOLING SAVINGS 34.2%

COOLING CONSUMPTION

HEATING CONSUMPTION

ELECTRICAL CONSUMPTION

POSITION: FUNCTION:	Morning							Afternoon							Evening
	5	6	7	8	9	10	11	12	1	2	3	4	5	6	7
DISTRIBUTION CLERK	7 SORT MAIL AND PLACE IN THEIR DESKS BY 8 AM.	7 PLACE 1ST CLASS CARRIER MAIL ON	9 P.O. BOXES;	9	9 SORT NON-PREFERENTIAL MAIL AND PAR-	9	9 READY MAIL	9 CELS------ FOR 12:30 PICK-UP	2	2 HANDLE PICK-UP--------	1	1			
MECHANICAL MARK-UP/ BOX CLERK			3 HANDLE PARCEL NOTIFICATION AT DUTCH DOOR AND MECH MARK-UP	3	3	3 AID DISTRIBUTION	3	3	3	3 MECHANICAL MARK-UP FOR CARRIERS RETURNING WITH NON-DELIVERABLES	1	1			
WINDOW CLERK					6 MAN SERVICE LOBBY WINDOWS; RETRIEVE	6	6	6 PARCELS; AID DISTRIBUTION	6	6	6	6			
SUPERVISOR CARRIER FOREMAN		1	1	1	1 OCCASIONAL	1 ROUTE INSPECTIONS AND	1	1 MANAGEMENT	1 FUNCTIONS						
SUPERVISOR STATION MANAGER					1 CUSTOMER SERVICE AND MANAGEMENT	1	1	1 FUNCTIONS	1	1	1	1			
CARRIER		50 SORT 1ST CLASS AND ROUTE MAIL ACCORDING TO PUNCH-IN	67 INDIVIDUAL ROUTES	67 PUNCH-OUT VEHICLE	0 DELIVERY ON INDIVIDUAL	0 ROUTES------	0	0	0 PUNCH-IN	67 SORT TOMORROW'S 2nd, 3rd CLASS MAIL TAKES NON-DELIVERABLES TO BOX CLERK DROPS OFF OUTGOING MAIL PUNCH-OUT					
CUSTOMER	BOX LOBBY ONLY	BOX LOBBY ONLY. PICK UP PARCELS			BOX AND SERVICE LOBBY PEAK SERVICE			PEAK SERVICE				PEAK SERVICE	BOX LOBBY ONLY		
MAIL DELIVERY 5 TON VAN		7 AM DELIVERY HOT SHOT REMAINING 1ST CLASS						12:30 PM PRINCIPAL PICK-UP		2:30 PM PICK-UP DELIVERY		4:50 PM PICK-UP			4:15 AM PRINCIPAL DELIVERY

Fig. 8.4 Occupancy load profile and activity description for a nonpeak workday (Jan. 1–Oct. 31); ten-year projection.

A second behavioral situation surfaced in discussions on facility use. Postal Service buildings traditionally provide for lookout galleries so that inspectors can observe carriers unobtrusively. These lookout galleries, with one-way glass, traditionally are suspended from the building structure. Inspectors can arrive unobserved, entering through a private entrance, and be in the building to oversee handling procedures without the carriers being aware of their presence. Breakout doors, so called, are traditionally provided for the unlikely instance in which an inspector finds a carrier acting illegally.

In visiting one of the typical prototype buildings, we found a number of behavioral/systems anomalies. First, the breakout door was completely inoperative—mail carts were stacked in front of it. More significantly, the aisles to be surveyed from the lookout gallery ran parallel with it. Instead of looking down each aisle, the inspector could see only the first adjacent aisle. Placement of the carrier aisles was left to the station manager, and he had placed the aisles to correspond with the direction of fluorescent lighting. In doing so, he had placed them parallel with the lookout gallery rather than at right angles to it. The fluorescent lights had been laid out without regard for the secondary effect of determining aisle placement and thereby circumventing surveillance! Moreover, suspending the lookout gallery from the roof structure created a concentrated load at midpoint of the span, making uniformly loaded roof systems impossible.

In the prototype plan postboxes were arranged in a sawtooth design. Postal Service personnel acknowledged that this sawtooth design created a series of dead-end areas not easily surveyed by management personnel. Since the served area is traditionally open 24 hours a day, it was clear that these unsupervised culs-de-sac were not ideal. A person arriving late in the evening to pick up mail would be anxious to know if other people were present in the facility. Unless each aisle was scanned, the presence of others would not be apparent. Our first thought was that the inconvenience to the served person was offset by the ease of loading the boxes from the rear. Investigation of the actual procedure determined that there was *no* compensating service advantage. The carrier filling these boxes from the rear used a mail cart which was pushed into the narrow

Fig. 8.5 Floor plan: Northshore station.

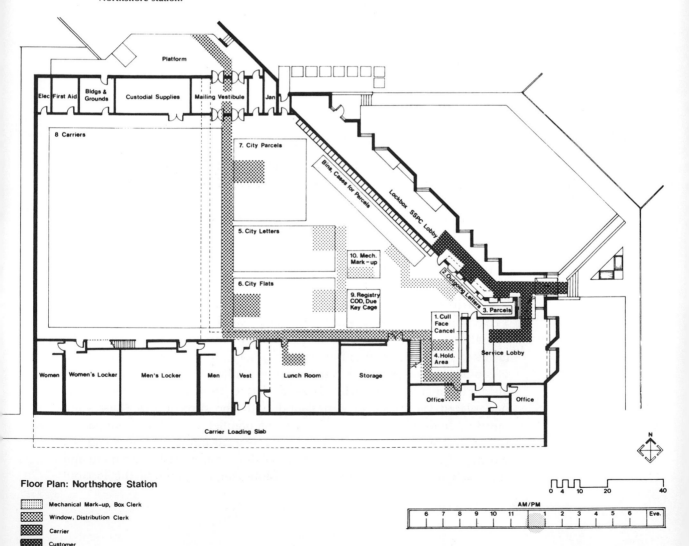

Floor Plan: Northshore Station

- Mechanical Mark-up, Box Clerk
- Window, Distribution Clerk
- Carrier
- Customer

confines of the service corridor, and then the carrier returned to the loading spaces periodically. It became apparent in discussions that a straight line of boxes would aid both the carrier and the general public.

One major reason for keeping the air conditioning at a working level during the full day was the arrival of mail in the middle of the afternoon. The placement of the loading dock required a person handling this mail to traverse the sorting room (Figure 8.5).

Our revised plan did four things:

1. It used a straight-line design for postal boxes rather than the saw-tooth design.

2. It relocated the service dock so that the sorting room would not have to be traversed in the afternoon.

3. It simplified the location of the lookout gallery, supporting that gallery with independent columns rather than having it suspended from the roof.

4. It rezoned the building on the basis of behavioral activity patterns rather than high- and low-bay areas.

Using a computer program developed by Timmerman Engineers, we ran a load analysis of the prototype and of our revised plan. This revised computer program documented the energy savings (Figures 8.6 and 8.7).

Fig. 8.6 Annual cooling consumption—total project.

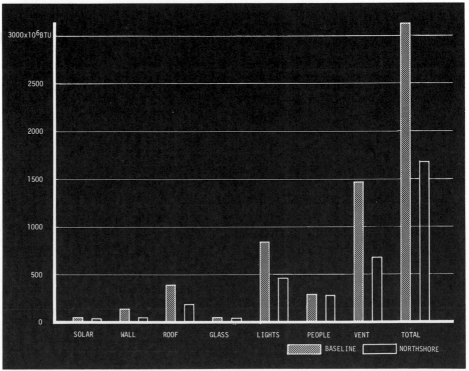

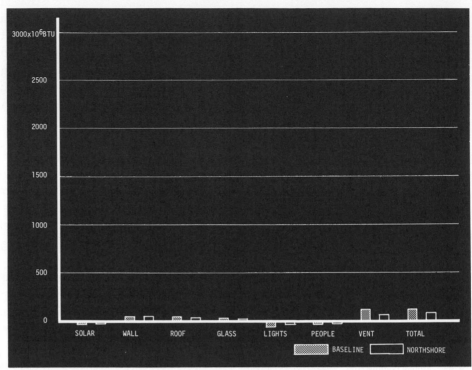

3000×10^6 BTU

BASELINE   NORTHSHORE

Fig. 8.7 Annual heating consumption—total project.

The revised building plan was approved by the regional Postal Service and is now under construction. In making the presentation we first showed a behavioral analysis of the prototype building and compared it with the behavioral analysis of our revised plan. This analysis, combined with the computer printout, justified our plan revision. A major saving in energy occurred by zoning the sorting room and radically diminishing the air-conditioning load in this area after 10 A.M.

Ancillary advantages accrue to the revised scheme. By removing the concentrated load from the ceiling system, it is possible to use a lighter, uniformly loaded structure. By separating the sorting room from other activity areas, the rear wall is left unobstructed for expansion. The revised plan considers orientation problems of the prototype. The glass at the public entrance and clerestory glass illuminating part of the service area are placed facing north in the prototype. If the building is reversed, the glass can be changed in orientation to provide north light regardless of the building's orientation.

Mitch Mize, a behavioral psychologist working with our office, developed the activity profile program. It became an essential document in directing the architects and consultants working on the building design. It is proposed that a feedback analysis be made of the building when completed to determine whether the theoretical savings in energy and implied efficiency actually occur as anticipated.

The significance of this study is the immediate application of behavioral architecture techniques to typical, average-sized architectural commissions.

Schematic Design

At the end of the Programming Phase a considerable body of information is available concerning the physical and social dimensions of the project. During the Schematic Design Phase it is proposed that specific solution statements be prepared to document the context and issues addressed in deciding on particular building configurations. These solution statements, in combination with the variable matrices prepared on a series of bases, should generate architectural alternatives. At the same time site information is determining systems data (see Figure 8.1). During the Schematic Design Phase and the development of alternatives, the site begins to carry increasing importance. The site will determine the issues of proximity to community, the parking and circulation patterns, and the space for expansion. The elements of expansion considered will determine the modularity of the project (see Figure 8.8). For example, apartment projects are often built in increments of 250 units; office parks are built in clusters of buildings; institutions often develop phasing strategies that move the facility in increments of at least one-fourth of the total facility. Staging strategies are essential, and they represent an important alternative in the Schematic Phase.

It is proposed that the systems components be completed during the Schematic Design Phase. Information of site conditions and expansion

Fig. 8.8   Hospital study—expansion modularity. (From "The Expandable Hospital," Progressive Architecture, October 1972. Copyright © 1972, Reinhold Publishing Company. Wolff, Zimmer, Gunsal, Frasca, Ritter, architects; Kaiser Foundation, sponsor.)

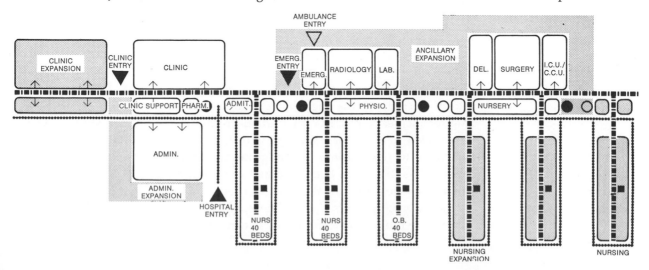

and modularity decisions have an impact on the structural system chosen. For example, the decision to develop a concrete structural system in the URBS dormitory project was predicated on fire code requirements.

High-rise structures will have more stringent fire code requirements, and the cost of such structures must be evaluated against the economy in land coverage. Again, parking structures, while conserving land, can approach one-half the cost of inhabited space. Clearly the variables to be considered in the actual schematic design are too numerous to outline here. What is important is that a series of viable alternatives are developed that can be evaluated as described in the Behavioral Design Process Model. (See the evaluation chart, Figure 7.14.)

The end product of the Schematic Phase is one scheme, evaluated against viable alternatives based on the subsystems proposed, the behavioral data compiled, and the cost requirements for the project. One valuable computer use is the development of a program that stores unit costs for elements of the concepts considered in schematics. Whether developed by computer or manually, this check is essential to be certain that the approved scheme meets budget requirements.

Defensible Space

It is beyond the scope of this book to develop in detail the areas of design that traditionally are accomplished in the Design Development and Construction Document Phases of building development. As mentioned earlier, the intent in introducing a behavioral design process is to alter the current process as little as possible, in the belief that significant redirection can be accomplished by specific additions to the process rather than by radical changes. Design development concentrates on human engineering factors: codes, furniture, security, requirements of the handicapped, and defensible space. These factors would be considered in any case, I believe, with the possible exception of defensible space.

The term *defensible space* was coined in an important study by Oscar Newman, under a grant from the National Institute of Law Enforcement and Criminal Justice of the U.S. Department of Justice. In essence the study documents the fact that certain configurations of housing have higher incidence of crime than other configurations. Since studies were conducted in adjacent buildings within the same community, Newman was able to relate crime to configuration rather than to the community mores. His thesis has been accepted as an important one by law enforcement agencies and by those concerned with developing high-density housing developments. As used here, defensible space refers to any building where individual territoriality is considered. For example, the exterior

Fig. 8.9   Access path—redesigned. [From Oscar Newman, Defensible Space (New York: Macmillan, 1972.) Copyright © 1972 by Oscar Newman.]

areas of a project generally are undefined; there is generally confusion between exterior areas that are to be unoccupied, those that are to be public in an active way, and those areas that are merely a setting for the building. The concept of defensible space as used here suggests that areas, particularly exterior areas, are clearly earmarked for public or private use. Simple techniques such as front stoops for houses, or retaining walls defining private gardens, or cul-de-sac courts adjacent to a group of entries all operate to establish symbolically demarcations of territoriality (see Figure 8.9). Interior configurations also can be developed for territoriality. Thought can be given to how an entrance is perceived by an outsider. Is there a significant demarcation before an entrance to a housing unit? In the case of nonhousing units, is there a clear central entrance which clearly establishes the point of control in entering? Is the entrance visible from the public corridors, both interior and exterior? (See Figure 8.10.) Defensible space as a concept must be related to security techniques, for the patterns of behavior expected in a project must anticipate disruption and the need for control. It is in the Design Development Phase that simultaneous-use diagrams are particularly effective (see Chapter 7). The process of presupposing movement patterns will quickly illustrate the areas of heavy traffic, the areas of entrance confusion, and the areas that can be earmarked for private use by occupants. The concept of defensible space suggests that a symbolic demarcation encourages the occupants to feel the

Fig. 8.10 Riverbend project. This is an excellent example of designing for defensible space. Territoriality is established at each entrance. Stairs are private. Most important, the corridors are single-loaded, and community surveillance is thereby greatly enhanced. (Davis, Brody & Associates, architects; Robert Gray, photographer.)

building is theirs, which in turn encourages their participation in maintaining security.

Occupancy Documents and Training

Through construction documents and building construction the project moves ahead very much as it would under the normal design process. Upon occupancy it is proposed that an Occupancy Document be prepared for the users of a project and a short discussion period be developed to show the occupants how the building was designed to be used. Traditionally at the time of occupancy architects give the owners the guarantees and little more. In complex social situations it is proposed that a series of meetings be scheduled prior to occupancy so that the architects can describe elements of flexibility built into the system and discuss in detail the management, security, and maintenance programs. It is difficult to direct an orientation program to the served occupants in the project, for there may be too many people to talk with on a personal basis. However, a pamphlet that welcomes them and lists data about the building can be prepared inexpensively and distributed to all occupants. Of particular value is a clear statement of what actions are to be taken in the case of common emergencies, such as fire, broken windows, injury, or suspected burglary. The behavioral psychologist working as a consultant throughout the project might well take charge of implementing this procedure.

Feedback

In Chapter 7 feedback was discussed as one means of data collection. The step must be stressed because the logic of designing for behavior requires that the assumptions made, particularly as documented in the Solution Statement (see Chapter 7), be checked against experience. Feedback is a new service of architects and will be approached in a variety of ways until a recognized format is developed and widely adopted. Only guidelines for feedback can be presented here since the documents will vary considerably depending on the complexity of the building under consideration, the funding made available by the owner or other sources, and the future usefulness of the document. It is hoped that a national clearinghouse will be established that will issue a format for evaluation and take on the responsibility for disseminating information collected. The following guidelines should be employed in preparing a feedback document:

1. A questionnaire directed to each role group within a project is the most useful feedback tool.

2. A behavioral psychologist must be involved in developing the

questionnaire, conducting interviews, and evaluating the findings. Whether it should be the same consultant who worked with the architect on the project or a second, independent consultant is open to question. I prefer to use the same consultant, considering that more is to be gained by continuity than is lost in a possible conflict of interest. The form of the questionnaire should be designed for computer compilation, if possible, so that cross-referencing will be feasible.

3. The owner should be active in developing the questionnaire and in considering the findings. It is hoped that the owner would combine the feedback phase with a management evaluation study to be certain that not only the building but the programs function correctly.

4. The feedback statement, when completed, should avoid self-congratulatory comments and concentrate on specific areas of assumptions realized and not realized.

5. Feedback should evaluate the alternative to build by projecting the alternative into the current time frame. For example, a decision to build may have been predicated on the difficulty of acquiring suitable existing space. It would be important to check whether or not that situation changed radically shortly after the decision to build or continues to be a problem.

6. Feedback should list specific suggestions for future projects facing the same building situations. These statements should address particularly the items outlined in the Solution Statement.

7. Until such time as there is a national clearinghouse, the document should be distributed privately as widely as possible. The AIA compiles a list of architects interested in feedback material and acts as an informal clearinghouse.

The Team

There is no question that collaboration between architects and behavioral psychologists is needed. Throughout the Behavioral Design Process Model it is essential, particularly on complex social buildings, that a trained consultant be an active participant of the team. There is precedent in the use of consultants: the architect today uses engineering consultants for structure, specialists in civil engineering, mechanical, electrical, and plumbing areas, and often consultants for graphics and interiors. Only a few of the largest firms have these capabilities on their staffs, and it can be argued that use of independent consultants creates a market of specialists with constantly renewed standards. Use of consultants underscores two things: the complexity of architecture, requiring specialists, and the role of the architect as the coordinator.

In referring to behavioral psychologists throughout the book I have intended that term as a description of anyone trained in social interaction. Such a person may be a psychologist, psychiatrist, social scientist, anthropologist, management consultant, or, increasingly, an architectural graduate with special training in the social and behavioral sciences. There is no licensing for these specialists, so they are known by their ability to perform, much as graphic consultants are. When the role they play is better recognized, it is possible that there will be some form of licensing; needless to say, their academic background serves much the same function, particularly for those receiving Ph.D.s in the related fields. It is possible, however, that in time behavioral training will be recognized as an integral part of architecture and there will be vehicles for training architects in this speciality. This will not alleviate the need for consultants, but it will produce a wider understanding of the issues throughout the profession. As mentioned earlier, there is a movement in this direction today with departments of architecture refocusing part of their curriculum. Currently the emphasis in such redirection is on ecological problems, as environment is seen in its human support characteristics. This essential overview has been long in coming and places the architect in the role of comprehensive planner. Increasingly, I believe, schools will take the next step and concentrate on the interface of buildings and behavior on the interpersonal level.

The behavioral psychologists must have a particular point of view to be helpful. First of all they must recognize the context in which they are asked to consult. Their peer group is in the academic community, and they are judged by their care in handling research. In architecture they are asked to work within a problem-solving, pragmatic, and immediate time frame. They will be asked to make judgments before these can be checked, and they will join with the architect in presupposing information that they do not have time, money, or technique to verify. Finally, they must be team members and must enjoy working with a vast array of building professionals, beginning with the owners and including the users, administrators, contractors, construction workers, and so forth.

In a real sense the role of behavioral consultant is a new field. Many academicians will find consulting a valuable adjunct to their major roles as teachers. As many more will develop firms, making consultation a major role and teaching a secondary one.

Where does an architect find such a consultant? The AIA has been active in promoting a liaison between architects and behavioral psychologists. The AIA will surely continue in its role of informal liaison. Major universities have programs in environmental psychology, the general term for behavioral architecture, and the professors actively involved with this program will undoubtedly be experienced, at least in significant research.

Finally, there are an increasing number of publications written by pioneers in the field (many are listed in the bibliography), and these authors are active in consulting work. The field is a broad one, and magazines cover aspects of design and behavior. A list of current magazines is included in the bibliography.

What specific roles does the consultant perform? In 1973 the AIA sponsored a conference to discuss in detail how architects and behavioral psychologists could work together. The conferees, four architects and four behavioral psychologists, met for 3 days and developed the Coolfont Model, named after the site of the conference. My major concern in the model as developed by the Coolfont conference is the continuation of programming as a subcategory under Schematic Design. The intent of the conference was implementation of liaison under the current design process, so the continuation of this sequence is understandable. The areas of involvement are to the point and have been included in the process model presented here. Those areas of involvement aside from the process model include:

1. Defining terms before beginning
2. Helping with client presentations
3. Suggesting site safety during and after construction
4. Working with interior programming
5. Developing the user manual and teaching program
6. Coordinating the feedback phase.

Who pays for the behavioral psychologist? Methods of payment to a consultant in the behavioral field are either on an hourly basis plus expenses or on a fixed-fee basis negotiated for particular increments of the work. There seems to be little justification in suggesting a percentage payment, and a contingency understanding (that is, one that reimburses the consultant only if a job goes through) is counterproductive, I feel.

There is considerable expense anticipated in a complex social building. However, in such a building the fee may be large, and some of the cost of the consultant can be partially absorbed if it can be shown that such work will bring solutions to fruition in a more logical and timely manner. But the issue of extra cost cannot be absorbed fully, except in simple buildings where the architect may use the behavioral design technique and presuppose solutions with little consultation. A fully developed questionnaire procedure may run to $10,000 or higher, depending on many factors, and computer time is costly. The consultant, as a qualified professional, will charge a high hourly rate. One of the major reasons I suggest strongly that programming be a separate and distinct phase, beginning with AIA contract documents, is to underscore the importance of information gathered at this time. Currently the architect requests additional payment for programming as an additional service to be performed *when the client requests it*. The AIA format places the burden of proof of need on the architect each time; if the AIA documents listed programming as a separate phase, the contract would contain a payment schedule including such work and the burden of proof would be on the client if it was not wanted. Programming costs should run on a sliding scale depending on the complexity of the social organization of a building; if related to percentage, the fee should run between ½ and 1 percent of the construction cost.

In a document entitled "Emerging Techniques to Architectural Programming," the AIA has this to say about reimbursement for programming as currently handled:

1. On jobs contracted with private, individual clients only one of five clients provided a written program. In 50% of the cases, the architect rated the programs of poor quality. On those jobs for which the programming was done by the architect, the average additional income for programming was reported to be about $800.00.

2. Institutional or corporate clients provided programs on one out of two jobs, and the architects rated 60% of these as good. On jobs where programming was done by the architect, the average additional income was about $4000 per job.

3. For Federal and State government clients, the survey indicates that programs are provided on five out of six jobs, and the architects rated 60% of these as good. On jobs where programming was done by the architect, the average estimated additional income was at $3,200 per job.

4. For local government clients, three out of seven projects included programs from the clients, 60% of which were rated good by the architects.[1]

This quotation points up a second flaw in the current AIA contract documents. These documents list the program as being the responsibility of the owner, suggesting strongly that the owner's staff can perform the functions, or many of them, listed in the Behavioral Design Process Model. The AIA documents are not to blame for the current design process; they merely reflect it. By doing so, however, they make proper reimbursement for services more difficult.

It looks very much as if the architect will be forced personally to sponsor the idea of programming and full use of consultants to the client in the next few years. The direction toward behavioral design is admittedly new; hopefully success in implementation and broad discussion of the issues will change the climate of opinion soon. Until then the architects involved in behavioral design and the consultants active in the field will probably find themselves underpaid. They will have to rely instead on the excite-

[1] Benjamin H. Evans and C. Herbert Wheeler, Jr., "Emerging Techniques to Architectural Programming," The American Institute of Architects, Washington, D.C., pp. 9–10.

ment of being involved in a new, open-ended field that has the potential of drastically changing the building professions.

How Precise? The peers for behavioral psychologists are their colleagues in the academic profession. They are trained to be precise in their research methodology and to express this precision in written articles and books. The scientific method suggests that two scientists working independently should be able to reproduce the same finding, given identical conditions. Working in behavioral fields where the variables are infinite and secondary effects are hard to judge, behavioral psychologists understandably become weary of generalizations, worried about proper definition of terms, and anxious to cross-reference and verify each conclusion.

The architect, on the other hand, is under continuing pressure to develop buildings in a given time frame. Architects must make a thousand decisions about every level of design from the location of a parking structure to the kind of magnetic hardware to be used on a closet door. They are fully aware of the complexity of their buildings, and they try to find a hierarchy for ordering them. In a sense architects begin a building with a blank sheet of paper and construct from a series of superimposed hierarchies the ordering that leads ultimately to the decision of push-plate hardware. Behavioral psychologists begin with the complexity of the interpersonal world of individuals. They work in the reverse direction, finding order out of complexity, and if they do not find order, they return again and again, each time changing their research format, tools, and definitions.

As earlier discussions indicate, there is a serious need for behavioral input in buildings, for architects build with or without behavioral data. In time the building partners of owner, architect, and government may change radically and allow significant periods of time for research before undertaking projects. Today, if behavioral architecture is to be implemented immediately, the process can be redirected but not precipitously changed. Behavioral psychologists, then, will be asked to change more of their way of doing things than will the architects. The context is the building situation as it exists today. The architect needs guidance but is not in a position to change the context in which that guidance must become useful.

Once the team members have been chosen and before beginning, it is suggested that a creative discussion be undertaken in order to develop not only the definition of terms to be used, but an understanding as to the importance of terminology in the first place. Terminology will always be far more important to behavioral psychologists than to architects, for it is the vehicle for communicating within their profession. Architects, on the other hand, know throughout the programming process that the document of words that is produced, however precise, however significant in creating accountability, will finally be turned into building form, and that cannot be verbalized.

Finally the owner must become involved. As the Coolfont conference indicated, one significant value in having a behavioral psychologist as a team member is that such a person can help clarify differences in goals between the owner, the architect, and the user of the building. A series of meetings early in the programming phase with the owner, the consultant, the architect, and representatives of the user will help set the ground rules for design and help reconcile differences before they become manifest in the building itself.

Who Does the Work?   One false view the general public holds of architectural firms is that they are homogeneous in skills and abilities. The principal who represents the firm may also be "on the board" doing the project. Just as likely, even in the average ten-person firm, the principal will be handling projects administratively, perhaps working in conceptual design, writing specifications, and performing job supervision. Much of the detail design on a project, including development of alternative schemes, is performed by two groups of architects, younger men and women recently graduated and older architects who have particular skills in preparing production documents. When my firm developed a design guide for the Corps of Engineers, we explicitly considered the team member who would use the guide. In developing a behavioral design process it is equally important that the workers be considered. Much has been said earlier about the need for a concise graphic language and, when words must be used, the need for making them brief but not cryptic. The rationale behind this is not only to enable communication between management professionals and presentation to the owner, but also to enable communication with the architect doing the work. It is important that the architect be included in the work sessions, and the architect will doubtless be party to many meetings that will provide a background to the approach. But the architect's job is a graphic one; it deals with the graphic two-dimensional vocabulary of drawings. The document that has the greatest utility is one that can be opened at a desk, like the space allocation diagram with pictograms of activities superimposed, as discussed in Chapter 7.

Along the same lines, meetings at the Coolfont conference were quick to point out that many behavioral psychologists do not know how to read drawings. If they are to be more than administrators, and they must be if they are to perform their full role as team members, it is necessary to discuss drawings with them and point out what they mean. I have found that a particular confusion to the nonarchitect is the proliferation of presentation techniques, each involving the same building. The schematic plan which is inked and pristine gives the impression of being the final design, while the working drawings that look anything but finished are construction documents.

The behavioral design approach to design must begin at home in the office that produces the work.

9
Frontiers

The book to this point has been involved with the practical applications of behavioral design today. Speculation concerning the implications of behavioral design on tomorrow's world, or on the theory of architecture, or on the professions of architecture and psychology has been kept to a minimum. Yet I feel that a behavioral design point of view once determined supersedes any other way of looking at buildings. There is a feeling of evangelical intensity in meetings concerning behavioral design. Many active in the field feel that behavioral design represents the seeds of a new architecture, as potent a movement for change as the Modern Movement was in the 1920s.

Tying behavioral design to systems logic has been the key to finding a means of quantifying behavioral indices in design, however approximately. One direction as behavioral design develops is improved techniques for expressing behavioral matters alongside physical ones. It is also certain that techniques for acquiring data will improve and behavioral psychologists will develop a vocabulary of terms that will move research forward. Hopefully such a vocabulary will relate to the common issues of buildings; in short, be in architectural language as well as in behavioral language.

But the increase in precision is not for me the frontier of behavioral design. Whether or not it can be shown that density or perceived congestion is the root cause of urban disruption is not a frontier matter, although it may be important. Again, the visual experiments in communicating behavior are fascinating but not the frontier issues. Christopher Alexander[1] in developing his *Pattern Language* has suggested a shorthand for design which is well worth watching. Lawrence Halprin in his motation study (Figure 9.1) has attempted to express such movement in time, using the techniques codified by choreographers. The weakness of such diagrams is their unfamiliarity. We are not accustomed to thinking in move-

---

[1] Christopher Alexander et al., *A Pattern Language: Towns, Buildings, Construction* (New York: Oxford University Press, to be published).

Fig. 9.1 Motation study—Nicolett Mall. (Lawrence Halprin & Associates.)

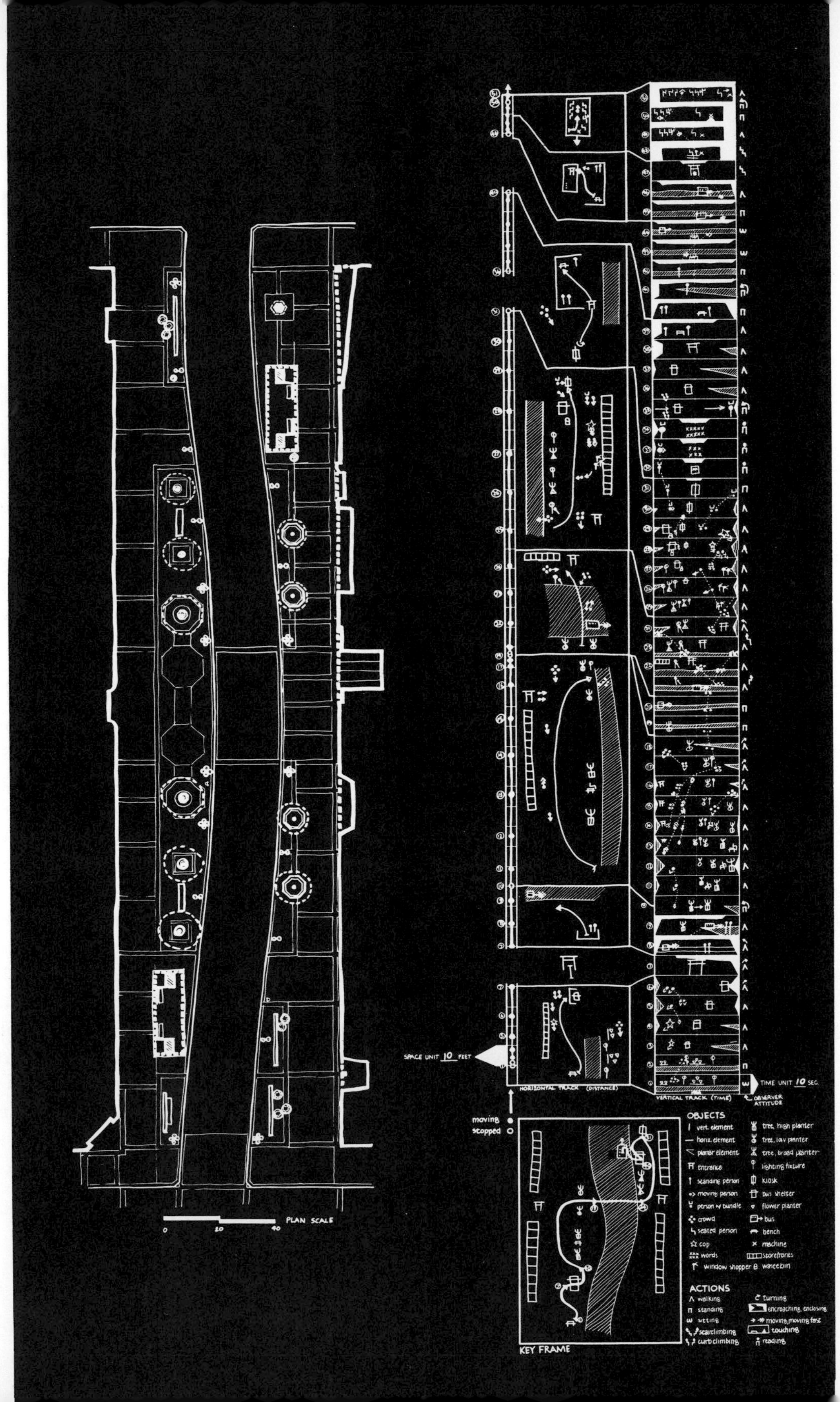

ment and time; therefore we are not accustomed to reading the diagram language necessary to plot simultaneous activity.

The root issues are more comprehensive, I feel. The root issues represent the frontier of thought. These issues may have been addressed thus far, but little has been said that solves them. The root issue is a society off-base with its values, believing as in a dream that technology, expressed through building, can replace the social fabric developed through centuries. The issue seems closely to parallel the use of natural resources, the fodder for the industrialized world. In just a few centuries we have used natural resources that were millions of years in forming. In a few generations we have "used up" social ordering that took centuries to develop. It is not primarily a physical situation that I am describing, but the physical expression of it is clear (see Figures 9.2 and 9.3). Let us not become romantic about the changes in Birmingham, England, for it would be invalid to suggest that pleasant market streets as in the 1900s represented a priori a higher quality of life than streets with traffic. Figure 9.4, however, displays the same pattern of place isolation in a thoroughly modern context, the regional shopping center. Like Birmingham it isolates and in so doing limits. This is the issue: limiting options in a world rapidly changing, limiting options and in the process destroying established social patterns.

Options/Value

The design of Milton Keynes, described earlier, was an advance on earlier new towns, for it allowed for change, albeit the changes were all antici-

Fig. 9.2 (below) Birmingham, England, yesterday. (National Monuments Record, Royal Commission on Historical Monuments.)

Fig. 9.3 (below, right) Birmingham, England, today. (The Architectural Review; Peter Baistow, photographer.)

Fig. 9.4 Shopping center.
(The Urban Land Institute.)

pated alternatives. Yet the difference may be imperceptible when the city is fully built, for the options are really options in the development strategy. For example, should a large or small school complex be built at an intersection? When the city is built, it will not be apparent that this ever was an option. More significant in new towns is the reliance on pedestrian ways, allowing the option of walking, biking, or automobile transportation, and tying a new town to business centers, as in Stockholm's new towns. Yet even the new towns, however responsive, are still creating the physical environment first and then asking the social group to adjust.

There simply is little respect for natural social ordering in the drive to solve the problems of the world technologically. Each new technological system is introduced, one upon the next, like raised sidewalks in Cincinnati to make the downtown more viable, but the shops on the natural street are doing badly. There just aren't enough people on the street to justify two sidewalk systems. Too bad—it was a good try.

There will be a new generation of coal-burning power plants surrounding major cities in the United States, each located in rural areas, each creating social disruption as it brings economic gain. The power plant announced by the Lower Colorado River Authority (LCRA), 2 miles from Fayetteville, Texas, will ultimately provide 3 million kilowatts of power.

The day after the plant was announced in the paper, the city council of Austin, Texas, 60 miles away, which had been previously involved in the decision making, ratified the location, since it would pay half the cost and use half the power. The city of Fayetteville, population 400, representing a surrounding community of some 2,000, had never been notified, or asked, or considered. Fayetteville is a natural resource in this country, socially. It has changed little in 100 years. It produces balanced citizens in an undisturbed rural setting. In the next years, $450 million will be spent on the Fayetteville plant alone. Nothing in the environmental impact statement is addressed to the cultural disruption such a change will mean.

Planners often do not seem to attend church or temple, so the religious traditions of a community seem superfluous. Many Americans today question the viability of the family. What intellectual derision is addressed to someone who would maintain the church or temple, the family, *and* the community! Yet it does not take a behavioral psychologist to make clear the sources of social cohesion which come from respect for church, family, and state. Fayetteville is a resouce, for people there quietly respect all three. Fayetteville is a resource where the social orderings come first, the configuration of the town comes second.

Because change has been imposed in industrial giant steps, the time for social evolution has passed. By scrupulously overlooking the obvious interlock between living, working, and schools, we play out our cards although we know we have lost the game—watching the whites flee the inner city, in Washington, D.C., for example, without changing the schools that might have kept them.

Why should it be so difficult for us to acknowledge the natural patterns that social groups develop? Doxiadis developed an exhaustive pattern book of human habitation, using the history of human settlements to suggest natural habitation configurations. Whether or not his ekistic interpolation (by which he found certain repetitive orderings universal) is accepted, the documentation of settlements he developed in support of ekistics is a resource of considerable value (see Figure 9.5).

Frontiers in behavior and environment for me are those ideas that restructure industrialization. First there are the experiments, made largely in protest. A rock festival puts people first and haphazardly forms a city for the hours and days of the ceremony. Communes, a big statement in the 1960s, dramatized alternatives to living patterns and built wonderful care-free homes and rediscovered the rural life. The Lama Foundation, where drugs, liquor, and promiscuity are out, being highly structured toward spiritual trips, may last (see Figure 9.6). Few others have.

The experiments in ordered living in China as in the U.S.S.R. will impress Americans for a short while, but like the experiments in rock

Fig. 9.5 Urban rural settlement in Kranidi, Greece.
[From Constantinos A. Doxiadis, Ekistics: An Introduction to the Science
of Human Settlements
(New York: Oxford Univer-
sity Press). Copyright © 1968
by Constantinos A. Doxiadis.
Reprinted by permission of
Oxford University Press.]

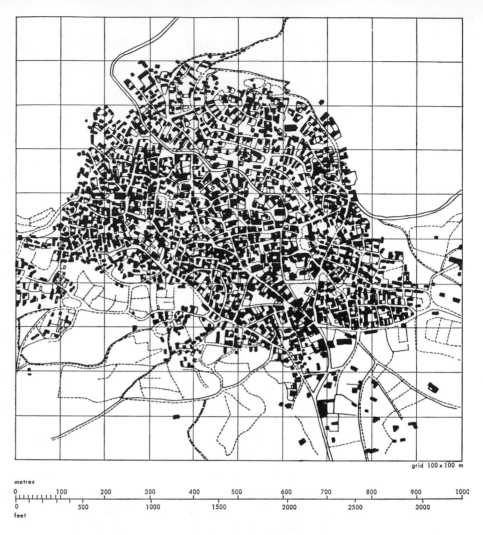

grid 100 x 100 m

Fig. 9.6 Handmade house.
(Bonnie Freer, Photo Re-
searchers.)

festivals, communes, or other media-induced interests, they will be short-lived in their influence, for their solution is essentially foreign to us and, however interesting, impossible to comprehend. We are left, then, with frontiers that have less zip and suggest no easy answers. The frontiers are those concepts that affirm the existing natural social groupings and assure that the physical environment will be supportive of these social entities, not disruptive.

Today the Sierra Club, Common Cause, and the consumer protection movements are groups questioning the way we do things. Essentially they are questioning three premises of industrialization: that size is efficient, that change is advantageous, and that industrialization is inevitable. In these movements are the seeds of real change, for the premise is social accountability in the last analysis for social decisions. It leads to participatory democracy—people questioning their government and by so doing guiding it. As on other frontiers today, perhaps the way forward is a reevaluation of what is past. The cynic who sees only failure in social action compounds the problem.

The frontier of behavioral architecture is summed up for me in a question I raised in Louisiana and have not answered. One weekend after being immersed in the low-income housing problems in St. Louis I flew to New Orleans and drove north through rural Louisiana. A black man with his children was fishing (Figure 9.7) for crawdads along the bayou, and I simply asked myself, where is the value scale?

Fig. 9.7 A natural activity pattern. What is its value?

Afterword

The book to date presupposes building as usual. The current building environment has been accepted uncritically; suggestions for introducing behavioral design have been tailored to the existing design process with as few changes as possible. Such an approach is essential, I feel, if any meaningful impact is to be made on the generation of buildings currently on the drawing boards. There is a euphoria and excitement about behavioral design that one feels at conferences on habitability, or at yearly conventions of EDRA (Environmental Design Research Association). Late into the night it is easy to believe that behavioral design represents as bold a new direction as the Modern Movement did in the 1920s, that EDRA is nothing less than a modern-day CIAM (Congres Internationaux d'Architecture Moderne), referring to the influential advocate of modernism that brought together leaders of the Modern Movement from all over Europe and America.

It is easy in discussions with newly found friends in a newly found field to believe there are endless parallels between today and the 1920s: CIAM published papers, EDRA publishes papers; the Modern Movement began as the world changed to industrialization, behavioral architecture begins as the world shifts to conservation and an ecological world view. Comparisons between today and the 1920s are largely fatuous, I feel, for the extent of change in the coming decades may be far beyond anything currently anticipated. Perhaps behavioral architecture is merely a step to a far more comprehensive design overview. Behavioral architecture suggests a synthesis of architecture and behavioral psychology; perhaps what is needed is a synthesis that adds economic theory, and perhaps metaphysics as well.

Change

The major premises of behavioral architecture suggest the complexity of people and the constraints of systems; it synthesizes people and systems into a technique for establishing alternatives and judging which alterna-

181

tive is most feasible. Yet the explicitly stated assumption behind this design technique is the status quo of building as we know it today. What happens when the process of building radically changes? What happens when the crises of ecology and energy force a drastic reduction in the rate of building?

It is hard for us to accept emotionally the end of the era of industrialization. The management generation in the United States and Western Europe grew up to believe that growth meant progress; it is hard to accept that the rapidly approaching end to fossil fuels will change all that. Success has come in ascending waves as preeminently exemplified in transportation and communications. For tens of thousands of years people moved at an average speed of 3 mph. All personal interactions were based on this speed of movement, generation after generation. With the advent of horses the speed became 10 mph, a dramatic increase. Yet the curve of speed against time changed radically from 1850 onward, from 65 mph with steam locomotion to 300 to 400 mph with propeller aircraft, to 500 to 700 mph with jets, and today to 1,500 mph with supersonic jets. And this increase in world travel pales beside the advances of space travel and the landing on the moon. Communication advances are no less remarkable. From the breakthrough of the Gutenberg press in 1441, a major step after tens of thousands of years of society, we find a galaxy of breakthroughs occurring during the last century: Bell's telephone, 1876; Marconi's telegraph, 1895; commercial radio, 1920; national television, 1950; and worldwide television today. Can a generation geared for these changes accept diminution of growth? The thesis of the book *Future Shock* is that people have difficulty accepting rapid change. I suggest that the shock of change is equally difficult either up or down the industrialization ladder.

Transportation and communications symbolize the successes of technology; yet the successes in medicine have been no less spectacular. These successes, in turn, have developed less benign advances, specifically in population growth. From 6000 B.C. to the Christian era the human population grew relatively slowly to 250 million. In the next fifteen centuries it doubled to 500 million. Then the growth curve rose dramatically, doubling again and again. By 1960 the population of the world passed 3 billion and by A.D. 2000 it may be 6 billion.[1]

In a real sense the surfacing of these statistics is an example of planning accountability on a global scale. This in itself is encouraging, yet the statistics compiled to develop a world view are anything but encouraging. The United States, with a sixth of the world population, uses 32 percent of

[1] Compilation from Stanford Research Institute Report, "Science and the Future of Mankind," ed. by Hugo Bayko.

all minerals and 39 percent of all oil products. How long can this continue? A Massachusetts Institute of Technology report to the Club of Rome in developing a symposium on the limits of growth projected known resources against use and time. Even if we assume five times the known amount of fuels and minerals, the answer was clear and unequivocal: the time is short, figured in decades for some resources, not in centuries.

I feel the world is rapidly approaching the symbolic end to fossil fuels, a moment in time that will transform profoundly people's thought patterns for centuries to come. The first tremor was the oil embargo of 1973; the symbolic end will be more dramatic and irreversible. The shortfall between the diminution of fossil fuels and the new power sources, be they controversial breeder reactors or solar generators, is a very sizable shortfall indeed.

Preparation for change, that is, change which does not imply growth, is surfacing in such books as *Small Is Beautiful* by the British economist E. F. Schumacher. Quite frankly he states we are using natural resources as income items rather than recognizing them to be capital items. In the process of industrialization, aside from depleting resources, we have conditioned ourselves to think in big configurations that tend to separate each of us from useful, productive employment. He suggests that only 3½ percent of the total "social time" available to us is actually used in producing goods under advanced cost- and energy-intensive technology. Using a very narrow definition of productivity, he argues that only one-third of all human beings are actually employed at any one time. Of these, only one-sixth are involved in actual production of food or material. Finally, only one-fifth of the total social time of these workers is actually spent in work, figuring holidays, sickness, absences, and so forth. He arrives at the startlingly low 3½ percent by multiplying $1/5$ by $1/3$ by $1/6$. The remaining 96.5 percent of social time is spent in support operations not directly connected with production. The result, as economist Schumacher sees it, is two worlds, one industrialized and cost-intensive, the other, the Third World, facing increasing population and scarcity.

Schumacher and others like him are rethinking the premises behind technological society. The issue is not how to build buildings humanely; the issue is the rate and type of growth itself. The premises of the technological societies must change if small is to be beautiful again and zero growth is to become a viable goal. Schumacher suggests that such change runs counter to the underlying premises supporting technology, premises that espouse evolution as a justification for natural selection and competition, that suggest nonmaterial goals have secondary value, that see all decisions as relative, denying all absolutes, and finally, that accept as valid knowledge only data collected through science.

Meaning Systems

The frontier is in meaning, for step by step in unraveling the motivations behind behavior one arrives at the meaning system the user lives by. Teilhard de Chardin, a natural scientist as well as a priest, suggests in *The Phenomenon of Man* that evolution continues in the mind and society of humankind with the ultimate goal of human beings' union with God. The ascendancy of Jung as a psychiatrist over the more doctrinaire views of Freud has produced a generation of followers espousing the unconscious as well as the conscious, something unheard of in earlier, less complex days of positivism. McLuhan suggests that the introduction of the rational is of recent origin: with the introduction of the printing press people felt that it was possible to match a direct statement against some complex inner state, creating the myth of casuistry.

Architects looking for a visual sign that meaning systems are being taken seriously again should ponder the successful Beaux-Arts exhibit at the Museum of Modern Art in New York in 1975. Needless to say, the Beaux-Arts represented what the Modern Movement rebelled against. John Lovell, in reviewing the exhibit in the *AIA Journal,* suggests that the Beaux-Arts considered the ordering of archetypal spaces and espoused institutional and individual values. He sums up the Beaux-Arts as a three-step process: form, function, meaning.

In this context of meaning, is it time to look again at the impact of religious architecture? Nelson I. Wu, writing in *Chinese and Indian Architecture* (New York: Braziller, 1963), suggests that in rock-cut chaityas the design was developed to come to life through the rite of circumambulation, the time-honored practice of translating a path into a religious experience. Again, he suggests that in the Great Temple of Madurai, in the "hall of a thousand columns," a worshiper measures his psychological penetration into the sacred sanctuary by the length of his passage, psychologically exaggerated by his countless turns.

Following Jung's idea of archetypes, Joseph Campbell has carefully reexamined the world of myths, both religious and secular. He is quick to point out that his use of the word *myth* in no way suggests falsehood; in his mind it is quite the contrary. He does suggest that myths must be understood both consciously and unconsciously as a complex meaning translation passed on from generation to generation. He points out that humans develop an open response to stimuli, unlike the closed response of insects. A child is born 12 years too early, he suggests. His open responses need to be learned within the family and the social group if he is to be whole, and promulgation of information includes myths one learns and uses in developing a mental image of existence.

Frontiers

In treatises on the future, alternative scenarios are developed, like the innovative Czechoslovakian movie shown at international expositions that allows the audience to choose the ending. Two scenarios seem to be forming. One scenario slows and controls industrialization and reaffirms the less cost-intensive and less energy-intensive configurations of society, specifically the rural. The second scenario conceives of space colonies, conveniently designed to match the overpopulation of the world (see Figure 10.1). I find these two concepts logically compatible if one adjustment is

Fig. 10.1   Behavioral design will be essential in space colonies. (NASA.)

made: the space colonies will develop an option for us, not become a uto-pian safety valve for overpopulation. The point is, whichever scenario is developed during the next centuries, it is clear that the role of behavioral design will increase in importance. Reestablishing natural behavior patterns will not be done in nostalgia; it will be done to overcome the two deficiencies of industrialized cities: the high-energy cost of maintenance and the lack of flexibility of pattern.

Surely in the reevaluation of less intensive life-support configurations and in judging those that could be transposed into space some methodology and visual language need to be developed to illustrate the actual behavior within the building or city.

The Visual Language

For me the search for a visual method of expressing behavior is a major frontier well beyond the first attempts presented in Chapter 6. But a beginning effort in this direction brings additional frontiers into focus. The visual language is immediate, elements can be read simultaneously rather than in sequence as is necessary with the written word. Signs and symbols have always had this immediacy, but signs and symbols suggest an image within the mind that can be compared with the image seen. The idea of signs suggests new knowledge of the inner sign within the mind; it suggests the unconscious image making as well as the conscious. Most significantly, it suggests the richness and diversity of the mind, not its simplicity.

A second frontier presents itself in searching for a visual language to express something as complex as behavior. There are considerable constraints to graphs and diagrams. They must have a top and bottom. There is an implied ordering in the hierarchy of graphic elements as they read from left to right, top to bottom. In struggling with visual equivalencies there is need to suggest time within the constraints of design patterns.

Yet the search for a visual language has all the aspects of adventure and growth. Such a language will not develop until those involved in the physical world and those involved in the psychological world learn to work much more closely together. The visual language is not an end in itself, but a culmination of research and experimentation in the issues to be considered: behavioral patterns, the constraints of geometry, the mental images of man, and the need for increased communication. In a real sense the issue is twofold. We must accept human complexity, and we must learn to communicate that complexity when we talk of the human environment.

Closed vs. Open Environments

It seems appropriate to end the discussion of frontiers where we began, with a consideration of closed environments. It was the closed environment of Webbe and the negative aspects of that environment that suggested this book in the first place. As a practicing architect, I thought it essential to have better tools within the existing building process to articulate the advantages and disadvantages of closed environments. The search has led to specific steps that can be taken at once within the status quo of the building process. The search leads as well to the limits of our knowledge, to the imprecision with which a world view is codified, to the imprecision with which secondary effects of closed environments are understood. It is in the fabric of current experimentation that answers will be found. Each new experimentation in life-style suggests meaningful arenas for research.

The charismatic movement represents such a grass-roots movement. Charismatics are deeply motivated Christians who give up their personal ambitions to live a choreography, if you will, of spiritual community participation. In Houston, Episcopalian charismatics have moved into a racially mixed part of town to be within walking distance of their church. Recently a Roman Catholic group took over a retreat house and properties to bring together those with a particular motivation for service. Yet the major area for research in natural patterns of human activity is in the socially healthy rural communities of America, where respect for family, church, and national origin still operate as balancing elements in social ordering. The activity patterns relate to nature and the production of goods.

In tomorrow's world basic behavior patterns surely will be understood and respected. The open environment will become a base line, that is, the natural ordering of the world about us. Closed environments, still needed and operational, will reinforce the internal meaning systems of the inhabitants. It is not too much to believe that humankind will use the parameters of its nature and physical surroundings to embark on the one great adventure facing us, existentially: understanding our life on earth and searching beyond our death.

Bibliography

Books

Alexander, Christopher: *Houses Generated by Patterns* (Berkeley Center for Environment Structure, 1969).

Ardalan, Nader, and Laleh Bakhtiar: *The Sense of Unity: The Sufi Tradition in Persian Art* (Chicago: University of Chicago, 1973).

Ardrey, Robert: *The Territorial Imperative: A Personal Inquiry into the Animal Origins of Property and Nations* (New York: Atheneum, 1966).

Banfield, Edward C.: *The Unheavenly City: The Nature and the Future of Our Urban Crisis* (Boston: Little, Brown, 1970).

Barnett, Jonathan: *Urban Design as Public Policy* (New York: McGraw-Hill, 1974).

Blecher, Earl M.: *Advocacy Planning for Urban Development* (New York: Praeger Publishers, 1974).

Burchell, Robert W.: *Planned Unit Development: New Communities American Style* (New Brunswick, N.J.: Rutgers University, 1972).

Burnette, Charles: *Architecture for Human Behavior: Collected Papers from a Mini-Conference* (Philadelphia Chapter of the AIA, 1971).

Burns, Jim: *Arthropods: New Design Futures* (New York: Praeger, 1972).

Campbell, Joseph: *Myths to Live By* (New York: Viking, 1972).

Canty, Donald J.: *The New City* (For Urban America, Inc.; New York: Praeger, 1969).

Chermayeff, Serge, and Christopher Alexander: *Community and Privacy: Towards a New Architecture of Humanism* (Garden City, N.Y.: Anchor, Doubleday, 1963).

Clarke, Arthur C.: *Profiles of the Future* (New York: Harper & Row, 1973).

Conant, James B.: *Slums and Suburbs* (New York: Signet, 1961).

Conway, Donald: *Social Science and Design. A Process Model for Architect and Social Sciences Collaboration* (Washington, D.C.: American Institute of Architects, 1973).

Cook, Peter: *Architecture: Action and the Plan* (London: Studio Vista, and New York: Reinhold, 1967).

Cutler, Laurence, and Sherrie Cutler: *Handbook of Housing Systems for Designers and Developers* (New York: Van Nostrand Reinhold, 1974).

Dahinden, Justus: *Urban Structures for the Future* (New York: Praeger, 1972).

Dattner, Richard: *Design for Play* (New York: Van Nostrand Reinhold, 1969).

Davies, Ronald, Leo Kuper, and Hilstan Watts: *Durban: A Study in Racial Ecology* (New York: Columbia University, 1958).

Davis, Morton D.: *Game Theory* (New York: Basic Books, 1970).

De Greene, Kenyon B.: *Systems Psychology* (New York: McGraw-Hill, 1970).

Downs, Anthony: *Opening Up the Suburbs: An Urban Strategy for America* (New Haven: Yale University, 1973).

Downs, James F.: *Cultures in Crisis* (Beverly Hills, Calif.: Glencoe Press, 1971).

Doxiadis, Constantinos A.: *Ekistics: An Introduction to the Science of Human Settlements* (New York: Oxford University, 1968).

Eiseley, Loren: *The Immense Journey* (New York: Vintage, Random, 1959).

Evans, Benjamin H., and Herbert C. Wheeler: *Emerging Techniques to Architectural Programming* (Washington, D.C.: American Institute of Architects, 1969).

Fraser, Douglas: *Planning and Cities: Village Planning in the Primitive World* (New York: Braziller, 1968).

Freedman, Jonathan L.: *Crowding and Behavior* (New York: Viking, 1975).

Friedman, John: *Retracking America* (Garden City, N.Y.: Anchor, Doubleday, 1973).

Gans, Herbert J.: *More Equality* (New York: Pantheon, 1968).

————: *People and Plans: Essays on Urban Problems and Solutions* (New York: Basic Books, 1968).

Gardner, John W.: *In Common Cause: Citizens' Action and How It Works* (New York: Norton, 1972).

Giedion, Sigfried: *Space, Time and Architecture* (Cambridge: Harvard University, 1954).

Gifford, Don: *The Literature of Architecture* (New York: Dutton, 1966).

Glasscote, Raymond: *The Community Health Center: An Analysis of Existing Models* (Washington, D.C.: American Psychiatric Association, 1964).

Goffman, Erving: *Asylums* (Garden City, N.Y.: Anchor, Doubleday, 1961).

Goldfarb, Ronald L., and Linda R. Singer: *After Conviction: A Review of the American Correction System* (New York: Simon and Schuster, 1973).

Goldfinder, Myron: *Villages in the Sun: Mediterranean Community Architecture* (New York: Praeger, 1969).

Good, Lawrence R., Saul M. Siegel, and Lafred Paul Bay: *Therapy by Design: Implications of Architecture for Human Behavior* (Springfield, Ill.: Charles C Thomas, 1965).

Goodman, Robert: *After the Planners* (New York: Simon and Schuster, 1972).

Greer, Scott: *The Emerging City: Myth and Reality* (New York: Free Press, 1965).

Gruen, Victor: *Centers for the Urban Environment: Survival of the Cities* (New York: Van Nostrand Reinhold, 1973).

Gutman, Robert: *People and Buildings* (New York: Basic Books, 1972).

Hall, Edward T.: *The Hidden Dimension* (Garden City, N.Y.: Doubleday, 1966).

Halprin, Lawrence: *The RSVP Cycles: Creative Processes in the Human Environment* (New York: Braziller, 1969).

Hardoy, Jorge: *Urban Planning in Pre-Columbian America* (New York: Braziller, 1968).,

Heimsath, Clovis: *Pioneer Texas Buildings* (Austin: University of Texas, 1968).

Howard, Ebenezer: *Garden Cities of Tomorrow* (Cambridge: M.I.T., 1965).

Huxtable, Ada Louise: *Will They Ever Finish Bruckner Boulevard?* (New York: Macmillan, 1963).

Jacobs, Jane: *The Death and Life of Great American Cities* (New York: Vintage Books, Random, 1961).

Jung, Carl G.: *Man and His Symbols* (New York: Dell, 1968).

Kaplan, Bert: *The Inner World of Mental Illness* (New York: Harper & Row, 1964).

Kepers, Gyorgy: *Module Proportion Symmetry Rhythm* (New York: Braziller, 1966).

Lamp, Paul: *Cities and Planning in the Ancient Near East* (New York: Braziller, 1968).

Lang, Jon, Charles Burnette, Walter Moleski, and David Vachon: *Designing for Human Behavior: Architecture and the Behavioral Sciences* (Stroudsburg, Pa.: Dowden, Hutchison & Ross, Inc., 1974).

Le Corbusier: *Towards a New Architecture* (New York: Praeger, 1970).

Leinwand, Gerald (ed.): *Prisons* (New York: Pocket Books, 1972).

Levine, Robert A.: *Public Planning: Failure and Redirection* (New York: Basic Books, 1972).

Lynch, Kevin: *The City Image and Its Elements: The Image of the City* (Cambridge: M.I.T., 1973).

————: *What Time Is This Place?* (Cambridge: M.I.T., 1973).

McClung, Lee Alfred: *Toward Humanist Sociology* (Englewood Cliffs, N.J.: Prentice-Hall, 1973).

McHale, John: *The Future of the Future* (New York: Braziller, 1969).

McLuhan, Marshall: *Understanding Media: The Extensions of Man* (New York: McGraw-Hill, 1965).

_____: *From Cliché to Archetype* (New York: Viking, 1970).

Masotti, Louis H., and Jeffrey K. Hadden: *Urbanization of the Suburbs* (Beverly Hills, Calif.: Sage Publications, 1973).

May, Rollo: *The Courage to Create* (New York: Norton, 1975).

Mayer, Robert H.: *Social Planning and Social Change* (Englewood Cliffs, N.J.: Prentice-Hall, 1973).

Menninger, Carl: *The Crime of Punishment* (New York: Viking, 1968).

Michelson, William: *Man and His Urban Environment: A Sociological Approach* (Reading, Mass.: Addison-Wesley, 1970).

Moholy-Nagy, Sibyl: *Matrix of Man: An Illustrated History of Urban Environment* (New York: Praeger, 1968).

Morrill, Richard L.: *The Spatial Organization of Society* (North Scituate, Mass.: Duxbury Press, 1970).

Myrdal, Gunner: *Beyond the Welfare State: Economic Planning and Its International Implications* (New Haven: Yale University, 1960).

Newman, Oscar: *Defensible Space: Crime Prevention through Urban Design* (New York: Macmillan, 1972).

Norberg-Schultz, Christian: *Existence, Space and Architecture* (New York: Praeger, 1971).

Public Health Service Publication: *Coping and Adaptation* (Washington, D.C.: National Institute of Mental Health, 1970).

Pass, David Vallingby, and Farsta Pass: *From Idea to Reality* (Cambridge: M.I.T., 1973).

Pell, Eve: *Maximum Security: Letters from Prison* (New York: Bantam, Dutton, 1972).

Perin, Constance: *With Man in Mind: An Interdisciplinary Prospectus for Environmental Design* (Cambridge: M.I.T., 1970).

Piaget, Jan: *The Origins of Intelligence in Children* (New York: Norton, 1963).

Proshansky, Harold M., William H. Ittelson, and Leanne G. Rivlin: *Environmental Psychology: Man and His Physical Setting* (New York: Holt, 1970).

Rapoport, Amos: *House Form and Culture: Foundations of Cultural Geography Series* (Englewood Cliffs, N.J.: Prentice-Hall, 1969).

_____: *Australia as Human Setting: Approaches to the Designed Environment* (Sidney: Angus and Robertson, 1972).

Reich, Charles A.: *The Greening of America* (New York: Bantam, Random, 1970).

Reidy, John P.: *Zone Mental Health Centers: The Illinois Concept* (Springfield, Ill.: Charles C Thomas, 1964).

Richmond, Mark S. (ed.): *New Roles for Jails* (Washington, D.C.: United States Bureau of Prisons, Department of Justice, 1969).

Rothstein, Fritz: *Beautiful Squares* (Leipzig, Germany: Edition Leipzig, 1967).

Rotkin, Charles E.: *Europe: An Aerial Close-up* (Philadelphia: Lippincott, 1962).

Rutledge, Albert J.: *Anatomy of a Park* (New York: McGraw-Hill, 1971).

Saalman, Howard: *Planning and Cities: Medieval Cities* (New York: Braziller, 1968).

Schumacher, E. F.: *Small Is Beautiful: Economics As If People Mattered* (New York: Harper & Row, 1973).

Seymour, Whitney North, Jr.: *Small Urban Spaces* (New York: New York University, 1969).

Smithson, Alison, and Peter Smithson: *Urban Structures* (London: Studio Vista, and New York: Reinhold, 1967).

Sommer, Robert: *Personal Space: The Behavioral Basis of Design* (Englewood Cliffs, N.J.: Prentice-Hall, 1969).

_____: *Tight Spaces: Hard Architecture and How to Humanize It* (Englewood Cliffs, N.J.: Prentice-Hall, 1974).

Stein, Maurice R.: *The Eclipse of Community: An Interpretation of American Studies* (New York: Harper & Row, 1964).

Subcommittee on Housing and Urban Affairs: *The Central City Problem and Urban Renewal Policy* (Washington, D.C.: U.S. Government Printing Office, 1973).

Sweet, David C.: *Models of Urban Structure* (Lexington, Mass.: Heath, 1972).
Teilhard de Chardin, Pierre: *The Phenomenon of Man* (New York: Harper & Row, 1965).
Toynbee, Arnold: *Cities on the Move* (New York and London: Oxford University, 1971).
Venturi, Robert: *Complexity and Contradiction in Architecture* (New York: Museum of Modern Art, 1966).
Volwahsen, Andreas: *Living Architecture: India* (New York: Grosset & Dunlap, 1969).
Von Hertzen, Heikki, and Paul D. Spreiregen: *Building a New Town* (Cambridge: M.I.T., 1971).
Wolf, Peter: *The Future of the City: New Directions in Urban Planning* (New York: Whitney Library of Design, 1974).
Wright, Frank Lloyd: *The Future of Architecture* (New York: Horizon, 1953).
Zeisel, John: *Social Science Frontiers: Sociology and Architectural Design* (New York: Russell Sage, 1975).
————: *Sociology and Architectural Design* (New York: Russell Sage, 1975).

Periodicals Regularly Dealing with Behavioral Issues

AIA Journal (The)
American Anthropologist
American Journal of Orthopsychiatry
American Journal of Psychiatry
American Journal of Psychotherapy
American Journal of Sociology
American Psychologist
American Sociological Review
Architectural Psychology, London
Architectural Record
Architectural Review (The), London
Archives of Environmental Health
Behavioral Science
Building Design and Construction
Built Environment
Engineering News Digest
Environmental Psychology
Environment and Behavior
Geographical Review
Hastings Center Studies
International Social Science Journal
Journal of Abnormal Psychology
Journal of Applied Behavioral Science
Journal of Consulting and Clinical Psychology
Journal of Educational Research
Journal of Experimental Research in Personality
Journal of Health and Social Behavior
Journal of Psychology
Journal of Social Issues
Journal of the American Institute of Planners
Journal of the American Medical Association
Journal of the Society of Architectural Historians
Progressive Architecture
Psychology Today

Index

Index